SUNY Series in Philosophy
Robert C. Neville, Editor

Nanzan Studies in Religion and Culture
James W. Heisig, General Editor

Hans Waldenfels, *Absolute Nothingness: Foundations for a Buddhist-Christian Dialogue*. Trans. by J. W. Heisig. 1980.

Frederick Franck, ed., *The Buddha Eye: An Anthology of the Kyoto School*. 1982.

Nishitani Keiji, *Religion and Nothingness*. Trans. by J. Van Bragt. 1982.

Takeuchi Yoshinori, *The Heart of Buddhism: In Search of the Timeless Spirit of Primitive Buddhism*. Trans. by J. W. Heisig, 1983.

Winston L. King, *Death Was His Kōan: The Samurai Zen of Suzuki Shōsan*. 1986.

Robert Morrell, *Early Kamakura Buddhism: A Minority Report*. 1986.

Tanabe Hajime, *Philosophy as Metanoetics*. Trans. by Y. Takeuchi with V. Viglielmo and J. W. Heisig. 1986.

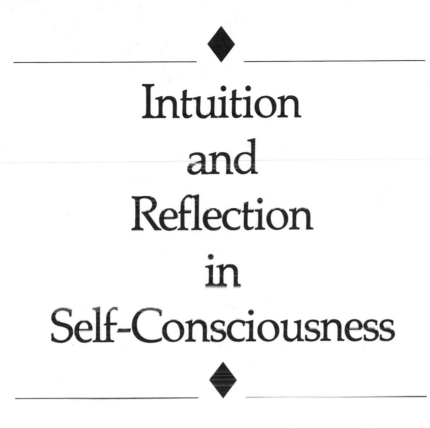

Intuition
and
Reflection
in
Self-Consciousness

Nishida Kitarō

*translated by Valdo H. Viglielmo with
Takeuchi Yoshinori and Joseph S. O'Leary*

State University of New York Press

Published by
State University of New York Press, Albany

©1987   State University of New York

For information, address State University of New York Press, State University Plaza, Albany, N.Y., 12246

Library of Congress Cataloging-in-Publication Data

Nishida, Kitarō, 1870–1945.
    Intuition and reflection in self-consciousness.

    (SUNY series in philosophy)
    Translation of: Jikaku ni okeru chokkan to hansei. 1941.
    Includes index.
    1. Self-consciousness.   2. Consciousness.
3. Meaning (Philosophy)   4. Experience.   I. Title.
B5244.N553J5513   1986   126   86–14538
ISBN 0–88706–368–3
ISBN 0–88706–370–5 (pbk.)

10 9 8 7 6 5 4 3 2 1

Contents

Foreword

It was apparently Swift's encounter with the Japanese syllabaries that inspired the following scene in *Gulliver's Travels*:

> These Bits of Wood were covered on every Square with Paper pasted on them; and on these Papers were written all the Words of their language in their Order. The Professor then desired me to observe, for he was going to set his Engine at work. The Pupils at his Command took each of them hold of an Iron Handle, whereof there were Forty fixed round the Edges of the Frame; and giving them a sudden Turn, the whole Disposition of the Words was entirely changed. He then commanded Six and Thirty of the Lads to read the several Lines softly as they appeared upon the Frame; and where they found three or four Words together that might make Part of a Sentence, they dictated to the Four remaining Boys who were Scribes....The Professor showed me several Volumes in large Folio already collected, of broken Sentences, which he intended to piece together; and out of those rich Materials to give the World a compleat Body of all Arts and Sciences....He assured me, that this Invention had employed all his Thoughts from his Youth; that he had emptied the whole Vocabulary into his Frame ....I made my humblest Acknowledgements to this illustrious Person

for his great Communicativeness; and promised if ever I had the good Fortune to return to my native Country, that I would do him Justice, as the sole Inventor of this wonderful Machine.[1]

Nishida may have a similar impact on his Western readers, who will find themselves tossed on a sea of words, in which any scrap of Eastern or Western philosophical, religious, scientific and literary diction may at any moment surface upon the churning squall of endless sentences and paragraphs, flicker suggestively, and before its pertinence has been more than dimly glimpsed abruptly disappear into the flood. However, unlike the word-processor on the floating island of Laputa, the Nishidian kaleidoscope, in its multiple formations and scramblings, permutations and combinations, is the product of a mind struggling with an ineluctable problem, that posed by the encounter of Eastern and Western traditions, and the perspectives it throws up suggest the immensity of the promise, as well as the treacherous pitfalls, that this encounter conceals.

"I have always been a miner of ore; I have never managed to refine it."[2] The sadness in these words reflects not merely Nishida's sense of personal limits, but also perhaps a realization that the task he had set himself, of pursuing philosophical speculation in a language so remote from Greek or German and so little oriented to logical definition and systematic development, was one for which the ground was unprepared. To make Japanese a philosophical language, and to express Buddhist insights in and against the philosophical jargon of the West, he had to spend a lifetime rummaging among untried linguistic and conceptual possibilities, rather than advancing with the assured scientific tread of his Western colleagues. If he made more progress in this endeavor than anyone before him, it is due no doubt to his strategy, stubbornly pursued, of focusing on a single central theme, one intimately attuned to Japanese language and sensibility as well as to the wisdom of Zen Buddhism, namely, the notion of "immediate experience."

In his phenomenally influential first book, *A Study of Good* (1911), he pursues this idea in a style inspired by Bergson and James. David Dilworth has pointed out that already in this work a fondness for arguments of a speculative and idealist tinge prevents Nishida from embracing the "radical empiricism" of James: "While Nishida, with Zen overtones, 'emptied' experience of all content to find a richer experience which he found no trouble in articulating in the language of Western idealism, James had actually pursued his own analysis of 'A World of Pure Experience' as a critique of transcendental idealism."[3] Bergson too becomes a fund of speculative rather than phenomenological insight in Nishida's reading, and the same may be said of his reception of Husserl, as the work here translated will show. Similarly, in 1933, he writes: "Heidegger's philosophy is not dialectical; it is merely an interpretative phenomenology."[4]

One wonders, however, if the complex dialectical language of Nishida's later attempts to approximate to the reality of immediate experience, the language of "absolutely contradictory self-identity" and the "self-reflecting mirror of self-identity," really served his purpose as well as a more strictly phenomenological approach might have done. One might express the same unease about the ambitious speculative language of Japanese philosophy as Lucien Price does about American music in remarking "that our composers, instead of beginning back where the Europeans began, in simplicity, have begun in complexity and tried to make it more complex. It is perhaps too soon to know whether this is a success or a failure."[5] Though Nishida's dialecticizing is inspired by the speculative legacy of Prajñāpāramitā and Hua-yen (Kegon) Buddhism[6] as much as it is by Hegel, it seems an unduly cumbersome vehicle for his insight into the way all experiences find their "place" in absolute nothingness (an Oriental equivalent of the Platonic or Neo-Kantian *mundus intelligibilis*); this insight may be more simply and effectively conveyed in his remarks on impressionist paintings or on the poetry of Goethe.[7]

Nonetheless, those who expect that the Buddhist philosophy of emptiness can meet and heal the religious and philosophical anxiety of the modern West will attend carefully to whatever insights prompted his struggle with the limits of Western logic. His dialectical proclivities are not very much in evidence in his second full-scale work, here translated. Neither does this work propound the speculative constructions of the world from the standpoint of absolute nothingness found in his later, increasingly daring writings. Even so, two celebrated Japanese authors, Akutagawa Ryūnosuke (1892–1927) and Tanizaki Jun'ichirō (1886–1965), found in it a Dostoyevskian revelation of the abysses of the human heart.[8] Indeed the work presents a small-scale enactment of the movement of Nishida's entire career, a movement from abyss to abyss. It originates from a Bergsonian-Fichtean abyss of immediate experience as self-consciousness and ends with a plunge into an Eriugenian-Schopenhauerian abyss of absolute will as absolute freedom. The argumentative infrastructure of this adventure may not always meet the highest requirements of logical cogency, but the reader is certainly taken on a wide-ranging journey, sharing the author's suspense as to the final destination.

Completed in 1917, *Jikaku ni okeru chokkan to hansei* (Intuition and reflection in self-consciousness)⁹ is the public diary of a philosophical education. It chronicles Nishida's eager search for a more sophisticated grounding of immediate experience in an account of self-consciousness loosely inspired by Fichte, as well as his long-drawn-out confrontation with the Neo-Kantian philosophers, Cohen, Natorp, Rickert, and Windelband, then at the zenith of their fame, but now, despite the reviving interest of a few historians, forgotten. During these years he was also reading Lotze, Windelband's mentor, who is credited with keeping alive the idealist tradition in the bleakly materialistic period between the death of Hegel and the raising of the cry "back to Kant" in the later 1860s by Otto Liebmann, Friedrich Lange, and Aloys Riehl, soon followed by Hermann Cohen. The Neo-Kantians saw Kant as constructing the rational foundations of Newtonian science and they aimed to streamline and purify this construction, by equating the "thing in itself" with the ideal imperative of the mind's desire to know, and reducing the Kantian categories to aspects of a unified thrust of noetic consciousness (Cohen, Natorp), or else by focusing on the "ought" of logical validity as the true foundation of knowledge (Rickert). This aim took them away from the critical radicality of Kant himself. Nishida too seems to have imbided serviceable Kantian doctrines, but not an effective critical method.

One might regret that Nishida devoted so much time to these increasingly scholastic epistemologists and so little to those of his authorities who had thrown off the yoke of Kantian jargon and embarked on the kinds of analysis which have prevailed in twentieth century philosophy: Husserl, Russell, Meinong, Brentano, Bolzano. It may be wondered why, given the obsolescence of the problems it deals with, this work should now be presented in an English translation. The misgiving cannot be allayed, I fear, by an appeal to the work's purely philosophical interest, for many an equally grandiose achievement in European philosophy of the same period now blushes unseen. But its historical interest, which is of more than one kind, may render its publication not unjustifiable. To students of European philosophy the present work offers a curious glimpse of the reverberations of Kant and Neo-Kantianism on a distant shore. For students of Japan this first document of a speculative struggle of a Japanese mind with Western philosophy may throw new light on the still unfolding story of Japan's absorption and transformation of Western culture since the Meiji period. Light is also thrown on the origins of the Kyoto School, which has recently become so well known in connection with the Christian-Buddhist encounter. Nishida's first work and several of the products of his later life are accessible in translations, summaries, and extracts in European languages; the present translation maps the transitional tunnel period connecting *A Study of Good* with the later works and at last makes a fully-rounded portrait of Nishida available to Western students. More than any other of his works, it reveals his anchorage in a certain constellation of Western ideas, and should serve both to temper claims about his uniqueness and originality and to locate his position in the history of philosophy more accurately.

The basis of the present publication is a complete, literal translation provided by Valdo H. Viglielmo, who in an unpublished essay gives this account of his work:

> When I turned to translate Nishida's second major work, . . . I was disappointed to discover that it lacked much of the grandeur and excitement of his maiden work. I was not prepared for the detailed epistemological analysis of this second work nor was I familiar with the many Neo-Kantian scholars from whose works Nishida quoted so extensively. Yet another difficulty for me was the frequency with which Nishida used analogies from mathematics. . . .My translation of the work proceeded extremely slowly, but after setting the task aside for long periods to concentrate on literary topics, I finally completed my draft translation, as I recall, in Hawaii in February 1965. . . .
>
> In the summer of 1963 I went to Japan for the entire academic year with my family. I had as my goal the completion of the translation of both *Jikaku ni okeru chokkan to hansei* and Natsume Sōseki's unfinished last novel *Meian (Light and Darkness*, London, 1971). Unfortunately I became seriously ill in the winter of 1963-64 and was unable to complete either translation at that time, but I did have occasion to meet with Professor Takeuchi in the late spring of 1964 at his home in Kyoto after I had recovered from my illness. At that time, and on numerous later occasions, he helped me considerably by reviewing my translation of *Jikaku ni okeru chokkan to hansei*, making valuable suggestions and corrections, as well as explaining to me various philosophical problems.

Upon reviewing the work with an eye to its publication, the staff of the Nanzan Institute of Religion and Culture enlisted my help in drafting a rather drastically edited version of the translation, allowing me to take bold liberties which at times amounted to a complete rethinking and paraphrasing of the text. This decision was not taken lightly. For one thing, it meant parting with the principles of translation under which Professor Viglielmo had labored. His reservations about the extent of the textual reconstruction were based on a fear that the reader would not be exposed to the true nature of Nishida's thought processes, with their characteristic redundancy and indetermination. For another, the Japanese academic world is not accustomed to the kinds of critical editing common in the West. In the judgment of the Nanzan Institute and its consultors, however, a literal and unabridged translation seemed impracticable at the present time if the work was to reach its intended audience. The editorial process of paring Nishida's composition in order to bring his essential arguments into clearer relief would of course have been impossible without the solid foundation provided by Professor Viglielmo's diligent and meticulous work in reproducing the substance and surface of the text.

Eliminating repetitions, ironing out the circuitous tentativeness of the style, which abounds in phrases like "it might be thought that..." and "one might also suppose that..." (though some praise this "meditative" style as reproducing the movement of the wondering mind), breaking up paragraphs, arranging sequences of ideas in more perspicuous order, and omitting fragmentary, opaque and inconclusive passages (while trying to avoid sacrificing anything of substance), I edited out a nimbus of vagueness, bringing the logical content of the arguments, insofar as I could grasp it, into clear view, so that they could stand or fall thereby. My aim was to "refine" Nishida's "ore" as much as was necessary to produce a more readable English text, one which might even be of help to those Japanese students who have found the work here translated a difficult hurdle to negotiate in their study of the philosopher. The results were carefully checked against the Japanese original (with much assistance from Jan Van Bragt and James Heisig). Our hope is that this abundance of cooks has for once enriched the broth.

The basic reason for the necessity of such editorial maneuvering is that Nishida wrote his philosophy *currente calamo*, adding section to section in the manner of a Japanese *renga*:

> Every morning he regularly wrote two or three sheets at a go, much as a novelist would work. Actually, I do not think Nishida wrote his essays with quite the same purpose as the creator of a literary work, for these daily installments rather served to chronicle his cogitations, a process which could have no end, just as it had no beginning. His books have a quite different flavor from ordinary ones with their ordered sequence of chapters. Rather than construct a book in this way, he wrote a series of essays, which accumulated to form a volume. Yet the result was never simply a collection of essays. When he had finished one essay he always immediately registered the feeling that

something was missing, and to supplement the lack he proceeded to add another. Like an artist, his work was never done.[10]

The breadth of Nishida's reading is a phenomenon worthy of note, and it may safely be assumed that no Western contemporary of his would have been able to explore a comparable range of Eastern sources. Reading German and English fluently, French and Latin with some difficulty, he imbibed influences from every major European literature, from the sciences, from German, French, English, and American philosophy, and from classical, patristic, and medieval sources. Somewhat in the spirit of a crossword-solver, I have tracked down as many of his allusions as possible, in the belief that the historical interest of the text would be enhanced by the provision of its dialogical context, the net of influences in which it is entangled. Though many details of influence and reference were left untraced, and many corners of Nishida's argumentation remain insufficiently enlightened, enough has been done to enable the reader to form a just estimate of what Nishida achieved in his long struggle with his sources and to survey his claims and arguments in a demystified perspective. In several places direct quotations replace Nishida's paraphrases, which serves to lessen the "thieving magpie" allusiveness of the text and identify its bearings in a more graphic way. Sometimes this may have compounded obscurity, for Rickert, Cohen, Natorp, and even the famed stylist Bergson are not always as lucid as their assurance would lead one to expect.

Rather than repeat Nishida's summary of his argument in the Preface, I shall merely make some suggestions as to how readers may most expeditiously find their way to the nub of the matter. It should be rewarding to pay critical attention to a motif which recurs everywhere, namely, Nishida's strategy, pursued in countless ways, of reducing the common dualisms of philosophical and common sense discourse to some immediately experienced reality which resolves the dualism and integrates both sides of it. Among the many dualisms targeted are those between intuition and reflection, subject and object, existence and value, the form and the matter of thinking, the universal and the particular, judgment and concept, quality and relation, logic and mathematics, the psychological and the logical, knowledge and will, mechanism and vitalism, body and spirit, *egressus* and *regressus*, rest and motion, past and future, being and non-being, the individual self and the greater (divine) self. It is clear that Nishida is carrying on his philosophical battle on a great number of fronts, crusading for a reduction of the jungle of received philosophical ideas and rigid dichotomies to the simplicity of the absolute, experienced in the here and now. The absolute is living, present Act; this Act, of self-consciousness, or will, or freedom, constitutes the full and ineffable reality which the scientific and philosophical language of self and world, past and future, matter and spirit, can grasp only in an abstract and objectifying way, leading to rigid dualisms and irresoluble antinomies.

This is quite Buddhistic, and was undoubtedly fueled by Nishida's Zen practice. But Buddhist philosophy is not explicitly drawn on, and even for his loftiest flights Nishida invokes such Western sources as Scotus Eriugena. Later, Nishida will satisfy his passion for unification and immediacy by integrating contradiction into his thought as the very texture of the here and now (in which both past and future are present only by not being present, or in which time exists only as the contradiction of space and space as the contradiction of time). But in the present work he indulges in syntheses more reminiscent of Western philosophy. In the early sections self-consciousness is the immediate instance which unifies subjectivity and objectivity, existence and value, intuition and reflection. In the middle sections the various sciences are unified as successive concretizations of the incomplete and abstract self-consciousness expressed in pure logic; the abstract form of self-consciousness calls for this fulfillment and through it returns to its own concrete truth. In the final sections absolute free will (which is both the immediate experience of the self and the ground of the cosmos) unifies knowledge and will, self and God, mechanism and vitalism, being and non-being, and provides a deeper ground for the results established in the entire preceding argument. Nishida himself recognizes that these sketches of a unifying ground could not satisfy his aspirations. For all the radicality with which they are successively sketched and occupied, each of these projections of the ultimate is derivative from some Western scheme. On finding his way back to the Oriental standpoint of absolute nothingness, Nishida must have sighed: "so near, and yet so far!" Whether he was later able to appropriate this standpoint lucidly, so that it overcame the accumulated jargon of the Western legacy, and showed through the serried abstractions of the prose meant to convey it, is a question on whose answer depends our final assessment of Nishida's historical status.

Perhaps the following sections may be recommended as most likely to repay attention: Section 1, which sketches Nishida's initial position, grounding knowledge, in its intuitive and reflective aspects, in unobjectifiable self-consciousness, an intellectual intuition in which the transcendental *Sollen* or "ought" actively recognizes itself; Section 10, which summarizes his views on the unity of consciousness and self-consciousness, existence and value, as worked out in a discussion of the judgment of identity "A is A"; Section 15, with its lucid account of the relation between sensation and cognition; Section 20, which attempts to capture the texture of the experiential world as a differential continuum underlying all other, relatively abstract, constructions of the world; Section 21, a characteristic piece of polemic against the objectifying psychology of Wundt; Section 29, which focuses the *élan vital* ("pure activity, reason-*qua*-non-reason, being-*qua*-relative-non-being, experience-*qua*-thought") whereby abstract thought hastens to its fulfillment in concrete intuition, logic calling for mathematics, arithmetic for analytic geometry, and so on; Section 37, in which from the foregoing meditations on the unity and interplay of subjective and objective in the Act of self-consciousness there begins to unfold a grand metaphysical vision of the relations between brain and consciousness, body and mind, mechanism and teleology, inorganic and organic, material and spiritual, relations founded in a vital unity whose core is the activity of the will; Section 39, which develops the notion of the living present as the center of gravity of reality, the apex of creative evolution, freeing us from the bondage of Newtonian time; Section 42, which surveys the world of knowledge from the final vantage point of a monism of absolute free will. If one begins by calling at these stations of Nishida's journey, noting the obscurities and unanswered questions encountered at each of them, and the possible implications of Nishida's claims at each point, one should enjoy a fairly adequate grasp of the scope and limitations of the work, which should make it easier to read in its entirety. The reader will, I think, find it advisable to pin Nishida down at the start in some such way as this, thus avoiding the risk of becoming lost in the flux of his wide-ranging discussion.

The reader should not pass over too lightly the pious remarks which strew Nishida's text, particularly in the later sections. Though at first these appear merely ornamentative, they may provide the essential key to the spirit of the work and the goal of its explorations. A tiny sprinkling of Buddhist allusions signals the realm of joyful detachment and freedom which Nishida aspired to capture in philosophical conceptuality. More portentous is the invocation of such figures as St. Paul, Basilides, Valentinus, Origen, Augustine, Pseudo-Dionysius, Eriugena, Saint-Cyran, Boehme. They orchestrate a monistic religiosity, wherein the self, as it touches its own depths, opens on to the paradoxical dimension of the absolute, grasped as a coincidence of opposites. Despite its derivation from a rather wayward selection of Christian sources, this line of speculation already reveals the characteristic lineaments of Nishida's religious vision, which later aquired fixed form in the notion of "absolute contradictory self-identity," a formula which becomes an almost obsessive ritornello in his later works.

Professor Viglielmo calls the conclusion of A Study of Good, the chapter entitled "Intelligence and Love,"[11] "a magnificent piece of literature, a kind of prose-poem on a par with the greatest religious poems of both East and West." While such a claim can scarcely be made for the present work, it nonetheless reveals a further stage in the author's nagging at the religious problem. Nishida's Prefaces are particularly interesting for their confession of how unsatisfied the religiosity of the final part of the work left him, and the reader may even find that the text itself conveys this dissatisfaction both by protesting too much in its presentation of religious ideas and by neglecting to pursue them with determination. No doubt the prevalence of the characteristic identities of idealism (between thought and intuition, between consciousness and self-consciousness, or even, it occasionally appears, between idea and existence) prevented him from attaining the more subtle and freely moving panentheistic outlook which is the core of the later "Nishida philosophy."

The present translation may claim to present a Nishida previously unknown to the West. The degree to which he appears as a compulsively *mimetic* philosopher—ever echoing the grave rumble of Kant, the tortured acrobatics of Fichte, or Hegel's dialectical flightiness—will remind some readers of analogous phenomena in contemporary Japanese life; I think of the youths at Enoshima clutching their cumbersome California surfboards as they paddle in a perfectly placid sea. Mimetic rivalry is also in evidence. One can hear Nishida purr with satisfaction as he shows, for example, that Husserl's careful distinction between the content and the object of perception falls short of the higher viewpoint in which "the object which transcends consciousness" is no more than "the internal unity of consciousness itself" (Section 25). These displays of knowingness are conducted in the key of suggestion rather than assertion, and in modest dependence on the authorities which he plays off one against another.

It must be admitted, however, that in spite of, or rather by means of, this mimetic dialectic (which the present rather homeopathic translation has compounded), Nishida emerges as a thinker of stubborn originality. Particularly in the last chapters, when he leaves off from shuttling from one Neo-Kantian category to another and forgets his minute preoccupation with judgments of self-identity and perceptions of straight lines, one becomes aware of a broader sweep, a more pleasing coherence, and a more determined thrust to this argument than its desultory progress had led one to expect. One finds oneself launched, unexpectedly, on the ocean of Absolute Free Will, which is identified with the very core of immediate experience before its conceptual moment has differentiated itself negatively from its matrix. The emergence of this theme, which combines the Hellenic quest for the absolute with the Biblical sense of God as creative will, and sublates both in a Buddhist wonder at the world which comes into being anew from nothingness at every moment, is refreshing like the explosion at the end of *Bolero*, assuaging the tedium of the professorial tone and the chagrin of interrupted arguments. These chapters mark a turning-point: behind them lies Nishida's long apprenticeship as an imitator of Western voices; before lie the grander themes of his later philosophy. No students of the Kyoto philosophy of absolute nothingness can afford to ignore these pages or their context (without which they cannot be understood). It is the interest of this genealogical revelation which most encourages us to present *Intuition and Reflection in Self-Consciousness* to the appreciation of a wider public.

Joseph S. O'Leary

NOTES

1. Swift, *Gulliver's Travels*, ed. Paul Turner, Oxford University Press, 1971, 183-84. James Heisig brought my attention to the theory that the Plate on page 181 is derived from a Swiss author's reproduction of the Japanese syllabaries.
2. Kitarō Nishida, *Intelligibility and the Philosophy of Nothingness: Three Philosophical Essays*, trans. Robert Schinzinger, Tokyo: Maruzen, 1958, preface.
3. David Dilworth, *Nishida Kitarō (1870-1945): The Development of his Thought* (1970), Ann Arbor, Michigan: University Microfilms International, 1977, 44.
4. Nishida Kitaro, *Fundamental Problems in Philosophy*, trans. David A. Dilworth, Tokyo: Sophia University Press, 1970, 95.
5. *Dialogues of Alfred North Whitehead as Recorded by Lucien Price*, New York: Mentor, 1964, 66.
6. Especially as conveyed by the writings of D. T. Suzuki. The influence of Prajñāpāramitā logic is particularly evident in Nishida's last essay, "The Logic of Place and a Religious Worldview." Two translations of this work are forthcoming, by David Dilworth (University of Hawaii Press) and Yusa Michiko (*The Eastern Buddhist*).
7. "Goethe's Metaphysical Background" in *Intelligibility and the Philosophy of Nothingness*, 143-59.
8. *Nishida Kitarō: dōjidai no kiroku*, Tokyo: Iwanami, 1971, 44-45.

9. The book comprises vol. 2 of Nishida's collected works, *Nishida Kitarō zenshū*, Tokyo: Iwanami, 1978.
10. Miki Kiyoshi, *Dokusho to jinsei*, Tokyo: Shinchōbunko, 1974, 137-38.
11. Nishida Kitaro, *A Study of Good*, trans. V. H. Viglielmo, Tokyo: Printing Bureau, Japanese Government, 1960, 185-89.

Preface

This work, consisting of studies contributed from September 1913 to May of this year (1917), to two journals, the earlier ones to *Geibun* and the later ones to *Tetsugaku kenkyū*, was originally meant to be a simple essay, but, as I pursued my thought to its finer reaches, doubt gave rise to doubt, one solution requiring another, and the pages piled up to form an entire volume. My aim was to rethink each dimension of the real in light of what I call the system of self-consciousness, and thereby to clarify a problem considered fundamental in contemporary philosophy, that of the connection between value and being, and between meaning and fact. Self-consciousness, in my usage, denotes the self-consciousness of the transcendental ego (close to Fichte's *Tathandlung*). This central conception, originally suggested to me, I think, by the Supplementary Essay in Volume I of Royce's *The World and the Individual*, was first expressed in my essay "Logical Understanding and Mathematical Understanding," included in *Shisaku to taiken (Thought and Experience)*, and the present work grew out of the attempt to investigate this idea thoroughly. If I have succeeded, I think I have shown that a new interpretation of Fichte can serve as the foundation of both Kantian and Bergsonian thought.

The first six Sections provide an outline of my views at the time I began this study. Here I clarified my understanding of self-consciousness, and aired the expectation of being able to explain the fundamental relationship between value and being in light of self-consciousness, in which meaning and existence are one, and which includes infinite development. (Later reflection showed me how problematic this project was, and forced me to state my doubts about it.) Reasoning that the real world is founded on the consciousness of an "ought," I saw the distinction between the worlds of meaning and reality as a relative one. I attempted a similar account of the distinction between universal and particular in Section 6, which now seems to me extremely inadequate in both thought and expression; the complete understanding of this idea must be sought at the end of the work.

In Sections 7 to 10, I tried to construct, as the foundation of my entire argument, a very formal system of self-consciousness on the basis of an extremely simple logical thought experience, the judgment of the law of identity. This judgment, I claimed, already encompassed in the most universal form the oppositions and relationships of value and being, object and cognitive act, form and content, and I thence attempted to clarify, in the most basic manner, the significance and relationship of each of these categories in concrete experience. In Section II, upon reconsidering the matter, I attempted to determine whether the empirical world can be explained as a system which is identical to that of the above formal thought experience, and I was forced to conclude that between these two stretch many chasms difficult to bridge. In Section 12, in order to clarify the transition of internal necessity from a merely formal system of logical thought to an experiential system having content, I ventured a fundamental theory, based on my previous discussion in "Logical Understanding and Mathematical Understanding," of how form acquires content, or how the abstract progresses to concreteness, as in the passage from logic to mathematics. Thus I clarified, with regard to the most abstract thought experience, the nature of the internal development of experience, or the *élan vital*. (This too is one of the basic ideas of this work.) Despite this elucidation, it proved difficult to move from the world of thought to the world of reality. In Section 13, I reduced the irrationality and objectivity of experience, as opposed to thought, to the fact that experience itself, like thought, is an autonomous system of self-consciousness, but the nature of this system, and the way in which it combined with thought, remained unclear. Sections 11 to 13, then, form a transition from the study of thought systems to that of experiential systems.

To show that systems of experience also are self-conscious systems, like systems of thought, and that all experiences, as systems of the same kind, are internal syntheses of meaning and reality, I needed first to prove that perceptual experiences are self-developing, self-conscious systems. I began with a general statement of the difficulties (14 to 16). I had become very interested in the original views of Hermann Cohen on "the anticipation of perception," which shed light on the *activity* of consciousness, but leave its *origin* unexplained. Cohen had thus, I felt, missed the key point at which the worlds of meaning and reality diverge; I was dissatisfied with an epistemology which did not open onto metaphysics.

From Section 17 the argument is chiefly concerned with consciousness, whose activity is grasped as the self-determining of an infinite idea. The relationship between unconsciousness and consciousness is characterized in the manner of Cohen as similar to that between dx and x; thus I viewed consciousness of a certain straight line as an infinite progression determining itself. In order to develop this insight into the way in which Platonic ideas descend into the real, I felt it necessary to examine carefully the psychologist's view of mental phenomena and to assess the significance and status of psychological analysis (18). As later explained, I do not see mental and material phenomena as independent realities, but as the two interrelated aspects of concrete experience. Immediate concrete experience is not the psychologist's so-called consciousness, but rather a continuum based on various a priori positions, whose unifying function is thought of as subjectivity, while that which it unifies is thought of as the objective; true objective reality is the continuum itself. In Sections 19 and 20, following Fiedler, I show that perceptual experience, in its pure state, is a formal activity, and that the continuous is the truly real.

In Sections 21 and 22, using the example of the consciousness of a continuous straight line, I discussed the opposition and relationship between subjectivity and objectivity in a creative system. Since to *perceive* a straight line is to be conscious of it as one determination of an infinite, continuous straight line which is an object of *thought*, I contended that this perception is a self-conscious system wherein a universal determines itself. By tracing this activity of determination to its source I hoped to throw light on the nature of consciousness. But the particular determination of a universal thought object in perception seemed an accidental event, extrinsic to this universal, and I was unable to discover an internal necessity of determination within the straight line itself as thought object. I attempted to evade this difficult point by proposing that the consciousness of an object of pure thought must include the experience of an activity, and that true subjectivity is a structural function of objectivity. Viewed from a more comprehensive standpoint, the unifying activity of a lesser standpoint appears as subjective, though constitutive of objectivity within that standpoint itself. Thus we are dealing with a dynamic fusion of subject and object which we may call both true subjectivity and true objectivity. However, the following problem arose: is not the lesser standpoint which is reflected upon from the more comprehensive one already an object? For if it were true dynamic subjectivity it could not be reflected upon, and that which is reflected upon is no longer dynamic subjectivity (24). At that time I had not yet discovered the standpoint of absolute free will explored at the end of this work; I was searching for something, and did not find it, so that the confusion of the discussion was unavoidable.

Abandoning the problem of the possibility of reflection, I discussed the qualities of the activity of consciousness (25), and invoked the notion of limit to shed light on them. A limit is a position of a higher order which cannot be reached from a lower one, yet which is the foundation of this lower position, providing the concrete basis to what is relatively abstract. In Section 26, I clarified this in light of contemporary mathematics, and tried to consider the various meanings of limit as qualities of activities. After making some observations on the distinction between objects of thought and objects of immediate perception (27), I used the idea of limit to study the union of thought and perception (28). I claimed that the union of number and perception in analytical geometry is not merely accidental, as a mathematician might think, but is based on the requirement of objectivity intrinsic to knowledge. Knowledge is an infinite developmental process, and its quest for objectivity is a quest for a concrete whole given at the outset, in which the union of thought and immediate perception is already given. (Later I described this truly concrete given as the unity of absolute free will.) This is the reason the objectivity of knowledge is attained through uniting thought and immediate perception (29). In Sections 30 to 32, I applied this idea to the relationship between number and geometric space, showing that in the transition from number to space the *élan vital* is again operative, and that the object of analytical geometry is the concrete base of both number and space. This helped me to focus the point of contact between thought and experience. Further reflection on the meaning of a geometric straight line as a self-conscious system (33) shed light on the opposition and relationship of spirit and matter, though this topic still remained extremely obscure (34).

From Section 35 on, I viewed perceptual experience as a self-conscious system similar to all thought systems, and unified all experience in accord with one principle. This permitted a clarification of the nature and relationship of spiritual and material phenomena. Having refuted the notion that the body is the foundation of consciousness, or that sensation arises from matter (36), I presented a teleological account of the mind-body relationship (37), and showed that only things which are ends in themselves are true concrete realities, that life is thus more concrete than matter, and spirit more concrete than life, that material phenomena are projections of spiritual phenomena, and that the material world is a means to spiritual development (38). I claimed that we can repeat past experience only in accord with a position of trans-cognitive will, and that this will is the true point of fusion of ideal and actual (39). The remaining chapters reconsider the main issues of the work from this final position. After giving an account of the primacy of the will (40), and after explaining that "absolute free will" is not merely formal will without content, but the activity of concrete personality (41), I discussed the relationship between thought and experience (42), the condition of possibility of the unification of all experience in a single system by reflection, and the nature and relationships of various realms of reality such as spirit and matter (43). Having thus established the principles of a solution of the problems which had so long detained me, I could undertake a final treatment of the problems of the union of value and being, meaning and fact, which were the first objective of this work, venturing an explanation of how, at a certain time and in a certain place, a certain individual can consider a universally valid truth.

The Postface consists of the lecture entitled "Various Worlds," delivered before the Philosophical Association of Tokyo Imperial University in April of this year, but since it sums up briefly the final position of this work, I have appended it here. Also, to facilitate the reader's comprehension, I have included a Table of Contents, but since this book was not written according to a preconceived plan, if one adheres too strictly to it, it may be more of a hindrance to understanding than a help.

This work is a document of a hard-fought battle of thought. I must admit that after many tortuous turns I have finally been unable to arrive at any new ideas or solutions. Indeed I may not be able to escape the criticism that I have broken my lance, exhausted my quiver, and capitulated to the enemy camp of mysticism. Nevertheless I have sincerely tried to clear the desk of my thought. Of course this is a work which I hesitate to present for the perusal of scholars, but if there are some who have problems similar to mine and who are similarly laboring over their solution, they may feel some sympathy even if they do not receive any enlightenment.

June 1917
Tanaka-mura, North Kyōto
Nishida Kitarō

Preface to the Revised Edition

This work is a product of the period when, after having been a high school language teacher, I first ascended the lecture platform of a university. The trend of my thought had already been set in *Zen no kenkyū* (*A Study of Good*). Now I began to study Rickert and the other Neo-Kantians, attempting to maintain an individual position on every point vis-à-vis this school. I opposed to their sharp distinction between value and being, and meaning and fact, an overall unity of the two pairs from a position of self-consciousness, which is an internal union of intuition and reflection. This position was close to that of Fichte's "Act," but not strictly the same, for I focused on the self-generation and self-development of concrete experience. At that time I was stirred by the works of Bergson, but again, despite my whole-hearted agreement with him, my ideas do not entirely coincide with his. The notion of absolute will, which is the final position of this work, may remind some readers of my present position of "the self-identity of absolute contradiction," but it is still very remote from it. I used the limit concept of the Marburg school to discuss the internal unity of thought and experience, and object and act, but the true final position, from which the problems could have been solved, though hinted at from various angles, continued to elude me, so that the work remained inconclusive. This is why I was forced to confess at the end of the first Preface that I had broken my lance, exhausted my quiver, and capitulated to the enemy camp of mysticism. Today, probably the only significance of this work is that it represents one stage in my intellectual development. Though I reread this work in preparation for the revised edition, it is so distant from my present philosophical position as to make it impossible for me to add anything. As I look back over this document of thirty years ago representing my hard-fought battle over several years, I cannot but have the feeling of exertion expressed by the famous phrase, "I have had fierce struggles, Descending into the dragon's cave for you."[1]

February 1941
Nishida Kitarō

Part One
Introduction

Self-Consciousness: Some Problems

Geibun, IV, Sept. 1913

1

Intuition is a consciousness of unbroken progression, of reality just as it is, wherein subject and object are not as yet divided and that which knows and that which is known are one. *Reflection* is a consciousness which, standing outside of this progression, turns around and views it. In Bergson's terms, it is that which refashions continuity in the form of simultaneous existence and time in the form of space.[2] But how, since we can never go outside the sphere of actual intuition, is such reflection possible? How can reflection be combined with intuition? And what is the significance of intuition for reflection?

I propose that what lights up the internal connections between these two is our *self-consciousness*. When in self-consciousness the self makes its own activity its object and reflects upon it, this reflection is the very process of the self's development and as such is an unending progression; it is not an accidental happening, but is the intrinsic nature of consciousness as such.[3] For Fichte the self is "the self acting on the self": "Thus to conceive or to think the self consists in the operation of the self itself towards itself, and conversely, such an operation towards itself produces a thinking of the self and absolutely no other thinking."[4]

The self's reflection on the self, its reflecting (in the sense of mirroring) itself, cannot be brought to a halt at this point, for self-reflection consists in an unending process of unification, and, as Royce saw, a single project of reflecting the self inevitably generates an unlimited series, just as, if one wished to make a completely adequate map of England on the surface of that country, each realization of this plan would immediately generate the project of another map including the previous one within itself in a never-ending process;[5] or just as an object placed between two bright mirrors must project its image infinitely. When we say that the self reflects on the self, or reflects itself, we are not dealing with something apart from the self in which the self is reflected as experience is reproduced in the form of concepts, but rather it is in the self that the self is reflected. Reflection is an event within the self, by which the self adds a certain something to the self, a knowing of the self which is also a process of self-development. Self-identity, correctly understood, is not static identity but dynamic development, and it is in this deployment of self-identity that the notion of an irreducible individual history finds a basis.

To psychology, when the self reflects on the self, the first self and the self which reflects on it are two chronologically distinct mental states, and though one may detect similarities between the two, one is finally forced to admit that they cannot be identical. They are united only by that feeling of self-identity which James compared to the brand on cattle belonging to the same owner.[6] What I mean by self-consciousness, however, is a much more basic fact of consciousness than those dealt with by psychology. For our ability to recollect the past and to think of it in historical concatenation is possible only because of a self-consciousness that already transcends time. The unity of different conscious states is possible only because there is a unifying consciousness transcending each of them. That which compares two mental states and judges the self of the first state and the self that reflects on it to be different can be nothing other than the self itself. The psychological view is a secondary one which approaches consciousness obliquely, and we should not forget that it too is in turn founded on a trans-individual self-consciousness. (In Kantian terms, the scientific standpoint has as its condition of possibility the unity of pure apperception.)[7] In any case the identity in self-consciousness of the first self and the self reflecting on it is not the identity grasped by psychology when it fixes them both as objects of thought. Instead the self which is thought and the self which thinks it are immediately identical, and self-consciousness is consciousness of the transcendental unity of the self. This unifying consciousness underlying the two consciousnesses in question takes the form of an internal "ought" *(Sollen)*.[8]

Now if self-consciousness is the unifying activity grounding all conscious unity, then *the subject of the activity can never itself become an object for consciousness;*[9] the self which is an object of reflection is no longer this active self, and so we are forced to the conclusion that self-consciousness, in the sense of the self reflecting on the self, is an impossibility! What is afoot when we reflect on or know our consciousness? It would indeed be impossible to reflect on and know the self if this implied, as is commonly supposed, that a past consciousness floats before one's vision, as an object is placed before the mirror which reflects its image. On this basis it would be impossible to reflect, not alone on the self, but on any past consciousness whatever, for even the consciousness of a second ago can never be repeated in the sense of a precise reproduction. This common notion of reflection may be associated with the dogmas of the epistemological theory of pictorial reproduction *(Abbildungstheorie)*.[10] Many thinkers since Kant, notably the exponents of the teleological critical theory,[11] have corrected this by insisting that knowing is not passive, but an activity of unifying and organizing the contents of consciousness by a priori forms. Thus to recollect or to reflect upon past consciousness is already in a certain sense to construct and order it. Indeed in every case reflection is construction, i.e., thinking. This is what the teleological critical philosophers have in mind when they insist that to know is to think. It follows that to know or to reflect on the self can only mean to think the self. This is what Fichte calls the self acting on the self, an action outside of which, as he insists, the self does not exist.[12] How is such an action of the self on the self, such a thinking of thinking, possible?

It is commonly imagined that that which knows and that which is known first exist separately, and that to know is the former's acting upon the latter; consequently, such a thing as the thinking which thinks thinking is considered impossible. But Fichte denies that the fact of our thinking arises on the basis of the prior fact of our existing and claims that, on the contrary, the latter is grounded on the former, for that which asserts that we must exist before we think is we ourselves, and this assertion is *our* thought.[13] As Rickert puts it: "Meaning precedes and surpasses all existence."[14] According to Rickert, the object of our cognition is not transcendent existence but is a transcendental "ought" and belongs to the realm of value.[15] Cognition is the recognition of this "ought" and our intellectual activity is the actuality of the appearance of this transcendental value within

5

consciousness.[16] (This is what stamps all our intellectual activity with the character of judgment.[17] The ultimate subject of this judging consciousness, the cognitive subject properly speaking, is only a limit-concept, the final standpoint from which all worlds of experience could be viewed as the content of consciousness, and as such it is not something which has any reality.)[18] The transcendental "ought" which grounds cognition is expressed in our intellectual experience by the necessity of a judgment or the satisfaction logical clarity creates. Rather than think of that which knows and that which is known as first existing and the former then acting on the latter to produce knowledge, we should derive both the subject and object of knowledge from this consciousness of value, of the "ought," which grounds all knowing.

Having clarified the conditions of possibility of our knowing, we return to the question: what is the condition of possibility of self-consciousness as the thinking which thinks thinking? The theory of knowledge we have presented obliges us to see the self knowing the self, thinking which thinks thinking, as value consciousness recognizing value consciousness itself, the "ought" recognizing the "ought" itself. Is this a tenable notion? I am prepared to maintain that the fact of the "ought" recognizing the "ought" itself is self-evident; the "ought" is based on the "ought" itself, not on anything else, for that which is founded on another thing cannot be said to be an "ought;" the "ought" is identical with the fact of recognizing itself. Windelband states that normative consciousness posits its own existence,[19] and Lotze has shown the impossibility of our not having recourse to the unavoidable circular reasoning such a position implies;[20] Rickert further argues that doubting already presupposes the existence of normative consciousness,[21] and Nelson, who held the opposite view, maintains that the objective validity of knowledge cannot be the object of proof.[22] Each of these arguments presupposes the same basis in a self-authenticating "ought."

In light of these reflections we conclude that self-consciousness is not originally a theme for psychological interpretation, nor can it be comprehended in the terms of an epistemology of pictorial reproduction wherein subject and object are in opposition and the former reflects the latter. Its significance and possibility can be elucidated only within critical philosophy on the basis of the "ought" recognizing the "ought" itself. Fichte argues that to be conscious of the self we must distinguish between the thinking self and the self which it thinks; and yet if we do this, this thinking self must become the object of yet another thinking self, and so on infinitely, so that we finally cannot explain the fact of self-consciousness; but nevertheless the fact of self-consciousness remains, and can only be explained as the merging of subject and object in what can only be called an intellectual intuition, an immediate and basic fact of consciousness which cannot be further explained.[23] If in this sense we can say that self-consciousness is intuition, intuition must be value consciousness recognizing value consciousness itself, the "ought" recognizing the "ought" itself; thus Fichtean intuition turns out to be an activity.

2

In the foregoing discussion of the significance and possibility of self-consciousness as I understand it, we have grazed a problem I should now like to discuss more fully. We saw that for Fichte self-consciousness, a phenomenon of immediate experience which eludes further explanation, resides only in the activity of thinking; to intuit the self means to actualize this activity.[24] But the problem is that this seems to be a thinking without a subject that thinks, an activity without an agent! Following the teleological critical philosophers we described this self-intuition as value-consciousness recognizing value–consciousness itself; if it is not this, Fichte can scarcely escape the charge of having fallen into the psychologism which attempts to derive value from fact. But to view self-consciousness in this way purely as the consciousness of an "ought" is inevitably to think of it as something completely unreal and as utterly unrelated to the phenomenon of our actual reflection, so that it no longer signifies an activity within the self as such. Windelband thinks that one is justified in interpreting Fichte's self in this way.[25] To overcome this difficulty I argue that along with thinking of the self as what grounds objective knowledge (Kant's pure apperception) one can also think of it as the basis of activity at the level of the actual, or in other words that the self in itself is operative at this level, as reflection or thinking, and that apart from this activity there is nothing we can call the self. In the case of an object other than the self, that which thinks and that which is thought are separate and the act of judging differs from its content. Only in self-consciousness, which is the self thinking the self, content thinking content itself, are these two one. (The aim of the present work is to locate the profound inner relation of intuition and reflection in self-consciousness thus understood.) But we must counter the suspicion that

7

this view of the activity of the self rests on a confusion of intellectual value and mental activity.

Truth is truth irrespective of whether we think it or not; value consciousness is a consciousness of universal validity, independent of our actual thinking processes. On this premise there is no intrinsic link between the self-consciousness wherein value-consciousness comes to self-recognition and the self-consciousness operative at the level of the actual, and the former must transcend the latter and be able to view it calmly as an intellectual object similar to all other phenomena. The best way to criticize this is to examine the arguments by which Rickert maintains a sharp distinction between intellectual value and intellectual activity. In the essay, "Judgment and Judging," he distinguishes three ways of looking at judgment. First, we can view judgment as merely one kind of psychological process, in which case it is simply one psychological event among others, arising in the individual consciousness and running its course in time.[26] From the logical viewpoint, however, judgment is the bearer of meaning and the psychological process of judging somehow expresses this meaning. Moreover, Rickert distinguishes the transcendent (objective) side of this meaning from its immanent (subjective) side, calling the former the "content of judgment" (Urteilsgehalt) and identifying it with what he terms value in his transcendental logic. This transcendent meaning, he claims, has no relation to the psychological activity of judging. For example, that two times two equals four does not have any relation to the act of judging whereby a certain person thinks this at a certain time and place. Transcendent meaning becomes immanent meaning when it has become immanent in the judgment act as its intended meaning, in which case it appears as the consciousness of a logical "ought."[27] Thus judgment presents the three aspects of psychological process, intended meaning, and logical content, which we must strictly distinguish and never confuse with one another.

While Rickert's distinctions undoubtedly have value at the level of academic inquiry, we must nonetheless ask whether consciousness of the "ought" is really so unconnected with conscious activity at the level of the actual. Does not the consciousness of an "ought" have the power to control our actual conscious activity? Is it not an activating force moving us from within? If not, it becomes something utterly without significance for us. When, for example, we think about a certain mathematical problem, mathematical necessity is the power which determines our combinations of ideas, it is a force in the realm of fact. In immediate experience, from the fact that we *must* think in this way arises the fact that we *do* think in this way, and an ideal which cannot have such effects at the level of actuality is not really an ideal. Once again it may be objected that these views rest on an egregious confusion of cause and reason;[28] but let us see whether behind such criticism there does not lurk a residue of dogmatism worth examining more closely.

Many, for instance, claim that truth has no intrinsic power to realize itself but becomes actual only when some individual conceives it, that is, only with the aid of a factual cause. But what do those who make this claim understand by "individual" and "factual cause"? Can these notions be formed without the prior unification of experience according to the forms of time and space? And if not, do they not already presuppose consciousness of the "ought" on which these forms are based? We maintain that all truth inherently possesses the power to determine our consciousness, and that its effectivity is not derived from another source. For example, when we judge that $2 + 2 = 4$, we comply with a requirement of reason which is a fact of actual necessity and which has no exterior source. When a certain system of consciousness develops on its own terms from within, this is a case of an "ought" which *is* an actuality, but when it does not so develop, the necessity to unify it according to the external forms of space, time, and causation has an extrinsic source. Usually we think of that which is unified according to the forms of space, time, and causation as real, whereas we think of a system of truth as ideal, but if the latter is not real, then we must say that the former, as being founded on it, is even more unreal.

I think that anyone who follows Kant's epistemology will allow that the thinking of experience in accord with the forms of space, time and causation, in accord, that is, with the categories of existence, is already based on an "ought," that is, on value, so that the truths of natural science can be seen as basically inventions of thinking. But this idealistic insight does not immediately provide an account of actual thinking, and the problem of the operancy of truth at the level of actuality still needs to be intensively discussed. It is clear, for instance, that from the mathematical necessity whereby two and two makes four we cannot infer the fact that a certain person at a certain time thinks this. Nor, even if physical knowledge were to reach a state of perfection and Laplace's god Intelligence were able to predict all happenings, could this ideal truth be immediately translated into physical fact.[29] In short, logical "ought" and fact can never blend, and though thinking according to time, space, and causation is based on the "ought," this cannot imply that the "ought" creates fact. But to clarify this difficult topic we must proceed to a more basic discussion of these notions.

3

We have seen that Rickert tries to distinguish strictly between logical meaning, or value, and the psychological function of judgment. But how is a judgment act which, strictly distinguished from meaning, is simply an event in time, able to think about meaning? How is it possible for transcendent meaning to become immanent as the meaning of the judgment act? When, for example, we think the truth of the law of self-identity, "A is A," from the continuity of two different independent mental images, even if they have identical properties, how is this judgment constituted? (According to Wundt, such "re-cognition" is not merely a repetition of an identical consciousness, but is a consciousness possessing a new significance, and for this reason he calls the relationship of psychological causation a *creative synthesis*.)[30]

It must be admitted that our immediate consciousness possesses meaning, that meaning is real as a fact of consciousness. One might attempt to reduce this consciousness of meaning to the status of a mere sensation or feeling, but the result of such analysis could no longer be described as *meaning*, any more than an analysis of its material could pass as an adequate account of a work of art. It requires no proof that phenomena of consciousness exclusively determined according to time, space and causation cannot be the bearers of universal meaning, any more than the matter of a work of art, without human consciousness of the aesthetic "ought" in its respect, can be the bearer of aesthetic meaning. If our consciousness of meaning were only fantasy, rather than an irreducible fact of immediate awareness, there would be no problem with an explanation of it in terms of the law of causation; but one cannot deny the reality of the consciousness of meaning, for to deny it already presupposes consciousness of meaning. When Rickert speaks of the consciousness of an "ought," it is probably not to be considered real; but neither can it be identified solely with his transcendent meaning, value as such, for it is that wherein value has appeared in the form of existence.[31] But, whereas in the case of natural phenomena one may think that their purposes are conferred on them from without, such a view is untenable in the case of consciousness, whose values are always intrinsically active processes, and thus belong indubitably to the real.

If the origin of the consciousness of meaning cannot be explained by the law of causation governing consciousness as psychological process, if between those two orders stretches an unbridgeable chasm, the problem remains: how is it possible that the consciousness of a particular person at a particular time and place conceives a particular meaning? Our conviction that the consciousness of meaning belongs to the real is largely based on the fact that we can conceive it in accord with the categories of existence. How is this conjunction of meaning and existence possible? If, as we have claimed, such things as time, place, the individual, and thinking presuppose the unification of experience according to an "ought," then the fact of our thinking a certain meaning, which implies the conjunction of meaning and existence, consists in our being able to grasp the relationship of a variety of aspects of consciousness. Immediate concrete consciousness is always embedded in relationships, it possesses a variety of meanings, and connections with other things in these meanings, and is thus capable of being unified from various aspects. Consciousness can be unified, for instance, under the aspects of truth, beauty and goodness, meanings based on an "ought," or under the aspects of time or individuality, categories of existence. If a chasm separates meaning and existence, it is hard to see how these different approaches to meaning can combine in one consciousness. I have glibly said that we view one consciousness from various aspects, but what is it that enables us to say that it is one consciousness rather than unrelated independent consciousnesses?

The riddle remains intact: How is it possible to combine existence with meaning? We can say that to think something exists is itself a consciousness of meaning, but were we to reduce the fact of existence to nothing more than a meaning in consciousness, then everything would become meaning, and existence and reality would utterly disappear. About what do we think when we think meaning? What is it that thinks meaning? Does meaning think the meaning of meaning? Even if meaning, as a fact of immediate consciousness, is real, can it become real by means of meaning only? Can meaning appear in the individual consciousness by means of its own power? Just as the consciousness of meaning cannot be explained from existence, must we also say that existence cannot be explained from meaning alone; or does the meaning termed existence cause the other meanings to exist? In which case, what is it that causes us to think the fact of existence? Does the meaning of existence cause itself to exist? Concerning other meanings, it suffices if we think the meaning and the consciousness of that

11

meaning, but concerning the meaning termed existence, we must think the existence of a thing, the meaning of the fact that this thing exists, and the consciousness of this meaning. In so far as the fact that a certain thing exists is truth as consciousness of meaning, a certain thing must exist, but this certain thing cannot be derived from meaning. It seems that unless we can solve these various perplexities we will remain unable to bring into view the unity of meaning and existence.

Meaning and Existence

Geibun, IV, Nov. 1913

4

We may begin our examination of the relationship between meaning and existence by looking at signs and symbols, which are commonly thought of as connecting the two. In *signs*, words for example, there is no internal relationship between the character of the indicating instance and the nature of the thing indicated; words indicate meanings as the sign of the cross indicates Christianity, by virtue of an extrinsic association of sign and signified. In the case of *symbols*, for instance the lily representing purity, we do find a degree of internal relationship between the character of the symbol and the meaning it designates, and the two things blend indissociably in a single significant form, as a matter of immediate experience; all the relationships a work of art has to the meanings it conveys are of this order. However, even the symbolic relationship is not a purely intrinsic one: we are inclined to say that the lily contains or evokes the feeling of purity, but this feeling might just as well be associated with another symbol, and there is no objective bond between the two things; the feeling is attached extrinsically to the symbol.

When we try to define the relationship between the psychological activity of judging and the content or meaning it expresses, we may think of judgment as a merely psychological reality, nothing more than the continuity in time of a cluster of concepts to which their meaning has been added from without in accord with the relationship between these concepts and the core of consciousness, the function of apperception, so that in every case the conjunction of meaning and existence is produced by the activity of the ego. This conjunction can then be conceived (on the model of the sign) as an accidental and arbitrary one, or (on the model of the symbol) as a necessary one, in which case necessity may be attributed to the determined character of the subject which is thought of as in a relation of necessity with the necessity of things. But no basis has been provided for this supposed necessary relationship. The two kinds of necessity commonly distinguished are logical necessity (necessity in the order of meaning) and causal necessity (necessity in the order of existence). The necessity here in question is clearly not the former, which is confined to meaning. Is it then the latter? Psychologists tend to think so and they reduce the subject as carrier of meaning to a thing that stands in a causal relationship with other things. But what is the nature of the necessity imputed to causal relationships? When two things are inseparably linked in our experience and their connection is found not to vary no matter how many times the same experience recurs, we come to believe there is a relationship of causal necessity between them. If meaning and existence are related in this way, then they may be seen as conjoined by the temporal form of simultaneity; what joins the act of judging with the meaning it expresses is the simultaneity of this conscious act and certain clusters of concepts (on which it stamps the Jamesian "brand"). But if the conjunction of meaning and existence thus depends on the form of time, what is time itself? It is undoubtedly the form that unifies our experience, but the ability to unify experience by means of this form derives from the unifying function of transcendental apperception; "time" is grounded on our consciousness of the "ought." Thus what links meaning—which in this merely psychological perspective is reduced to the status of an existent—with other existents, turns out to be the consciousness of meaning! If we think the conjunction of meaning and existence in this way as the temporal association of one existent with another, we remain absolutely unable to make this conjunction really intelligible.

5

Let us put the question: What does it mean to say that something exists? If we think in strictly experiential terms, that a certain thing exists means no more than that an identical experience can recur many times. Stricter reflection obliges us to doubt whether an experience repeated in time can really be the same experience, and not merely a similar one. This reduction of existence to experience implies the idealist view that there is no indubitable and immediately given existence apart from our subjective self and that the existence of things outside consciousness is only a fabrication of our mind. Still stricter reflection takes us to the further conclusion that even the existence of the self is in turn merely the recurrence of identical, or to be precise, similar experiences, so that we are unable to give any stronger grounds for the existence of our psychological self than for the existence of things!

If we reduce the meaning of existence to unchanging self-identity, it turns out that what corresponds to this definition in immediate experience is neither the thing nor the psychological self but the consciousness of the logical "ought." When we consider consciousnesses which differ temporally to be non-identical, this judgment already presupposes consciousness of an identical, unchanging "ought." Rickert might object that what is identical and unchanging is not the consciousness of an "ought," but the "ought" or value itself, and that as a psychological phenomenon consciousness of an "ought" can have no claim to unchanging self-identity. If existence is unchanging self-identity, then that which most indubitably exists is pure value or principle, not this phenomenal world but an ideal world of a Platonic order. Rickert in fact rejects this peculiar definition of existence as inadequate, and rigidly distinguishes the world of cognition objects as a domain of value from the world of existents.[32]

Reviewing these arguments, we find that the recurrence of identical or similar experiences does not in fact yield the notion of existence, but merely permits these experiences to be unified under a common rubric. Windelband's sharp distinction between "identity," a category of existence, and "sameness," a category of reflection,[33] forbids us to confuse the similarity or sameness of qualities of experience with the identity of things. But what is the significance of Windelband's distinction and on what is it grounded? We can distinguish between the contents of consciousness and the process which synthesizes and unifies them. Sometimes the contents can be freely combined, the same content appearing in different relationships and the same relationship occurring among different contents, but sometimes this is not possible and we stumble instead on a resistance of these contents to free manipulation by the subject's unifying activity. May we not view this resistance as the distinguishing mark of existence? When the connections of the contents of consciousness are already inscribed in these contents and the synthesizing function of consciousness does no more than repeat them, these connections are objective. When the categories of the synthesizing function, which is the basic characteristic of our consciousness, appear as categories uniting contents independent of this function, they are, in Windelband's terms, categories of reality, but if they unite contents which the synthesizing function can combine freely, they are categories of reflection.[34]

This account raises several questions. Is it not in effect a reduction of the fact of existence to the independent self-identity of certain contents of consciousness? And is the distinction between the two kinds of content not the same as that between the content given in immediate perceptual experience and that which is the product of free reflection? Does the distinction between sameness of qualities and identity of things permit a clear line to be drawn between independent contents and those which can be freely combined, or between the unity of immediate perception and the unity of thought? These distinctions lean heavily on the free synthesizing function of the subjective self, yet the content of consciousness is never unified extrinsically by this function, but always by means of its own qualities. When, for example, one compares the qualities of two things and judges them to be identical, this judgment is determined by the qualities of the contents of consciousness themselves and by no other force. First there is an intuition of the identity of the qualities, a consciousness which has self-identity, and the synthesis of judgment is established on this. This integrated view of the matter can correct the above theory which assumes the possibility of freely synthesizing what is given in experience and overlooks the independent synthesizing function which the content itself always possesses.

If we really want combinations of contents of consciousness which cannot be freely manipulated, does not that which has relations of internal necessity, a mathematical principle for example, best exhibit this quality? Is it possible to apply the categories of existence to these, instead of reserving them for combinations according to the forms of time and space? Since the resistance to manipulation here is due to an internal or logical necessity of the content itself rather than to an external combination of things, the categories of existence are not considered applicable, whereas external combinations are considered to be based on what is independent of subjectivity. If we continue to think thus, Windelband's distinction too can mean no more than a distinction between internal and external combinations of contents of consciousness.

6

If one can view the existence of things as combinations of contents of consciousness according to the forms of time and space, what are these external combinations, and are they such that they can always be distinguished from their internal counterparts? How are combinations according to time and space related to consciousness of an "ought"? Clarification of these problems may help us to grasp the relationship between meaning and existence.

Suppose one has spent several days solving a mathematical problem, or completing a painting. From within, each of these activities would appear as the unfolding of a single consciousness, under the sway of a single meaning, but from the outside, seen merely as psychological processes without reference to their meaning, they appear as merely temporal combinations of discrete experiences. However, the latter too can be seen as based on a certain internal meaning. Indeed, we can say that the internal syntheses, in which contents of consciousness are combined in accord with a single meaning, do not differ—essentially from combinations according to space and time. The two differ only in that in the latter the contents of consciousness are viewed under their most universal aspect, that of space and time, which permits each of our continuous, heterogeneous experiences to be viewed as homogeneously as possible. The difference is simply one between homogeneous and heterogeneous, universal and particular. Of course, not every unification of experience under a homogeneous aspect is effected by means of time and space. Universality and spatio-temporal homogeneity cannot be immediately identified. Nor is it easy to find an intrinsic connection between the subjective unification of experience according to universal characteristics and the objective combinations of time and space. Yet without the ability to view experience universally, we could not unify it according to time and space, though the latter unification adds something to the former. There is a necessary internal relationship between the thinking subject's universalization of experience under general concepts and the intuition of the homogeneity of experience according to the forms of space and time. Immediate experience, like Bergson's pure duration, is a single internally unified experience wherein each part has a particular position and significance. Such a unity requires no addition of universal concepts, any more than would the union between the parts of a work of art. Nonetheless, by projecting these continuous, heterogeneous experiences on a homogeneous medium, and by separating each part and considering it as independent, one establishes the universal concept, which, based on their similarity, universalizes them. If this reveals a necessary relationship between the universalizing view and the unifying of experience through a homogeneous medium, it does not however fully clarify the relationship between universality and homogeneity. What is the significance of this unifying of experience through a homogeneous medium, and how is it possible?

Kant saw the forms of intuition as having a source entirely foreign to thought, and though he regarded the unity of pure apperception as the basis of all unifying functions, he still ascribed a separate foundation to intuition.[35] Similarly Rickert argues that to form the concept of number we must add an extraneous, alogical element to a purely logical concept, so that, for example, the logical object "one" and the number "one" are wholly different concepts. He says that we form the concept of number through substituting a homogeneous medium for the heterogeneous medium in which such logical distinctions as that between "one" and "the other" are formed.[36] Is the homogeneous unity which many Kantians see as the basis both of the concept of number and of space and time something which is in no way included within thought?[37] If, as Hegel claims, judgments are acts of internal necessity wherein a universal develops itself, so that even the apparent tautology "A is A" expresses the subsumption of a particular under a universal,[38] and if the mutuality of the distinctions between A and B and between B and A presupposes a universal unifying the two and permitting these distinctions, then at the foundation of thought we must posit an intuition of unity, and this must be the basis of the homogeneous medium also. Kant would reject this attempt to found the continuity of lines and numerical series on the relationship between the universal and the particular, pointing out that the relationship between a certain space and all of space is that of part to whole, not particular to universal, that the principles of geometry cannot be derived from universal concepts, and that while space is intuited as infinite no concept can embrace infinity.[39] Yet, strictly speaking, our comprehension of a single geometric straight line does not depend on a simple, immediate perception, as Kant seems to presuppose, for the straight line of intuition is a mere symbol of that which geometry constructs.

Poincaré's distinction of perceptual space from geometric space and his account of the experiential bases of the homogeneity of space are suggestive in this context:

Suppose that, by an external change α we pass from the totality of impressions A to the totality B, then that this change is corrected by a correlative voluntary movement β so that we are brought back to the totality A.

Suppose now that another external change α′ makes us pass anew from the totality A to the totality B.

Experience teaches us that this change α′ is, like α, susceptible of being corrected by a correlative voluntary movement β′ and that this movement β′ corresponds to the same muscular sensations as the movement β which corrected α.

This fact is usually enunciated by saying that *space is homogeneous and isotropic.*[40]

If we ponder the fact that the homogeneity of geometric space is based on the correspondence of repeated voluntary movements which correct an external change by returning to the original position, might we not be able to say that this is ultimately based on the activity of self-consciousness whereby the self, returning to itself, recognizes itself? There is no reason to anticipate as inevitable the possibility of something that can be called an identical movement, and the possibility of a return to an original position by an identical movement must derive from the requirement of self-identity. Thus, the homogeneity of geometric space is grounded on the activity of self-consciousness. Moreover, if, as I have argued in "Logical Understanding and Mathematical Understanding," the order or infinity of numbers is based on a system reflecting a system within a system, that is, on the self reflecting the self within the self, then the order or infinity of a geometric straight line must have the same foundation. We conclude that there must be a homogeneous medium behind the heterogeneous medium wherein one thought object is distinguished from another, and that it is this homogeneous medium which grounds relations of quantity.

In the course of his critical rehandling of the Kantian categories (quantity, quality, relation, modality) as "the logical foundations of the exact sciences," Natorp makes the following observations:

Quality and quantity . . . present the original process of the synthetic unification of a manifold in general in its two aspects, which belong together inseparably, namely, its outward and inward, or its peripheral and central directions. We recall Kant's distinction of extensive and intensive magnitudes: in the former whole precedes parts, in the latter parts precede whole, that is, he relates the former to an external division, only subsequently unified, and the latter to an inner, rooted unity, which is subsequently divided up in the manifold; accordingly, he associates the former with discreteness, the latter with continuity[41]

19

....Quantity arises when, in the basic logical correlation between unity and the manifold to be united, one focuses on the latter, and clarifies the form in which it must necessarily be conceived.... Differentiation belongs as such to quality; but it posits, on the side of quantity, plurality. These two modes of apprehension—differentiation and plurality—are so rigorously correlative, that every effort to pull them apart is bound to fail. This does not prevent the abstract separation of the purely quantitative determination of plurality as plurality...from the qualitative one of differentiation as differentiation.[42]

Natorp reduces the difference between quantity and quality to one of emphasis, and claims that qualitative relationships, especially that between particular and universal, lie at the basis of quantitative relationships. But if the qualitative relationship is so to speak without content, if it is so extremely universal as to be merely an object of thought, then from the vantage point of concrete unity it appears as a purely *quantitative* relationship, and it is this which provides the basis of the homogeneity of quantitative relationships. Kant claims that space and time are non-conceptual, but if one confines the universal concept of space to what can be derived from the sensation of extension which defines perceptual space, no geometrical principle can be established (for geometric space is quite distinct from intuitive space). To provide a basis for the principles of geometry, we must conceive the universal quality of geometric space in purely logical terms, in the way I have just proposed.

The relationship between universal and particular is usually thought of as merely qualitative, for a particular is that wherein a certain quality has been added to a universal. The traditional syllogism is constructed on this basis. But if we adopt Lotze's view that there must be a system at the basis of all syllogisms,[43] or, as Bosanquet puts it, that the basic condition for deduction lies in a system, in other words, if the universal which is the foundation of deduction must be seen as a system,[44] then the true relationship between universal and particular lies in the internal development of this system. This definition can be verified at the purely qualitative level, for the notion of a particular color subsumed under color in general can be interpreted as the internal development of the experiential content of color in general (of the Husserlian intuited essence of color),[45] and the system of colors arises in this way. (It might be objected that this is to substantialize a concept, but as long as the color universal can be discriminated intuitively, it must be recognized as an independent experiential content. If one calls it an abstract concept, one must for the same reason say that red and green are abstract concepts, and so on indefinitely.)

20

To refer to qualities of things is to unify statically a system of experience, to unite experience about a center, in Natorp's inward direction. Every system of experience, even numerical systems, can, I believe, be unified qualitatively in this way. Universalization is often understood superficially as a method whereby an originally indivisible system of experience is divided quantitatively into independent and static elements which are then recombined. Should we not rather think that all systems of experience are identical in form and different in degree, from systems of contentless thought objects such as numerical systems and the system of time and space based on them, through systems with increasingly richer content, all the way to experiences of pure internal unity, thought of directly by means of their content itself?

Part Two
Properties of
Systems of Experience

A System of Pure Thought

Geibun, V, March 1914

7

As I have argued in the preceding section, the difference between the two perspectives on the existence of things, namely, that in which immediate experience is unified from the outside by the forms of time and space, and that in which it is unified directly from within, must be seen as no more than a difference of degree, and the absolute distinction which the Kantians make between them cannot be maintained. Bearing this in mind, I wish now to present the claim that *existence and value (the "ought") are two inseparable aspects of experience.*

The judgment of the law of identity, "A is A," expresses the fact that we have fixed a certain thought object, and the idea that this thought object is self-identical. It does not consist merely in the thought of something called "A," nor in an elucidation of the content of consciousness "A," nor does it assert the existence of A, but it expresses the logical "ought" on which our faculty of judgment rests. It spells not a repetition of the same consciousness in time, but the emergence of a new consciousness, the consciousness of an "ought" which is of a higher order than what can be apprehended in mere temporal continuity. Yet, paradoxically, the higher consciousness this judgment expresses cannot in fact be embraced in a single moment, but must needs appear in a temporal continuity of consciousness. Dilthey tells us that mental representations are not fixed facts but living impulses possessing a force of their own, which come to be, develop, and then disappear.[46] Judgment, too, is a lived experience belonging to the flux of consciousness. We experience it immediately from within the developmental process of consciousness, a process characterized by internal necessity, in which consciousness realizes its meaning and purpose. Since this process is an activity, indeed the most fundamental activity, judgment, too, is intrinsically active. Thus, in the judgment "A is A," the "A" which we first think of is not static and isolated, but must bring along with it "is A;" it is not simply "A," but it is "as for A." The identical here expressed is neither the subject "A" nor the predicate "A," these being merely the means whereby it manifests itself. "Judgment is the concept in its particularity, as a connexion which is also a distinguishing of its moments. . . . The copula 'is' springs from the nature of the concept, to be self-identical even in its self–externalization."[47] Mutual relationships can sometimes be set up by external causes, but in judgment the relationship is always one of internal necessity, the spontaneous unfolding of a living thing. If we reflect on the implications of the consciousness of a logical "ought," I think we are obliged to see the matter in this way.

In light of this we may re-examine the relationship between logical value, or transcendent meaning, and the internal development of consciousness itself, or the act of judgment. Rickert claims that transcendent meaning depends in no way on an internal development of consciousness; the form this meaning takes in the event we are conscious of it has no relation to the meaning itself. To keep this distinction clear he maintains that we should not speak of an "ought" but use the term "value."[48] Now it is true that if one focuses as a mere psychological happening the act whereby a certain individual thinks a certain meaning at a certain time and place it has no relation to the meaning itself. But this is not the true consciousness of judgment, which can only be brought into view as an internal development of consciousness experienced immediately from within. I maintain, against Rickert, that there is an inseparable relationship between what we could term the phenomenology of judgment and meaning itself. Rather than saying that judgment is an expression of meaning, we should say that it is its activity. It does not determine meaning extrinsically, but is the particularizing act necessary for meaning itself, apart from which meaning cannot be conceived. When we focus the experience of judging as a psychological happening in time, meaning itself seems to transcend it, but judgment is a far more basic fact of consciousness than can be brought under the category of time, consisting, as it does, in the unity of two objects of thought, or rather, in the self-differentiation of a single object. In Rickert's view the transcendent meaning is the signifying intention of a temporal psychological activity, which is teleologically oriented towards this meaning. But the internal development of consciousness cannot be such an amalgam of two instances. It must be still more immediate and fundamental than temporal relationships, for these are in fact grounded on it. The experience of the internal development of consciousness in the activity of judging must transcend time, with the consequence that the consciousness of judgment cannot be confined to the class of psychological acts, but enjoys an immediate and indissociable relationship with meaning itself, and together with it constitutes one concrete logical consciousness. This is surely what Hegel meant by describing judgment as "the concept in its particularity."

We have seen that "A is A" does not elucidate the content of consciousness "A" (for "B is B" expresses the same meaning), nor does it properly express the self-identity of an object, though it can be understood in this way. Purely logically, "A is A" merely indicates and fixes a certain content of consciousness. Now to abstract and fix a content of consciousness, for example "black," is to universalize it, which means to consider the various particular blacks as differentiations of universal black. Whether or not one is conscious of it, without such a subsuming or differentiating activity it is impossible to fix a content of consciousness. Next, if we fix the singular content "this is this," no matter how many times we think "this is this," its meaning remains the same. The phrase might be taken to mean that the "this" itself, the object in question, is to be thought of as objectively single and invariable, but properly it expresses a demand of thinking, an "ought." Even if the "this" is a singular and unrepeatable fact, its assumption by our consciousness as an object of thought gives it universal meaning, as an internal "ought" of our experience of thinking, which is indefinitely repeatable. We must undoubtedly distinguish the universal ("black") from the singular ("this") contents, but they function identically when they provide the basis for the universal validity of the internal "ought" of judgment. This being so, we cannot think the law of self-identity, "A is A," in abstraction from the internal development of consciousness, the lived experience of thinking, and logical meaning is unintelligible except on the basis of an experience—Kant's synthetic unity of apperception, or Natorp's "unity of the manifold"[49]—which is one with that meaning.

27

Admittedly, when we think a certain meaning, as long as we do not reflect on it, we are probably not aware of the experience of thinking as a transcendental synthesis. The mathematician thinking of a mathematical problem is not necessarily aware of the character of the cognition which grounds mathematics (which is why mathematics and physics could develop without waiting for Kant's epistemology). But this does not mean that these two levels of consciousness are essentially independent, for they are inseparable aspects of one experience. When Rickert distinguishes the perception "white" from the act of perceiving white, he neglects to note that the perception is grounded on our experience of perceiving and that apart from this the sensation "white" has no basis. When he insists that truth does not depend on whether human beings think of it or not, he overlooks the fact that we cannot think apart from an immediate experience of thinking, and that a truth which totally transcends thinking can have no meaning for us.

8

If I have correctly characterized the relationship between the experience of thinking and logical meaning or value, we can now go on to ask what is the relationship between the experience of thinking and its objective referent, the existing thing.

Usually it is supposed that the object of thought lies outside and beyond the subjective activity of thinking, and is self-identical and invariable, and that the objectivity or truth of knowledge consists in the subject's conforming to this transcendent object. But does this not imply the arbitrary assumption that subjectivity and objectivity are separate and independent? To be able to think an objective referent independent of the subjectivity of the self, subjectivity itself would first have to be raised beyond individual subjectivity. That is why Kant, arguing that the unity objects require is nothing other than the formal unity of consciousness, sought the objectivity of knowledge in the synthesis of pure apperception: "It is only when we have thus produced synthetic unity in the manifold of intuition that we are in a position to say that we know the object."[50] That subject and object are separate and independent is a species of dogmatism deeply engrained in our minds, but I am inclined to agree with Natorp that their opposition is a relative one:

> When I see a particular color (red, green), at a naive cognitional level the red, or the green, is already the object. . . . At a higher level of

cognition of the object, I view this object as merely subjective . . . realizing that in these expressions of quality (red, green), a rigorous, firm unity and identity, an "object" in the strict sense, was not attained, and in fact ought not to have been sought; whereas a firmer and, consequently, at least relatively objective determination can be attained in a physical apprehension of the said object, for instance as a particular velocity of vibrations of light. But at a still more advanced stage, this formulation, too, may turn out to be imprecise, or at least incomplete and inconclusive; hence arises, once again, the demand for a relatively objective determination, over against which the one heretofore taken as objective now, once again, exhibits a (relatively) subjective complexion. Thus, no attainable "objective" determination can ever claim this objective status except conditionally, and it is apparent that absolutely every determination of an object, without exception, when compared with the higher determination which emerges every time (whether as actually attained, or as a task), can and must once again be regarded as "subjective." Likewise . . . no consciousness can be called subjective in an absolute and exclusive sense, for each in turn represents the objectivization of another, be it at the lowest level. . . . The process of cognition can be understood either as an infinite process of objectivization or as one of subjectivization, depending on how one thinks its path is described. And indeed one can say that the direction of objectivization, that is, of unification toward the center, represents the plus-direction of the path of knowledge (for knowledge as such aims at the unity of consciousness), while the direction toward the manifold (the undetermined, but to be determined, which as requiring central unification is relatively peripheral) is its minus-direction.[51]

If the opposition of subject and object is relative, such statements as "There is something" or "Something exists" no longer refer to things existing beyond and apart from immediate experience, for the world of existence is one department of the world of objects of thought. It is unified according to the forms of time and space and perpetually has to be thought in that way. We have seen that such pure objects of thought as mathematical principles cannot be identified with the existents with which the natural sciences deal. Yet the objectivity of the latter is based on the objectivity of the former; the objectivity of existence is based on the objectivity of an "ought." When we are obliged always to think in the same way of a certain mathematical truth, it can be said that this truth "is so," though no doubt this sense of "is" does not directly denote the "existence" natural science registers in saying that such and such a thing exists; a mathematical truth exists in the elementary sense of having an unchanging self-identity. Rickert's

29

"ought" which precedes existence is another instance of what exists in this broad sense, and as such provides the basis of the unchanging self-identity of natural existents.

The consciousness of an "ought" is the most immediate and concrete experience we have, most immediate because it precedes and founds the distinction between thinker and what is thought, and most concrete because it includes within itself various fundamental relations. This is the Act, or *Tathandlung*, which Fichte tells us "does not and cannot appear among the empirical states of consciousness, but rather lies at the basis of all consciousness and alone makes it possible."[52] If we mentally discriminate the content of consciousness "A" from the concrete experience "A is A," the content "A" can seem self-sufficient and without relation to the consciousness of the "ought" "A is A;" for example, the content "red" and the idea that "red is red" seem to have little to do with one another. But on closer consideration it appears that we cannot think the content "red" as independent and self-identical without presupposing the "ought" which obliges us to conceive it thus, so that it is not by the extrinsic imposition of the principle that things must be self-identical that the judgment "red is red" is arrived at, but it is established by the force of the content of consciousness "red" itself. We commonly contrast particular contents with universal relations which unify them, and we are apt to think of the contents as isolated fragments which of themselves cannot engineer the establishment of any relation; hence the distinction of the matter and form of knowledge. In immediate concrete consciousness, on the contrary, the relation between one moment of consciousness and another (expressed in judgment) is set up by the content itself. (Hence Natorp can say that "quality represents the synthetic unity [the basic cognitional act] not as the unity created by peripheral encompassment [as quantity does], but as central unification, or rather being-one.")[53]

The distinction between relation and quality too is only a difference in the way of viewing a single content of consciousness. We usually think judgments of identity are founded on a relation, but when we view what is related as one thing it is a quality. Thus to think "red" as an independent, unchanging thing and to be conscious of the "ought" whereby "red is red" are two sides of an originally identical experience. In immediate concrete experience there is only the self-development of a certain content of consciousness. When we are conscious of the basis of this content in its static aspect, it is thought of as an existence transcendent to us, and when we are conscious of it in its aspect of dynamic unfolding, we think of it as the consciousness of an "ought," or else merely as a subjective psychological activity. But since there is no objective referent of thought separated from the subjective unifying function, the unchanging self-identity of the object consists precisely in this act of transcendental pure apperception. As concrete total experience, as true reality, there is only the spontaneous act "A is A." Rather than imagine that subject and object are mutually opposed, and that our thought experience arises from their interaction, one should see them as aspects of this single experience, or Act. The distinctions and relationships between matter and spirit could be shown to arise in much the same way as those between subject and object. The possibility of reducing these basic concepts to aspects of a single activity is most effectually shown from the contentless thought experience "A is A" for here the experience and the object of thinking are immediately one in the Act.

When Rickert says the "ought" precedes existence, if we broaden the sense of "existence" beyond temporal and spatial existence to include whatever is identical in itself, then we can surely say that the "ought" and meaning exist. Existence and the "ought" are two aspects of one experience and this unity of the two resides in self-consciousness, as radically understood. Fichte's "If A exists, then A exists"[54] attempts to reduce the necessary relationship between "if" and "then" to the fact of self-consciousness, but we may go further and claim that the fact of self-consciousness is itself rather based on the consciousness of the logical "ought" "A is A." Indeed Fichte himself notes that the judgment "I am I" is coterminous with the fact that "I exist;" the consciousness of the logical "ought" which it expresses founds the fact that I exist.[55] Similarly, "A is A" includes as one of its aspects the fact that A exists, and this fact includes as one of its aspects the "ought" "A is A." The form "A is A" gives rise to the content "A" and vice versa, in contrast to the usual distinctions of form and content. This unity of activity and result, form and content, is the basic characteristic of the Act, which is our most immediate and concrete experience. In its aspect of unity this is the object of thought, and can even be thought of as existence, while, opposed to this, the aspect of the original experience can be thought of as psychological activity. We can comprehend the true relationship of these two aspects intuitively only within the Act, and if one doubts the reality of this Act, it is already by means of it that one doubts.

Geibun, V, August 1914

9

We have seen that what is most immediately and concretely actual for us is the internal development of the contents of consciousness themselves in the judgment of identity, within which various fundamental categories and their relationships are included, and that it is a merely abstract view, narrowly focused on one aspect of reality and excluding the other, which would see this as an "ought" separated from existence or as form separated from content.

When a certain content of consciousness simply "comes to mind" and is captured in an isolated state prior to reflection, when Bergsonian pure duration is cut into separate independent forms by the homogeneous medium, this process can be thought of as the "presentative consciousness"[56] (on the subjective side) of existence in the natural-scientific sense (on the objective side). But subject and object are no more than two different ways of viewing the same content of consciousness, at one time in its aspect of separateness and independence, and at another in its aspect of internal development. (Some distinguish the content of consciousness from the object of thought, but these are different perspectives on an identical thing, and it is meaningless to think of a content of consciousness which cannot become an object of thought of some kind.)

That a certain content of consciousness possesses its own quality means that that consciousness must be self-identical, A must be A, and one's awareness of this self-identity is not extrinsically imposed, but comes about through the force of consciousness itself as its spontaneous development. Hegel calls identity "reflection within itself,"[57] and the necessity of thinking a certain content of consciousness as self-identical denotes a reflexive return of that consciousness within itself, a transition from the form of simultaneous existence to that of pure duration, in Bergson's terms, or from abstract to concrete existence. Or we can say that mere existence, through its association with an "ought," returns to itself. When an abstracted content of consciousness is grasped in its subjective aspect as "presentative consciousness," this is a similar transition to concreteness and "subjective" here denotes consciousness returning to itself. Subjectively "A is A" is consciousness of judgment; objectively it denotes the independent self-existence of an object transcendent to us. Thus the object "A" which has simply come to mind as an object of "presentative consciousness" can itself be seen as subjective, as a phenomenon of the noumenon "A," or an index of the meaning "A." The reason that what was previously viewed as objective must be viewed from this new position as subjective is that it first appeared as individually independent but is now seen as able to maintain its objectivity only within certain relationships. The truly objective now becomes the transcendent reality or meaning which holds these relationships together. (This account also entails that the world of natural science and the world of subjective mental process are the abstracted subjective and objective aspects of a single judging consciousness. The natural scientific world is established by the synthesis of transcendental apperception, which also roots that "objective world" in the original experience thereof; conversely, the "subjective mental process" is produced by abstracting the self-realization of transcendental apperception from that which it concretely synthesizes.)

To say "A is A" is at first merely a matter of our reflecting on "A." But if we shift the focus to "A" itself, it also expresses the consciousness "A" returning to its own foundation, the intuition of a unifying "A" underlying the isolated "A" of our reflection. Thus reflection which links isolated items opens onto intuition of a more profound unity, and what is subjectively the deepening of reflection is objectively the unfolding of a greater reality. Our initial reflective consciousness of "A" is a synthesizing activity of a high order, but from the vantage point of a still higher unity this activity itself can become the object of reflection. Behind this reflective consciousness (which, as Bergson says, appears at the point where the vertical line of pure continuity intersects a horizontal transverse section)[58] a still deeper intuitive consciousness is operating (or is creating itself) in the form of pure continuity. Reflection on "A" is "A"'s returning to its own foundation or, as we can also say, its self-realization. This self-realization is not dependent on another force: "A" itself develops itself and indeed the true "A" consists in this development.

How is it possible that the static self-identity of "A" and the dynamic "ought" of "A is A" can combine in one experience, wherein what is subjectively the activity "A is A" is objectively the self-identity "A," and vice versa? The unity here is not that of two sides of a thing, but has the deeper meaning of an autonomous living unity. In consciousness knowing is immediately one with existence, and subjective activity is one with objective fact. We can find the basis of this unity only in *self-consciousness*, wherein the fact that "I know myself" immediately means that "I am," and vice versa, a self being by definition that which knows itself. This form of self-consciousness underlies all consciousness, and thus "A is A" likewise directly implies that "A is." It is only because we ascribe to the "I" a special existence separate from such thoughts as "A is A" that we miss seeing this. (If it is objected that ordinary consciousness is not established by recognition as self-consciousness is, I would reply that psychological conceptions of re-cognition are of no relevance here; they are mere derivatives of the fundamental re-cognitive activity whereby all consciousness maintains and develops itself, and which is nothing other than self-consciousness, which I see as the basic structure of all consciousness.)

Self-consciousness is never passive. It is an activity of reflection identical with the self itself. It is not a mere registering of the self's identity, leaving the self unchanged, for all reflection brings about some development of the self. Reflection is intuitively given as the stuff of self-consciousness, but it is also the constant activity whereby self-consciousness develops itself. What is grasped as a given, as an "is," turns out immediately to be an "ought," and the "ought" in turn is always immediately an "is." The self-maintenance of the self, whereby "the past is preserved by itself, automatically,"[59] is an "ought" embodied in a living process of development, a veritable creative evolution, the motor force of our personal history. This is not confined to pure self-consciousness without extraneous content, though most easily discerned there, but is the core of all concrete consciousness in its autonomy and spontaneity. Artistic intuition, for instance, though it appear simple and unreflective, is never without an element of reflection, and its obedience to the "ought" of reflective self-development can involve a strenuous and painful effort. There is no advancement of consciousness without reflection, and the dynamic unity of consciousness which reflection maintains is not repetition, but constant development.

10

All consciousness can be seen either as objectively given existence or as subjective activity governed by an "ought," and the unity of these two aspects lies in the structure of self-consciousness, wherein subject and object, "ought" and existence, are immediately one. It seems that no existent can acquire autonomous reality, can be self-caused (causa sui), except through self-apprehension. As Hegel remarks, the Delphic "Know Thyself" has a philosophical as well as a practical upshot.[60] In the natural world, in which the idea exists outside itself,[61] knower and known are separate, for the knower is objectified as the psychological subject, and the true, transcendental subject, Kant's consciousness in general,[62] does not appear. Thus separated, neither subject nor object can enjoy autonomous reality. Again, when perception and sensation are objectified as pre-reflective consciousness unaccompanied by self-consciousness, their concrete reality is missed, for they cannot have autonomous reality without self-apprehension. Empirical consciousness, concretely considered, must include the knower within itself. Or one can say that, at a certain depth, empirical consciousness becomes consciousness of an "ought" and that this in turn is recognized as self-consciousness. Self-consciousness is not a later consciousness copying an earlier content, but is the internal development of empirical consciousness. Thus, independent, self-existent, concrete consciousness, or immediate experience, in both its basic structure and its process of development, takes the form of self-consciousness. Both the perceptual and scientific worlds, as they concretely exist, are structured in this way, so we can say that there is no objective, material world separate from the subjective, spiritual one: our world always has self-consciousness as its core and as the law of its development. We illustrated this by showing how the simple unreflective consciousness "A" develops itself and returns to its foundation in the reflective "ought" expressed in the formula, "A is A," which gives the concrete state of the consciousness "A." One might object that the unreflective consciousness cannot become the reflective one without something being added. This objection is plausible only on an abstract plane. Concretely, we cannot escape seeing that there is an immediate and internal link between the content of immediate intuition and the subsequent reflective apprehension thereof; the unity of these two is far deeper than theories of "pictorial reproduction" can account for, and they must be grasped as aspects of one and the same reality.

"A is A" also distinguishes "A" from "non-A." An activity of differentiation accompanies the act of identification, which can thus be seen as the positing of "non-A."[63] We may further deduce that "A" and "non-A" can be seen as the self-differentiation of an underlying identity, and that their differentiation is not extrinsically established but originates in self-reflection, identity itself including difference, as in Hegel's logic. Only in self-consciousness, where the reflecting self and the self reflected on are identical, is identity clearly and immediately one with difference. Self-consciousness thus provides the concrete foundation of logical self-identity.

The content of consciousness "A" in isolation is objective; when it is opposed to "non-A" it is put in relation with an other and caught up in a developmental flux, wherein it appears as subjective; but it can again be grasped as objective from the standpoint of a still more comprehensive "A." Grasped in its unity the flux of consciousness appears as objective; grasped as developmental advance toward unity it appears as subjective. In all consciousness the totality first arising in an implicit or latent form aspires to-

35

wards its full development; its latent and manifest states are not immediately identical, but their relation can be expressed in the syllogism, which is the form wherein a universal dissolves itself and again reconstitutes itself, "the reconstitution of the concept in the judgment, the unity of concept and judgment,"[64] and which is the form not of subjective thought only, but of all reality: "The Syllogism is the reasonable, and everything is reasonable."[65] If one thinks of the universal founding the syllogism as objective and the process of its development, the syllogism itself, as subjective, one falls into the error of dissociating subject and object and of objectifying subjectivity itself as psychological subjectivity. (Psychology, with its abstract faculties of knowledge, will, and feeling, divorces the process of development from its objective content and cannot apprehend the lived experience of the self-developing whole wherein subject and object are one.) Immediate experience is the spontaneous development of an infinite whole. When it is united from a given center within it, the objective world is established. Subjective activity thus sets up a system separated from the whole, but at the same time this subjective activity is what connects that system with the whole. Take the instance of a single straight line: if we examine this objective system we find that it includes separation and connection within itself and reveals itself to be founded on the structure of self-consciousness. The subjective activity which conceives a finite line fixes one system within the unending progression of self-consciousness, objectifies experience, determines the finite within the infinite: and this can also be grasped as the process whereby a universal is determining itself. The line determined as objective is produced by a subjective self-determination of experience itself. If with Dedekind we see infinity as the projection of a system within a system and number as a series of such infinities, then the activity which projects the system within the system is a subjective process and the finite number is its objective correlate, and one may equate actual infinity, the discovery of the infinite within the finite, with experience.[66]

I hope this extremely rough argument has indicated how the consciousness of the simple law of self-identity includes the oppositions and mutual relationships of subject and object, existence and "ought." If one objects that this law is merely formal, I answer that form and content too are but different perspectives on an identical experience, and that pure logical form is an unmeaning figment if sundered from the unfolding of immediate experience. To distinguish the determined, the object of thought, as the matter or content of self-conscious experience from the process of development which determines it as its form, is an unfounded procedure, for all consciousness can be grasped indifferently as form or matter. Red, for instance, is as much a consciousness of relations (as in the judgment "This is red") as a content of sensation. To say this color awareness is particular in relation to the universality of logical judgment is to forget that this particular system is itself universal in relation to still less universal systems, and that the distinction of universal and particular is thus only a relative one. One cannot divide the concept "red" from the sensation "red" for within the sensation the concept is operative; the particular sensation is a self-determination of the experience of red in general while the conceptual judgment "This is red" is a self-articulation of the sensation.

Transition from a System of Pure Thought to an Experiential System

Geibun, V, Nov. 1914

11

In Sections 5 and 6 we saw that the notion of *existence* could be derived from the unification of immediate experience according to the forms of time and space. We showed that this external unity cannot be distinguished absolutely from the internal unification of experience effected by its *meaning*, and that the various syntheses of the contents of consciousness—whether logical consciousness, or aesthetic consciousness, or that structured according to time and space—differ only in their degree of unification or relative universality. I shall now give a more detailed account of this difference, and then I shall revisit the problematic of Sections 5 and 6 in light of what was worked out in Sections 7 through 10.

We can distinguish several ways in which experience is unified. Experience unified according to the transcendental forms of time and space constitutes *empirical knowledge. Natural scientific knowledge* is a further unification of experience according to the transcendental logical "ought" underlying scientific law. In contrast to this external unity of experience according to the categories of existence, *esthetic intuition* is a unity of pure internal meaning (based on a transcendental esthetic "ought"), as is the *logical consciousness*, found in mathematical knowledge for instance, whose purely formal and a priori character may forbid us to speak of it as unifying *experience* at all. Esthetic intuition and natural scientific law are alike in that they unify experience according to a transcendental "ought," but differ in that the "ought" bears on subjective significance in the first case, and on objective fact in the second. Esthetic intuition, which does not conform strictly to the objective data of experience, but simply disposes of them as its material, is in this respect more closely allied to mathematical knowledge, whose content is also a creation of thought lacking objective existence.

We can further clarify the characteristics and relationships of these modes of unification of experience by examining that which stands over against the "ought"—immediate or pure experience, and the world of fact structured according to time and space. If time and space, as the Marburg philosophers argue, can be adduced logically,[67] then that which stands over against the "ought" within temporal and spatial experience cannot be these basic principles of construction themselves, but only the experiential content which they unify. What does it mean to say that this experiential content opposes the "ought" and is, as it were, irrational? Sometimes experiential content can be divided a priori into its possible forms (a triangle, for instance, must be equilateral, isosceles or scalene), but in other cases this is not possible (one cannot determine a priori how many varieties of color can be distinguished); the former division is necessary, the latter contingent. The relation between two contents is necessary if based on an "ought," accidental if it depends on experience alone; we do not seek a rationale for the particular combination of shape, color, smell, etc. in a given thing. Even in experiential knowledge constructed according to a transcendental "ought" we cannot derive content from form, and we can determine which content of consciousness will combine with which only from "the witness of our senses."[68] It is through such facts as these that we are brought to recognize the irrationality of experiential content in contradistinction to an "ought." This permits a division of the objects of knowledge into three groups: those wholly determined by an "ought" in their content as well as in their form (e.g. the objects of mathematical knowledge), those whose content comes from experience while their unity is conferred by an independent "ought" (e.g. the objects of aesthetic intuition), and those whose content and unity are equally derived from experience (e.g. the objects of natural scientific knowledge).

12

Running through the distinctions made above is the problem of the apparently unbridgeable gap between what comes from an "ought" and what comes from experience. In Sections 7 through 10 we showed how within the consciousness of a pure ought, as in the logical law of self-identity, the oppositions and mutual relationships of existence and "ought," knower and known, form and content are already to be found. That discussion, I recognize, remained incomplete. Let us now carry it a step further, with a view to shedding light on the above problem.

What does it mean to say that certain *material* constitutes knowledge by conforming to a certain *form*, or that we unify the experiential content in accord with an "ought"? The logical "ought" is form at its purest. In comparison with it, the formality of mathematical knowledge is relative. Mathematics cannot be reduced to logic, for in its construction something is added, which must be called its material or content. Logic is more formal and more universal than mathematics and the laws of mathematics are established in conformity to those of logic. This relationship between the two disciplines reveals the opposition of form and content in its most elementary state. Kant located the alogical factor essential to the constitution of mathematics in pure intuition, which he saw as utterly different from the understanding. Poincaré locates it in "the affirmation of the power of the mind which knows itself capable of conceiving the indefinite repetition of the same act when once this act is possible."[69] Rickert, building on Kant, posits the *homogeneous medium* as the basis of mathematics, in contrast to the heterogeneous medium which is the basis of logic. While there is much to be said for these accounts, they leave unanswered the question whether the factor distinguishing mathematics from logic is added to logic purely extrinsically, or whether it has some necessary relationship to logic.

What is the nature of the relationship between the homogeneous and heterogeneous mediums distinguished by Rickert? Natorp provides a clue to the answer, when he claims that quality and quantity (heterogeneous and homogeneous) are the correlative aspects of a single activity of thought. The qualitative self-identity "A is A" implicitly distinguishes "non-A" from "A," and when "A" is contentless, this is the same as distinguishing "A" from "non-A." This reversibility and identification of the one and the other founds the notion of mathematical one, as in $1 = 1$. The unity in mutual opposition of logical objects which arises in this way, according to the reciprocation of thesis and antithesis, corresponds to Rickert's homogeneity and founds the relationship $1 + 1 = 2$.[70] The activity which thus unifies mutually opposing objects in the homogeneous medium can itself be seen, from another viewpoint, as numerical one. This activity which both distinguishes and unites is that of self-consciousness, which reproduces the self within the self and thus founds the possibility of an infinite numerical series. To restate this in terms of form and content: When the content of logical judgment is nil, and we can reciprocate thesis and antithesis, Rickert's homogeneous medium is set up. Thus that which is thought of as standing over against logic in the constitution of mathematics is not given from without. Number is a system of thought objects considered in abstraction from their content. When the development of the contents of consciousness (which constitutes immediate experience) is viewed formally, in abstraction from the contents themselves, both logic and mathematics are founded. The self-identity of a certain content of consciousness, viewed in this formal way, gives rise to the purely logical form "A is A." When this self-identity is reflected on from a more comprehensive standpoint, which transcends "A" to bring "A" and "non-A" into opposition and to reverse this opposition, the mathematical standpoint of the homogeneous medium is established.

Though mathematics is thus more concrete than logic, that which is added to logic in its construction (be it pure intuition or the homogeneous medium) is actually the creative activity whereby logical consciousness develops itself. If, as we argued earlier, the concrete is the foundation of the abstract, and the progress of something from an abstract to a concrete state is thus a return to its foundation, then logic is one aspect of mathematics, and mathematics underlies logic. The common view that logic is the more subjective form[71] can be given a foundation by our earlier thesis that when seen from a higher unity the process towards that unity appears as a subjective form. Here the acquisition of content by subjective form consists in the self-development of that form. The content does not come from outside but from the creative unity which extends behind form as its background. Both logical and mathematical consciousness may be seen either as form or as content, depending on whether they are viewed under their static or their developmental aspect.[72]

Now let us go on to ask, in light of the above: what is the relationship between logic and time and space? These are the forms of thought which unify the material of experience (and are not of course given by means of perception). Mathematics cannot be constituted by these forms, as Kant thought, for the forms of time and space themselves derive from the homogeneous medium which is the basis of mathematics. The homogeneous time and space of mathematics, based on the homogeneous medium, have no real existence, whereas the time and space of physics cannot be reduced

41

to mere products of thought, since they are combined with the content of experience, and compose one system with it. It is of the latter that Natorp is thinking when he claims that time and space cannot be considered to be mere products of thought, as number is, and that they include non-thought elements, Kantian intuition. He points out that the order of time and space, while it coincides in one respect with the order of number, must be distinguished from it insofar as it has a relationship with existence (whereas mathematical judgments are never judgments of existence).[73] What is the added element which distinguishes the order of time and space from that of number? When we speak of the pure forms of time and space as acquiring reality by combining with the content of experience, or of the numerical order as acquiring reality by being determined by experience, we imply an objective independence of experience from thought as the source of this reality. But what does it mean to call experience objective, or to say that thought conforms to or is determined by experience? For Natorp existence is a concept of pure thought, and arises from the qualities of thought objects which demand to be completely determined.[74] Undoubtedly, the existence determined in time and space is a form produced by the demands of thought. Yet the content thus determined does not emerge from within but comes from without. We must now turn our attention to this extrinsic factor, to the irrationality, or objectivity, of experience vis-à-vis thought.

13

We can distinguish immediate experience to which no activity of thought has been added from experience whose content has been constructed according to the categories of thought, experience in the Kantian sense. For Kant, "there are two conditions under which alone the knowledge of an object is possible, first, *intuition*, through which is it given . . . secondly, *concept* through which an object is thought."[75] Objective knowledge is constituted by the "constraint" of intuition. But whence comes this constraining power of intuition, and what is its nature? From the standpoint of critical philosophy, objective reality, or existence, is grounded in the synthesis of transcendental apperception: "The relation to a transcendental object, that is, the objective reality of our empirical knowledge, rests on the transcendental law, that all appearances . . . must stand under those a priori rules of synthetical unity."[76] Our thinking of the content of knowledge is determined by the prior demands of thought, but we cannot say that this content itself is also supplied by them. Not to recognize any rights to the content in the constitution of empirical knowledge is to think of the content as being in itself only an unsynthetized manifold, mere material put at the free disposal of thinking. But even if there were no order among the contents which provide the material of knowledge, one could still not ignore the nature of the material itself as one necessary element in the constitution of knowledge. Even though it can be freely viewed from any aspect, or divided up according to any formula, the fact that it is viewed from a given aspect, appears in a given way, is divided up according to a given method, presents itself in a given formula, must depend on its own nature; this is what Kant means by the constraint of intuition.

For example, in the factual judgment "This thing is black," the subject, "this thing," is established by the formal determination of time and space, and the judgment is constituted in conformity with the categories of the understanding. Nevertheless, both the content of consciousness "black" and its combination with the content "this thing" also depend on "the witness of our senses." It appears that judgment is not constituted merely by the combination of two representations, as formal logic might lead us to imagine, but is always grounded in a prior synthesis and results from the analytic explication of this synthesis.[77] Thus, the judgment "This thing is black" arises from the analysis of a synthetic totality which is first given. The content "black" which is its predicate is not an isolated, fixed concept standing outside the subject, but is the constructive power of immediate experience, which Hegel calls "the dynamic leaping-point of life."[78] It is not through the conformity of content to a form which utterly differs from it that judgment is constituted, as Kantians think, for the judgment "This thing is black" is constituted by the force of the content "black" itself which imposes itself as a Husserlian essence. This Act founds the objectivity of factual judgments, just as a similar Act founds the knowledge of logical form, and it also entitles the content of knowledge to claim its own rights over against form. Immediate experience, that which is truly given, is the self-deployment of the content of consciousness, and it is this Act which concretely constitutes judgment. That is why for Hegel "all things are a judgment,"[79] and the forms of logic are not the forms of subjective understanding alone, but the forms of concrete experience itself.

In pure logical consciousness, whose experiential content is nil, the systems of its development constitute logic and mathematics. As these are grounded in the experience of logical consciousness, so the systems of color and sound are grounded in visual and aural experience. Just as the physicist structures the world as a system of dynamics, so to the painter or musician it appears as a system of color or sound, which may suggest that the senses, usually thought of as passive, have a spontaneous organizing function like that of thought. If thought of abstractly, sense data have no vital power, but in the concrete texture of immediate experience sensory content is a living force, which deploys itself according to an internal a priori in what we call the development of sensation. Only an oblique approach, starting from the conventional premise that sensation arises from the operation of external things on the sense organs, leads us to think of sensation as given from without, or as resulting from the evolution of the sense organs. Just as logic and mathematics are built from the most universal a priori structures of pure thought which exclude all content, the system of sensory knowledge has its basis in certain a priori structures of a sensory order. This a priori, self-developing sensory system is the condition of the possibility of distinguishing qualities by means of the sense organs and of discovering by introspection such structures as the psychologist's system of sensation. We must avoid the illusion of a faculty psychology which thinks of the activity of consciousness apart from its contents, remembering that this activity is always the process whereby a universal is determining itself. If thought is the process whereby the logical a priori determines itself, sensation can be seen as the self-determination of the sensory a priori, the sense organs being only the material expression of this process of self-determination. Thus no phenomenon of consciousness is a mere quantitative aggregate, but each is a "creative synthesis," and the abstract Kantian view of sensation as a manifold of miscellaneous elements is contradicted by its concrete texture.

The Kantian view that empirical knowledge is constituted through a structuring of content by a priori forms presupposes that formal knowledge is autonomously established, while empirical knowledge arises in conformity with it, that logic and mathematics, for example, autonomously set up the laws which natural science must follow. But has the form of empirical knowledge then no intrinsic relation to its content? Can form ever be more than merely one abstract facet of concrete experience? Can there ever be a formal judgment which lacks all content? Even logical knowledge is derived from the nature of objects of thought in general, and mathematical judgment presupposes mathematical objects. Judgment, then, is not constituted by form, but should rather be seen as a development of the content of experience, and as constituted by this content. If the addition of form to content constituted judgment, then such a judgment as "A triangle is a quadrangle" (which pays no respect to the constraint of intuition, but cannot be faulted on grounds of form) would be true, and such tautologies as "A is A" would qualify as the most satisfying instances of formal truth. But it is meaningless to speak of formal truth. Judgment is constituted by content. Its content is its foundation.[80] Of course, this content is not the isolated subject or predicate, but the unity which conjoins the two, or rather the unity existing prior to their distinction. Nor is content something basically different from form, for originally, in what Hegel calls their absolute relationship, form and content are "mutually transformed into one another."[81] A content is *understood* not by some external operation, but in virtue of its own self-deployment, and when it is understood, it turns out to be not mere content, but a kind of "ought," already possessing the power to constitute judgment.

We may conclude that the constraint of intuition in regard to thought does not reside in mere formlessness, but that, rather, the opposition of form and content is the confrontation of the two a priori structures which constitute knowledge: a system of form and a system of experience. The apparent independence of the experiential basis of factual judgment from transcendental a priori forms derives from the fact that experiential content inherently itself constitutes a system. Because it is inherently systematic, and because it also belongs within a larger system which comprises the logical system too, experience can constrain logical form. Let us proceed to an examination of the similarities, differences, and relationships between these systems.

A System of Perceptual Experience

Geibun, VI, Jan. 1915

14

To clarify these relationships, let us examine some systems of experience and their interconnections. Let us take a simple sensory experience, supposing for the moment that such an experience can be found in an independent form. We note first that to feel a certain sensation is to discriminate it from others, a discrimination which may be qualitative or quantitative. But the quantitative distinction of sense data already presupposes the notion of external stimuli, and in immediate experience there are, strictly speaking, only qualitative distinctions, of which quantitative distinctions are one variant.

Next, we meet the important problems raised by the distinction between sensation and the judgment based on it. A sensation cannot be identical with the judgment which compares it with other sensations, and registers the similarities and differences, for pure sensation must be prior to judgment. But does this pre-judgmental pure sensation exist, and how is it to be understood? Stout, following Stumpf, makes the following observations:

> Within limits we can vary a stimulus without producing any perceptible difference in the object cognised. If this variation in the stimulus is

accompanied by variation in the sense-experience, then we have a variation in the sense-experience which makes no difference to cognition ....We may vary the physical conditions on which the pitch of a musical note depends, so as to produce a graduated scale of notes. increasing or decreasing in pitch. Symbolize the series by P1, P2, P3, P4, P5...Pn. Now if the variation of the physical conditions is sufficiently gradual, P1 may be quite indistinguishable from P2, and similarly P2 may be quite indistinguishable from P3, and P3 from P4. None the less P4 will be perceived as distinctly different from P1.

Thus, we have sensations which we do not identify. Stout goes on to show that most of our sensations are of this kind:

> At this moment I am thinking about psychological topics. I receive at the same time a multitude of diversified impressions from surrounding things which certainly enter into my total experience. The room is well lighted, and the sun is shining in at the window. But, with my thoughts otherwise occupied, I do not notice this....The kind and degree of illumination modifies my consciousness, even though I do not take cognizance of it.[82]

This difference between "sensation as cognitive state" and "sensation as cognised object"[83] can also be shown from the fact that differences in the distance of an object are not consciously registered as differences in its size, despite the changes in size of the image projected on the retina. In everyday life we attend only to the pragmatic aspects of sensation, leaving it to the artist to note its subtle gradations and express its inner character. Psychology focuses a level of sensory experience to which cognition has not yet added anything, and further indicates that it is only when this is cognized, and its qualities conceptually expressed, that we acquire sensory knowledge of "red" or "green." Another form of non-cognitive consciousness is James's "psychic fringe," which cannot be brought to explicit awareness, although its existence and its influence on consciousness cannot be denied.[84] (One might attempt to explain this as an aggregate of faint sensations, but if James is right, these sensations must be related to one another and cannot therefore be a mere aggregate; otherwise they lose their character as a subconscious system on the fringe of the psyche.)

This leaves unanswered the philosophical question of the relation between these conscious states and the cognition to which they stand opposed. How is it possible to perceive a non-cognitive pure sensation? When we are aware of the sensation "red" and designate it as "red," it is commonly supposed that the sensation is reproduced in a representation which is a dim copy of it. But can a later consciousness reproduce an earlier one? Bergson does not think so:

> Consciousness cannot go through the same state twice. The circumstances may still be the same, but they will act no longer on the same person, since they will find him at a new moment of his history. Our personality . . . changes without ceasing. By changing, it prevents any state, although superficially identical with another, from ever repeating it in its very depth. That is why our duration is irreversible. We could not live over again a single moment, for we should have to begin by effacing the memory of all that had followed. . . . All our belief in objects, all our operations on the systems science isolates, rest in fact on the idea that time does not bite into them. . . . [But] the universe *endures*. The more we study the nature of time, the more we shall comprehend that duration means invention, the creation of forms, the continual elaboration of the absolutely new.[85]

Accordingly, Bergson would say that conceptual knowledge provides no true grasp of the real, and that pure sensation cannot be cognized in judgment. One might counter that the *formal* unrepeatability of time does not rule out the possibility of repeating its *content*. It might then be objected that any identity of temporally distinct contents of consciousness would be compromised by the influence of the earlier content on the later. To this one might reply that, if influence is understood in terms of mechanical causality, it does not exclude the possibility of the reappearance of identical elements. But Bergson is best answered by calling for a scrutiny of the notions of the passage of time, and the transformation of consciousness, which underlie his arguments. For it is impossible to make these notions intelligible except on the basis of a trans-temporal consciousness (just as for Kant the intuition of time and space is founded on the unity of transcendental apperception). Only a narrow focus on the phenomena of consciousness as events arising temporally and ordered according to the form of time makes it seem that, by virtue of the unrepeatability of time, a sensation which is delimited by a certain moment cannot be repeated in the order of time. What is unrepeatable here is a sensation on which we have already reflected, not the original concrete sensation itself. This very argument that consciousness cannot be repeated presupposes as its foundation the possibility of trans-temporal consciousness. Some may claim that the consciousness of time is itself determined within time, but a little reflection shows that a consciousness of time which does not imply the transcendence of time is self-contradictory.

Rickert represents a second line of argument against the possibility of the cognition of sensation. He correctly insists that cognition is a constructive activity, and that even when we recognize our own consciousness it cannot be said that this cognition is reproduction. But he confines cognition to the realm of value, as recognition of an "ought," and denies that it is a union with the real. Rickert argues that when we are asked "Is the sun shining?" and answer "Yes," this "Yes" affirms neither of the representations "sun" or "shining," nor the relationship between them, but a fourth element already implied in them, the consciousness of judgment. The representations of contents of consciousness must not be confused with judgments made in their regard.[86] There is some validity in this fine distinction of viewpoints, but in concrete terms is there such a thing as a consciousness which does not contain this fourth element at all? Even Rickert himself does not think so. It is in constructing that which stands over against the "ought" that Rickert comes up with the notion of a content of consciousness which is completely devoid of this "ought" element. The logicist epistemology of Rickert (and of the Marburg philosophers) sharply distinguishes between consciousness, seen as determined by time and space, and thought. But what is determined by time and space is not real consciousness, but an abstraction of psychology. Even individual consciousness does not, strictly speaking, exist, for it too is an object of consciousness, just as desks or trees are. The very fact that Rickert considers the act of cognition to be the recognition of an "ought" testifies to the impossibility of confining consciousness to space and time.

15

Having parried these arguments against the cognition of sensation, we must now attempt to discern the true relationship between the two.

I hold that all consciousness contains its objects within itself, and that, since sensation is consciousness, it too must include its objects within itself, just as the consciousness of time, or of judgment, does. (In allowing no place for the immanence of the objects of cognition in consciousness, the Marburg school puts itself in an impossible position.) Sensation is commonly thought of as a particular unique consciousness determined by time, space, and quality, but this is an abstract account of sensation, a construction required by thought, rather than what is concretely given in immediate experience. Sensation as concrete consciousness, or as experience, is the *process*, a kind of *fieri*, whereby a certain concrete universal determines itself.

According to the Marburg school, sensation is *given* as *something to be determined*, and this determination is nothing other than the limit reached by the process of determination at a given moment. A given sensation is determinate in comparison with one that is less so, and still in need of determination when compared with one that is more determined. The determination of sensation resembles a mathematical limit, to which one can come nearer at will but never attain. A given sensation is like a sum added up to a certain point. For Cohen and Natorp, what is given to thought is not imposed from outside as something alien to it *(denkfremd)*, but is required by thought itself. It is given as that which is to be discovered or to be determined, like the x in mathematical problems, or the data *(dedomena)* in Euclid's sense. To be given and to determine are simply two mutually related but opposing aspects of consciousness, like the positive and negative in mathematical number, so that there is nothing either absolutely given or absolutely determined, and even the sensations least determined by thought have already been determined to some degree by the mere fact of being contents of consciousness. Moreover, all knowledge is based on some hypothesis, but the hypothesis cannot be based on a void; the nothingness prior to hypothesis is not *ouch on* but *mē on*, not mere nothingness, but "relative nothingness." It is "what most insistently calls for justification," for thought always and everywhere demands the securing of its foundations, a demand Cohen calls the law of origin. Thus even the cognition of a single sensory quality demands to be founded in something universal, and this cannot be the transcendent meaning of Rickert or Husserl, but must be immanent in experience. It must be related to what it founds as dx is to x in mathematics: as dx is the basis of a finite x, so a certain sensory characteristic is a determination of a continuous whole.[87]

We may now give an account of what happens in the cognition of a present sensation. When one cognizes the consciousness of a moment earlier, the earlier and the later consciousness are not independent actions succeeding each other merely chronologically, nor does the later reproduce the earlier, for that is logically impossible. If however we think of the given sensation in the way suggested above, then what grounds the later cognition is also what grounds the earlier sensation. While it would be nonsense to say that the earlier consciousness is established by the later one, it can be said that cognition transcends time, and goes to the foundation of consciousness. The judgment "A is A," for example, does not express a cognition of the first A by the second, but a consciousness of the "ought" which founds their identity. Likewise, to cognize the quality of a certain sensation is to unify it from a deeper position, and to view it as the self-determination of a concrete universal. The consciousness of cognition is not different in kind from that of sensation. Sensory consciousness is a particular instance of cognitive consciousness, and the latter, though it seems chronologically later, is prior to sensory consciousness in the realm of value. On the common assumption that the order of time is the only form of reality this statement is nonsense, yet the spatiotemporal order, no less than that of sensory quality, must have as its ground the unity of internal quality.[88] That our experience develops in conformity with time is a secondary consideration, since the most basic form of the development of experience is the deployment of internal meaning. Our various experiences develop from their respective centers, which in turn originate from still more fundamental centers. If we grasp this basic unity we can transcend time, and take our stand in an eternal now, from whence we can see that sensation and cognition have the same foundation, or rather that cognition is at the foundation of sensation. The ability to go back in memory and compare a present sensation with a past one may also be grounded on this.

All this can be greatly clarified by a study of Cohen's profound reflections on Kant's "principle of the anticipations of perception." Since, for Cohen, what is given to thought is what thought intrinsically demands, sensation is not yet the real, but merely the index thereof, and cannot of itself be an object for thought; it is "one form of the relationship of consciousness to its content, with a view to the determination of this content as object."[89] In consciousness of what Kant calls "the unity of the manifold," the objectification of sensation, and the securing of its objective reality, necessarily take place according to the "principle of intensive quantity." In other words, it is by considering sensation as intensive quantity that we are able to move toward the "real things" which are the objects of physics. Kant did not sufficiently clarify the idea of intensive quantity, and it is to Cohen's great credit that he disentangled it from extensive quantity, clarified its significance, and recognized its strategic epistemological function. In extensive quantity one proceeds from part to whole, from *unity* to *plurality* and to its unification as *allness*, whereas in intensive quantity one proceeds from whole to part, and its unity is not the unity of a plurality, but the determination of a unitary whole according to the category of *limitation*. Intensive quantity is the quantity of "continuous and uniform production,"[90] that is, it is nothing other than "differential quantity." When thought raises

51

sensation to the level of objectivity, it transforms it into an extensive quantity, according to Kant's "principle of the axioms of intuition."[91] But extensive quantity is formed by the comparison of similar contents, and such a "comparison quantity" requires as its fundament the thing which is the matter of the comparison.[92] The extension of a perceived red object must be based on the extension of a *qualitative* red. It is by being anchored in this qualitative fundament underlying perception that our knowledge is knowledge of reality.

The forms of intuition and understanding do not suffice to produce empirical knowledge, but merely indicate its possibility; even space, if not seen as the conditioning of phenomena, is "a mere figment of the brain."[93] Empirical knowledge is constituted only when these forms combine with empirical content, with the sensation which provides perception with its fundament. But where does this reality of sensation come from? If we trace it to the things themselves of the external world, we destroy the transcendental method. If it is to enter a system of empirical knowledge as that which has been required by thought and as capable of being thought, and as that which must be recognized as the real which founds experience, then we must think of it as a qualitative unity, or as intensive quantity. If sensation were something whose qualities were purely diverse and held together by no continuity whatever, then it would not be qualified to function within a system of empirical knowledge as the guarantor of its reality, and would be unintelligible even as a mere psychological quality. The sensation of red, for example, has no claim to independence or objectivity unless it is the determination of a qualitative unity, and the sensation of heaviness can be the object of physics as a real thing only if it is the determination of the intensive quantity called gravity. This qualitative unity must be thought of precisely as intensive quantity, which, proceeding from whole to part, is the determination of a whole, and is thus not an aggregate but a continuum. When Kant says that the real has a degree, the degree in question must be intensive. Continuity, "the property of magnitudes by which no part of them is the smallest possible,"[94] is the mark of the qualitative, and the idea that the qualitative can be discontinuous is due to a confusion of intensive with extensive quantity. Thus it is only as qualitative unity, or intensive quantity, that sensation is qualified to be an object of cognition, and an instance of the real within the system of experience. Qualitative unity, intensive quality, and continuity are one. This unity is precisely reality, and it is by means of it that empirical knowledge secures its objective foundation. As Cohen has insisted, the unity of transcendental subjectivity on which empirical knowledge depends is not that of understanding nor that of intuition alone, but must be a unity which has combined form and content, the unity envisaged by the synthetic principles.

Geibun, VI, March 1915

16

Sensation, since it is not the real, but only one form of the relationship between consciousness and its content, is similar in this respect to intuition and to thinking. It becomes objective by our thinking it as the determination of a continuous unity, and it is then qualified to function as an element of knowledge within the system of experience. Cohen distinguishes sensation as mere awareness *(Bewusstheit)* from the knowledge of its objective reality as consciousness in the proper sense *(Bewusstsein)*.[95] He sees the difference between the two as one of degree in the development of experience, claiming that in the actual contents of experience there is nothing either purely subjective or purely objective. Or rather, consciousness as index and consciousness as the real are not different consciousnesses at all, but simply two aspects of a single concrete consciousness.

Consciousness is an unending development, in which the answer a certain problem elicits becomes itself a problem seeking further answers. When a certain problem has been solved on the basis of a certain hypothesis, we have to ask on what this hypothesis itself is based, and to justify it on the basis of another more fundamental hypothesis. So thought advances indefinitely from hypothesis to hypothesis towards its foundation. Cohen, inspired by Leibniz's "principle of continuity," sees this infinite advance of thought as constituted by a law of continuity, the "law of operations" whereby thought operates from itself: "The adventurous route to the discovery of the origin requires a compass. The concept of continuity provides this." "In virtue of continuity, all the elements of thought, insofar as they may qualify as elements of knowledge, are generated from the origin."[96] Thought, says Cohen, is "the unity of a plurality," which does not suppress that plurality, but sustains it. This two-faceted unity is precisely that of judgment, and it can be considered both as the unity of knowledge and the unity of objects.[97] But we focus this unity only by fixing one moment in the ongoing process wherein this unity advances indefinitely according to the law of continuity.

While admitting the profundity of Cohen's interpretation of sensation from the Kantian standpoint, I feel that there are still some flaws in his basic position, notably in his claim that in thinking "the production is itself the product."[98] He is unclear on the opposition and relationship of subject and object, and his account of the relationship between sensation and its object also seems to me to be incomplete. He says that thought is creative, that its productivity is that-which-is-produced, and that its unity is precisely its multiplicity, but how does the one produce the many, and how can productivity be directly identified with the produced? If we are not allowed to say that thought, which is "the goal and object of its own activity,"[99] is acted upon from without, how can we explain its inherent creativity?

Here is where the ideas developed in Sections 9 and 10 may come to our aid. There we saw that the true structure of the creative activity of thinking is the form of self-consciousness, in which reflection is both a fact and an activity of creative development, fact creating development and development in turn becoming fact, and in which the self maintains itself by reflecting on and developing itself. In self-consciousness, therefore, productivity is directly that which-is-produced, and vice versa; the "I" which is one is the "I" which is disrupted in reflection, and vice versa. Cohen, who keeps as close to Kant as he can, regards Fichte's self-consciousness as metaphysical, and from the standpoint of the critical philosophy sees it as a reversion to the Cartesian position.[100] If, proceeding from the necessity of self-consciousness, one insisted on the transcendent existence of the self (*cogito ergo sum*), this might indeed be a regression to a dogmatist position. But as I have shown, existence and the "ought" are the two sides of one Act, and self-consciousness, properly understood, is simply that which reveals this concrete reality.

While I do not wish to assume the role of an apologist for Fichte, I should like to note that his account of self-consciousness also provides a foundation for the logicist approach to meaning. Rickert's stress on the priority of meaning to existence is a valuable corrective to dogmatic realism. But by limiting "existence" to the sense it has for such realism, the merely secondary existence with which natural science deals, rather than classing this existence as a derivative from "existence" in the higher sense of the autonomous self-identity of meaning, he confines thought to a world of value, and makes it impossible to understand how there can be a cognition of the real, or how the Platonic Ideas can appear at the level of the actual. The unchanging self-identity which constitutes the existence of a thing is founded in the self-identity of meaning, as are the most immediate phenomena of our consciousness. When Fichte says that "the existence of the self is nothing more than the fact that you yourself are posited by yourself"[101] and that "*self* and *self-reverting act* are perfectly identical concepts,"[102] does he not already found existence in meaning in a way that solves Rickert's dilemma?

Rickert might say that the fact of the trans-temporal identity of the ego has no relation whatever to the acts which bring it to consciousness, and that, since meaning is prior to existence, the identity of meaning is in turn a much more basic fact than the existence of an unchanging self. But in the phenomenon of consciousness the immanence of meaning is its essence. There is no consciousness which does not possess meaning in some sense, and the unity and identity of meaning are necessary conditions of the constitution of consciousness. Rickert might argue that no matter how many times we think of an identical meaning, the meaning itself is unaffected, for there is no relationship between the identity of meaning and psychological occurrences which belong to time and space. But as one piece of evidence that the relationship between a content of consciousness and the fact of our being conscious of it is not a purely extrinsic one (like that between a triangle and the representation of it), I should like to quote the following remarks on the consciousness of time: "The 'now' in which consciousness experiences a content as present must belong both to phenomenal and objective time. . . Time is a form of consciousness, since it is a form of the content and vice versa; it is the form of givenness itself."[103] The consciousness of time reveals the same union of meaning, act, and existence as that implied by the fact that in self-consciousness the ego is conscious of the ego in the ego.

SECTIONS 17 TO 20
Problems of Consciousness

17

A study of the relationship between conscious and unconscious may help us to deal with these issues in a more satisfactory way. If consciousness were only a surface accompaniment of stimuli to the cerebral cortex, this relationship could be grasped in materialist terms as one between a material substrate and its epiphenomenon.[104] From an epistemological point of view that would be unacceptable. Yet if we claim that consciousness is distinct from matter, and cannot be thought to arise from it, we may be led to the view of Maupertius and Diderot, that there is an elemental consciousness even in the atom and that our consciousness evolves from this (or from the "tiny perceptions" of the Leibnizian monads).[105] But to grasp conscious and unconscious as stages in such an evolution involves a purely hypothetical construction of the unconscious, and the apparent contradiction of a conscious unconscious.

Let us approach this issue in light of our remarks on finite and infinite towards the end of Section 10. In antiquity a point was defined as the end of a line, but

> following a suggestion of Kepler, the point in a tangent has come to be determined as the productive point of a curve. The concept of direction pertains to this productive significance....This is incompatible with the ancient definition according to which the point is the *limit* of

the line. Now the point has another, positive significance. It is no longer only the end, but rather the beginning of the line. The curve is produced from the point which it shares with the tangent.[106]

The finite segment of a curve is the integral whole of tangent points, arising from what is infinitely small, as x from dx. May we not also think of the unconscious underlying finite consciousness as similar to dx in relation to x?

When we are conscious of a geometrical curve, the particular curve of which we are conscious is a determination of an infinite series; it is our determination of an infinite whole, or rather, our being conscious is the self-determination of this infinite whole. Psychologists may dismiss this as a speculative fantasy. Apart from the school which deals with "elementary thought processes" no psychologists are prepared to admit a consciousness of a geometrical curve or straight line apart from sensation, or to add such an element to their table of psychological sensations. Rather they associate the geometrical concepts with perceptions of movement, and attempt to reduce these perceptions to elements which can be classified in the table of sensations, such as pressure sensation, muscular sensation, or articular sensation, which they see as the exclusive constituents of all concrete consciousness.[107] But does not sensation, too, result from the determination of a certain color or sound on the basis of a qualitative unity? Is not consciousness of a given sensation always the self-determination of a certain whole? Does not the consciousness of a sensation thus reveal the same structure as we would claim for the consciousness of a geometrical curve or straight line?

To pursue this argument, it is necessary to examine the theory that consciousness is a combination of "elementary mental processes" (comprising "pure sensations" and "simple feelings").[108] Wundt and his colleagues do not go so far as to identify directly concrete consciousness with the elemental mental processes. These are rather the result of a scientific analysis, and it is only when combined that they constitute concrete consciousness, whose simplest forms are the "mental formations," composite components of immediate experience.[109] This notion that mental processes which are not themselves conscious combine to give rise to consciousness is a highly problematic one.

Is this analysis of consciousness into its elements a *material* analysis or a merely *conceptual* one? In conceptual analysis we are free to choose the standpoint from which to proceed, and consequently it is not necessary that the results of this analysis, the elements, should actually exist. Bracketing the reality of the thing analyzed, we view it merely under the aspect of meaning and analyze it into elements of meaning. If I analyze conceptually the books on my desk, classifying them according to color, shape, or size, it is clear that the elements thus arrived at need not have physical reality, nor even mental reality; it suffices that they can be *thought of* as distinct concepts. In conceptual analysis there is no difference between analyzing a real thing and analyzing an ideal object, such as a triangle, into its even more ideal elements. If the psychologist's analysis of consciousness is of this kind, then the phenomena of consciousness are not intrinsically affected by it, and the claim that consciousness arises from a combination of elements turns out to have a much weaker sense than a scientist's claim that a certain substance can be analyzed into its elements. Indeed this conceptual analysis would be incompatible with the psychologists' dedication to scientific method. (Some scientists now see atoms and molecules as explanatory hypotheses rather than as independently real, but it remains true that the only form of analysis accepted as scientific is one that reduces a phenomenon to the quantitative relationship of simpler elements.) In any case it is hard to see what light such a conceptual analysis can shed on the origin of consciousness and its relationship to unconsciousness.

However, if the analysis is to be taken as a material one, it remains unclear how consciousness can arise from a combination of elementary mental processes. There are of course instances in the world of natural science of a new phenomenon arising from a combination of elements. But when, say, hydrogen and oxygen combine to produce water, a phenomenon quite different from them, this difference is only an impression of our senses. A strictly scientific viewpoint (even if not fully attained as yet) would ideally reduce everything to quantitative terms, such as the number and position of electrons, for when Planck says that the goal of physics is "liberation from anthropomorphism"[110] it is just such a reduction of the heterogeneous to quantitative, homogeneous relationships that he has in mind, and the fact that the homogeneous is the basis of science spells the elimination of the qualitative. Thus the emergence of a new quality from a combination of elements is a phenomenon apprehended by our consciousness but not recognized by science, and a psychological analysis presupposing such an emergence goes against the trend of scientific method.

Geibun, VI, June 1915

18

All the phenomena of consciousness, according to Wundt, are complex or composite, and an elementary mental process can be arrived at only by analysis and abstraction. Suppose that the elementary process a is combined with b, c, and d, in one case, and in another with b', c', and d', we arrive at the idea of a as one element by abstracting it from these combinations.[111] Have these elementary processes any reality at all, and if they have, in what sense do they have it? If they have none, where shall we seek the reality of consciousness? However much the psychologists may wish to distinguish their methods from physical analysis, they are unlikely to accept that their analysis is merely conceptual. They would insist that mental phenomena are real, and that the elements which compose them must be real too, in a sense different from conceptual constructs such as points and lines.

We can interpret the analysis of consciousness, or the relationship between consciousness and its elements, in different ways. For instance, one could proceed on the assumption that the elementary processes are real, though not experienced in their independent state in immediate introspection, and one could take them to be the components of concrete, temporally constituted experience, components which are combined, either simultaneously or successively, to produce our consciousness. While one cannot be conscious of a pure sensation, say of red or blue, as an independent reality, one can regard it as a component of concrete consciousness having a reality comparable to that of molecules in material phenomena. Or again one might adopt the view of many contemporary psychologists that phenomena of consciousness are unitary events possessing their own individuality, and one might say that what is real is the totality of each such event. But in this case, if we wish to see the elementary processes as more than the abstract product of intellectual analysis, we must define their reality in another way, for we can no longer regard them as "atoms" of concrete consciousness.

In seeking this new definition of their reality, we may be helped by the realization that, as Wundt shows, all phenomena of consciousness are qualitative. He sees the elementary processes as having the attributes of quality and intensity. Differences in "intensity" are qualitative and not amenable to scientific quantification (and even the additional attributes of extension and duration which Titchener confers on the elements are not to be identified with the space and time which the physicist measures; the qualitative duration of phenomena of consciousness has nothing to do with the quantitative measurement of time).[112] Moreover, the two kinds of elementary process, pure sensation and simple feeling, are not independent of one another, but are the constituents of a single experience, and thus even the simplest mental phenomena contain both, with their attributes of quality and intensity.

It must further be noted that the phenomena of consciousness can be seen both as physical and as psychological. While the perception of the colors red and blue and of their distinction is a matter of immediate experience, a mental phenomenon, it can also be apprehended in physical terms as vibrations of light. In what does this difference of perspective consist? If the distinctive feature of mental phenomena is that they can be immediately experienced, can we not say, adopting the standpoint of naive realism, that physical phenomena, too, can be immediately experienced? However sophisticated the physical sciences become, we shall undoubtedly never quite be able to leave behind us this naive conviction that red and blue things really exist. But the psychologist's insistence that mental phenomena are facts of immediate experience is based on a no less naive belief that the objects of consciousness exist within consciousness, and on a forgetfulness of the distinction between "the thing of which we are aware" and "the actual awareness itself" or "the mental act of apprehending the thing" (Russell). Since the thing of which we are conscious does not exist within consciousness, the possibility of viewing sensory qualities as psychological does not undermine the validity of also viewing them as physical. The fact of red or blue is in itself neither psychological nor physical.

The ability to distinguish sounds or colors qualitatively is a given of immediate experience. But for a particular red to be distinguished from other particular reds, there must be a comprehensive totality at their base; before distinction there must be synthesis, and before the distinction of particular qualities the consciousness of a universal must be operating. The consciousness of the universal is immediate, and simultaneous with the consciousness of the particular qualities. Qualitative distinctions and quantitative distinctions, knowledge of the subjective world and knowledge of the objective world, are equally necessary and equally immediate constituents of experience. To think that only psychological phenomena are immediate is the result of a deduction which proceeds from the distinction of the worlds of mind and matter as independent realities and sees sensation as more basic than thought. Immediate experience, which is the self-development of the content of consciousness itself, can be interpreted physically, in its aspect of unity, or psychologically, in its aspect of development. Thus the single experience of the color red enfolds: 1. the quality, or what Husserl might call the essence, of red; 2. the objectively existing red thing which possesses this quality; 3. the sensation of red; 4. the act which is aware of this sensation (the act of sensing). When the logicists distinguish content and act, pointing out that the perception "red" is not red, what they call a psychological act is nothing more than the developmental aspect abstracted from its experiential content. But as Natorp observes, "I do not hear my hearing, I hear only the tone; and it is I who hear it, that is, it is there for me, it is a component part of my (present, taken into view for now) consciousness, and therewith is ordered into the concrete unity of this my experience."[113] To hear a sound means that the sound belongs to the unity of our experience. The psychological act is only that function whereby partial content is integrated into the unity of the whole. In ordinary psychology the center of sensation and movement is the ego, which from a central position unifies experiential content. The experiential content belonging to this center is thought of as produced by the consciousness of the individual, which is imagined to create the quality "red" when a certain vibration of the ether is felt by the eyes. But in reality "red" itself is neither physical nor psychological, and our consciousness of it should not be thought of as adding to or changing a prior physical datum. It is not the case that a new quality arises by means of consciousness; the very idea of a certain person's being conscious of something is one that is added after the event.

19

In his book on modern painting, Max Raphael claims that the straight line of art is not that of mathematics, but is one that expresses in every point "a merging of the straight line and the curve," and embodies "a tension of the dimensions." He argues that the artistic use of color can be described in similar terms.[114] Another writer observes:

> In a chapter of his *Theory of Colors*, Goethe speaks of a "sensual-cum-moral impact of colors." What he understands by this is that the impression of a colored thing is not exhausted in sense experience, but rather each color calls forth in addition a special affective mood. This secondary impression is strongest when one fills the eye entirely with a single color, for instance by looking through colored glass....These impressions may be called mood-differentials, from which the mood builds itself up....While sensation appears as a foreign body to the subject, as given to him "from the outside," these mood-elements come forward as something belonging to one, and *they lie near the sphere of*

activity. . . . Their close connection with activity is seen most clearly in certain particularities, which again can best be observed in colors: blue *requires* orange as a complement, purple requires green, and so on. This . . . can only mean that in the mood-impression of a color something like an energy or a striving is involved, and that this striving attains its *fulfillment* through the impression of another specified color.[115]

Conrad Fiedler, who sees the artist's activity as the development of the visual faculty and the work of art as the expression of this development, claims that one absorbed in seeing immediately senses the developmental possibilities of visual perception, and this leads naturally to the activity of expression.[116] Matisse, according to Max Raphael, would look at the same object for weeks or months until it compelled him to create it.

I propose that these statements about artistic intuition reveal the veritable character of all experience. We say that science is ratiocinative and art intuitive, but science is also founded on a certain creative a priori element, and it is pure to the degree that the scientist becomes one with this element, becomes wholly absorbed in thought as the artist is wholly absorbed in visual perception. What corresponds to the artist's visual object in this case is the Idea, in Plato's sense, or the hypothesis, "that which is pure," which the Marburg philosophers identify as the foundation of science.[117] But if something like artistic intuition underlies science, it is also true that artistic intuition itself is not necessarily limited to that which emerges at one stroke, and many works of art, like Albrecht Dürer's "Gate of Triumph," have been created like a mosaic through the efforts of voluntary thought (Hirt). We are dealing then with a qualitative difference within a single, transcendental, creative a priori. The pattern here discerned holds true, I believe, of all experience and allows us to glimpse the creative system in which reality itself consists. Every reality, we surmise, is a constituent of a system organized by some a priori, and the degree of purity of the system determines the degree to which that reality imposes itself as indubitable. In this sense, both the world created by the artist and that explored by the scientist have an equal right to be considered real.

We have seen that for Cohen the *infinitesimal* is the basis of reality and sensation acquires reality only when it takes the form of *intensive quantity*. But these forms of continuity can ultimately be ascribed only to such a creative system as we have described, which develops dynamically and embraces contradictions within itself. What actually is continuity? Russell explains continuous motion as follows:

In a continuous motion, then, we shall say that at any given instant the moving body occupies a certain position, and at other instants it occupies other positions; the interval between any two instants and between any two positions is always finite, but the continuity of the motion is shown in the fact that, however near together we take the two positions and the two instants, there are an infinite number of positions still nearer together, which are occupied at instants that are also still nearer together.[118]

This is to interpret continuity as the infinite possibility of analysis, or as an ideal demand charging thought with an infinite task of analysis. But this infinite possibility of analysis presupposes a creative system capable of autonomous development from within, and only such an autonomously active entity can be continuous in the above sense. Thus it was that Spinoza's *causa sui* was able to develop into Leibniz's monads, whereas finite things, which are not self-sufficient and cannot be thought of except as connected with other things, have no such capacity for such vital (infinite) development.

Contrasting ancient science with that inaugurated by Kepler and Galileo, Bergson remarks: "ancient science thinks it knows its object sufficiently when it has noted of it some privileged moments, whereas modern science considers the object at any moment whatever."[119] Galileo, in other words, studies movement itself. Thus, a force is only extrinsically characterized as finite and discontinuous; as defined in modern science, force has its own autonomous vitality, is continually active, and possesses acceleration. In contrast to the idea that concrete, immediate experience must be finite and discontinuous, modern science suggests that the immediately real is an infinite continuum. If we try to grasp immediate experience as a finite and discontinuous system we end up with something very like a dream, in whose reality we cannot believe. The experience which we know as real has been constructed according to categories, and the sciences are constructed from a vantage point permitted by this categorical order. To adopt this vantage point is not to depart from the given, as Kantians think, but to come nearer to the real, like Galileo.

I have argued that to consider the real to be the infinitesimal presupposes a self-generating, self-developing system. Conversely, every developmental progression from within is differential, and must be a continuum in the strict sense of mathematics and physics. Scientific reality is constituted from one vantage point within the self-developing system of experience, and artistic reality is constituted from another.[120]

20

When Cohen says that the infinitesimal, or continuity, expresses reality, he comes close to the insight that the most immediate, concrete reality for us is a system of self-generating, self-developing experience. But if we think of continuity negatively and extrinsically, as Russell does in defining continuous motion as what can be subjected to infinite analysis, the continuum thus sighted is still dependent and lifeless, not yet autonomous and free reality. Only that whose continuity is internal, that which has within itself the motive of its development, in other words, only that which knows itself and is self-conscious, can deserve the name of autonomous, free reality. Anything that can be an object, or appear as an object, is still divisible. The reflecting self alone is that unity which is indivisible in itself and able to operate infinite division.

We think of the existence of the material world as independent not only of our knowledge or ignorance of it, but even of whether or not we exist. But in reality this world does not exist apart from the subject, for it is constituted by the unity of Kant's pure ego. Conversely, even individual consciousness has an objective world corresponding to it, at least in the sense of Brentano's claim that all consciousness necessarily contains an immanent object.[121] The objective natural world is simply the further development of this objective world of individual consciousness, or, as Poincaré says of the relationship between a mathematical continuum and a physical one, the former is the rationalization of the latter.[122] The mathematical physical world of the physicist is one in which the objects of the experiential world have been developed. The progress from the experiential world to the mathematical physical one is generally thought of as a departure from immediate experience, but from another angle could it not be seen as the deepening or the developing of this experience?

Even the experiential world is never something merely given, but is more an incomplete world grasped in a limited perspective. With our present visual powers, for instance, we can distinguish shades of color only up to a certain point; yet the experience of the reality of a color must intrinsically contain a capacity for infinite development, or in other words must be differential. That is why when a painter is absorbed in a visual perception he finds curves within straight lines, and a tendency to black and white in all colors. The sensation of a determined color is an abstract concept. It might be objected that an infinitesimal quantity of a color-stimulus is not that color at all, and that there is also a maximum limit to the development of a color-sensation. Nonetheless, I maintain that the experience of the immediate reality of a color is effected only by the operancy of infinitesimal quantities of that color. For quality can maintain and develop itself only on the basis of quantity. Independent concrete experience arises from the interplay of quantity and quality. Living things are those in which quantity has become a moment of quality. It is this differential development of experience which makes possible the "anticipation" of new perceptions.

Poincaré, distinguishing between law and principle, tells us that the differential equations whereby Fresnel expressed the relationship among optical phenomena will always be correct, irrespective of the truth of the particular theory they were meant to prove.[123] The mathematical physical world (which is a rationalization of the experiential world) is the one mapped in such perpetually valid differential relationships. When, for example, physicists analyze movement in terms of vectors, they are thinking of movement as a continuum at each infinitesimal moment; unless they could do so, Zeno's arguments against the possibility of movement would be irrefutable.

When we say that experience is discontinuous, we already presuppose the continuity of the self; without consciousness of continuity we could not conceive discontinuity. We imagine that we can be conscious of the position of a moving thing at each discontinuous moment of its movement, but that we can only think the unity of these moments as a continuum, not actually perceive it. Yet the fact that we know these moments are not discontinuous already presupposes consciousness of a continuum. The mathematical axiom of continuity is intelligible only on the supposition that continuity is given intuitively. As Bergson has shown, if we were not conscious of movement immediately from within, we could not recognize movement at all.[124] Discontinuous experience is an abstraction; real experience is always continuous because always containing within itself a unifying ideal.

I have claimed that the natural world is elaborated from the object world of individual consciousness. Individual consciousness cannot be absolutely distinguished from Kant's pure apperception. A consideration of "subjectivity" may make this clearer. In medieval times *subjectum* meant substratum or substance (*hypokeimenon*), while "object" meant that which has been objectified in consciousness, the present-day "representation." In modern times however, objectivity denotes the real while subjectivity is thought of as phenomenal or illusory (though the logicists, following Bolzano,[125] separate objectivity from reality altogether and locate it in purely epistemological objects, unchanging meaning or value, which then transcend "subjective" activity all the more). One reason for this etymological shift may be that formerly the "holder" of phenomena was thought of as real, whereas now it is the unchanging relationship among phenomena which is considered real. Yet some modern thinkers have distinguished between the act and the content of consciousness, and think of the content as unreal and subjective and the act as real and objective, while the subject of the conscious acts is also considered to be objective.[126] Thus, when Twardowski distinguishes act, content, and object, he sees only the content as subjective, while ascribing reality to the act and locating the object in Rickert's world of meaning.[127] When, at the beginning of modern philosophy, Galileo distinguished between primary and secondary qualities, he implied that subject and object were causally correlated as phenomenon and noumenon, so that the object which had been the content of the subject in medieval philosophy now became an independent reality including even the subject. In opposition to this one might attempt to maintain consistently the Berkeleyan *esse est percipi* with the result, as in contemporary monism, that the material world is seen as an unchangeable combination of concepts, and object and subject are opposed as the unity and disunity of the contents of consciousness.

Kant, seeking to overcome relativism from the standpoint of idealism, located the objectivity of knowledge in the a priori synthesis of cognition, and thus contrasted subjectivity and objectivity as the unity of the pure transcendental subject and the unity of an individual subject delimited by time and space. Contemporary Kantians have developed this idea fully, presenting objectivity as universal validity based on a transcendental "ought." But from another angle whatever unifies experience from some standpoint, albeit a trans-individual one, represents a subjective and abstract aspect of the totality of concrete experience. The "ought" may have a fundamental status in regard to existence delimited by time and space, but there is a wider totality of experience, which, though it lies beyond the ken of our cognition, we must think of as true objective reality, and within this totality the opposition of subject and object may be that between the totality of experience and a part of it, between concrete and abstract.

Consciousness of Rectilinearity

Geibun, VI, Dec. 1915

21

I turn now to a study of the relationships between subject and object within a creative system of immediate experience, as exemplified, once again, in the consciousness of a continuous straight line. Psychologists explain this consciousness as a conjunction of the sensation of eye muscle movement and visual perception. Yet a continuous straight line, as mathematics defines it, is very different from this. A continuum in the strict sense is currently defined as something the totality of whose elements belong together, in other words, as a set; not merely a set which is *everywhere dense* (one containing another element between any two elements however small the interval between them), but a *perfect set* in Cantor's sense (wherein all asymptotic limits belong to the set itself and all of its members can be such limits).[128] I propose that the straight line of visual perception, as conforming to Archimedes' axiom, can be thought of as a continuum in this strict sense.

Psychologists may deny that there can be a single conscious perception of mathematical continuity, since they define the field of consciousness in function of temporal acts of attention, and measure it by the number of items it can embrace. But the field of consciousness, like all the presentations of subjectivity in experimental psychology, is an abstraction. Through the use of a tachistoscope, one determines the maximum span of attention, or what can be perceived in a single instant, as six simple sense impressions, and by similar experiments the field of consciousness is found to embrace between six and forty simple impressions.[129] But these findings are arrived at by studying consciousness under special conditions: the objects of attention are meaningless lines and numbers, and the experimenter is careful to remove all elements of significance. Only so is a quantitative measurement of the field of consciousness possible. Clearly, this method cannot measure the *meaning* apprehended by consciousness. One can count the number of letters, as meaningless impressions, which consciousness can embrace, but one cannot measure its grasp of the meaning these letters convey when intelligibly arranged. A written sentence may appear as a string of visual impressions; read aloud it may be no more than a succession of auditory representations; yet when understood as a sentence, not only it, but each of the words which compose it, are bearers of meaning; it expresses a "proposition in itself" and each word expresses a "representation in itself."[130] The consciousness of meaning is no less real a phenomenon of consciousness than visual and auditory perception, though its object is so different. Brentano's account of the "intentional immanence of an object"[131] as essential to consciousness suggests that all mental phenomena intrinsically include meaning. Can one really succeed in removing meaning completely, so as to study consciousness purely psychologically? When attention grasps the impressions of six lines or letters, are not these lines and letters immanent in consciousness as meaning? If the object of thought is meaning, we can say that the object of perception too is a species of meaning. When psychologists whittle consciousness down to mere perception, this is no longer real, concrete consciousness, for it misses the awareness of meaning which always underlies perception. The experimental psychologists consider consciousness to be fragmentary and limited to a given time and space, failing to see that consciousness always belongs to a continuum, stands out against a wider background, and is the focus of a totality of relationships.

Thus, even if we concede that consciousness of a straight line in the strict mathematical sense cannot be a single consciousness in the psychological sense, we can still say that it is a single consciousness as possessing a single meaning or object. Cohen's "unity of knowledge" is the true field of consciousness. Our habit of distinguishing knowledge from consciousness needs to be corrected. The visual perception of a straight line is not a composite of lesser elements, but is founded on a unified grasp of continuity like that of the mathematician.[132] When we take a visual straight line as standing for a mathematical straight line, a prior consciousness of the latter is operative in our thinking as Cohen's "method." True, we have to distinguish the mathematical straight line from the visual one, but unless there were some underlying identity, what we intuit could never be grasped as a straight line. I submit that the creative system of concrete experience, autonomously operative, is what fundamentally constitutes consciousness of a continuous straight line, and that this system is most exactly illustrated by the mathematical definition of continuity. Perhaps Fichte had glimpsed this when he observed that "the ego which intuits itself as active views its activity as the drawing of a line."[133]

22

Consciousness of a particular straight line is clearly only an impure form of the consciousness of rectilinearity. But, as already noted, we are conscious of a finite straight line as one determination of an infinite, continuous straight line, which can extend infinitely and which is also infinitely divisible. Since we deny an absolute distinction between an immanent and a transcendent object of consciousness, this finite, subjective determination of the infinite straight line appears as contingent and extrinsic. What is it that thus contingently determines the consciousness of a straight line as subjective? It may be that the mathematical straight line itself contains the potentiality of being determined at will, or even requires such determination. But this potentiality does not suffice to explain the actual fact of determination. There is no apparent reason why a mathematical straight line should require determination, or that someone be conscious of it in actuality. In awareness of a straight line a notion of rectilinearity is implicit, and the mathematical definition is elaborated from this. Continuity is an ideal demand within our experience, and mathematical continuity in the strict sense is fully intelligible only as the experience of a self-generative, self-developing system. Thus the mathematical straight line is unintelligible apart from the experience of a determined straight line. The understanding of the straight line as pure object of thought is grounded in an experiential act. (This accords with Husserl's teaching that particular significations are but the ideal moments of the signifying act, and that the most immediate reality is intentional experience.)

If we grasp the intuition of a finite straight line in the abstract terms of experimental psychology, it can have only an external relationship, if any, to the mathematical straight line (also viewed abstractly). But if, with Brentano, we assert that meaning is essential to the constitution of consciousness, and inconceivable apart from the activity of consciousness, then we can no longer regard an object of pure thought as an abstract universal without the slightest activity in itself, but must grasp it as a concrete universal containing within itself the impulse toward development, or as a self-conscious system. The emergence of pure thought is an intrinsic dynamic of experiential content, and this dynamic, or concrete, universal possesses within itself the activity whereby it is known; it is "absolute activity."[134] Thus when, in regard to a particular line I draw, I am aware that this line can be extended infinitely and divided infinitely, what is operative in this awareness is precisely the idea of a mathematical straight line. The principle of this operation is expressed in Fichte's remark that by knowing one is blocked by a wall one transcends it.[135]

If knower and known are represented as separate realities, the universal and the individual are independent of one another. But the individual thus objectified cannot be the real subject, for as the constructive unifying activity of consciousness, this cannot be made an object of reflection. It is rather the maintainer and the center of the objective world. Thus the etymological primacy of "subject" as the foundation of "object" is restored. Kant, however, still thinks of the unifying activity and the unified content (or what Husserl would call the material and the quality of the act) as separate. If one transcends this abstract dualism to apprehend the inherently dynamic character of the content of consciousness in immediate concrete experience, one can see the synthesizing process of subjectivity as nothing other than the act whereby the content of consciousness develops itself. In the real world of immediate concrete experience, thus, the subject is a genuine dynamic development, the knower includes the known within itself, and subject fuses with object in a dynamic unity wherein subject is immediately object and object is immediately subject.

Within this self-conscious Act, what is the significance of the opposition of subject and object? If we set content and activity over against one another, the activity of synthesis can be regarded as subject, and the synthesized content as object. But if we contrast both of the instances thus abstractly separated with the dynamic development in which they are one, then each of them can be seen as subjective, while this development itself is the only true objective reality. In Hegelian terms, the contrast between subject and object is that between the universal concept as simple unity distinguished from its determinations, and judgment, which is the concept's state of differentiation; but true reality is found only in their unity, the syllogism, which is "the essential ground of whatever is true."[136] The subject-object opposition is only a moment of this concrete reality, and the true *subjectum* in the medieval sense is this activity in which the opposition of subject and object is submerged. In Section 20 we saw that there is objective content even in the subjective world of individual consciousness, while behind the trans-individual objective world there lies a subjective unity, and that it is merely when viewed from the standpoint of this objective world that the world of individual consciousness is thought of as subjective. From the standpoint of a comprehensive synthesis, a lesser one, as still in a process of development, appears as subjective. Thus the relation of subject and object changes according to the synthesis which is the standpoint: to natural science the world of intuition may be subjective, but from an aesthetic viewpoint it is the natural scientific world that is subjective. Whatever appears as impure or imperfectly worked out from a given standpoint is subjective in terms of that standpoint.

Husserl interestingly distinguishes various worlds according to "spontaneities of consciousness": when we are in the mathematical attitude, the world of mathematics is there for us; when we adopt the natural attitude, the natural scientific world is there for us; and all these worlds are embraced by a Cartesian cogito.[137] These various worlds are based on the common standpoint of what we call the objective world, but when we develop this standpoint in a pure and thoroughgoing way we do not depart from subjectivity. When, for instance, a mathematician thinks of a straight line in the strict sense, he does not become trans-individual, but attains purity as mathematical subject: the purification of the object is the purification of the subject, and conversely what is impure or imperfectly worked out may be due to a confusion of standpoints.

23

Although as actually perceived a straight line can never acquire mathematical purity, the fact that we are conscious of it as straight shows that a mathematical cognitive subject is operative behind this perception, or that the ideal of a mathematical straight line is in some way implied. When we think about a geometric straight line by means of a line drawn on the blackboard, the inevitable slight crookednesses will not affect our consciousness of geometric rectilinearity.[138] Unless the mathematical ideal is in some sense implied in the intuited straight line, consciousness of a mathematical straight line is an impossibility.

We saw that for the Marburg philosophers what is to be determined is subjective and what has been determined is objective; and the opposition of subject and object is a relative one between two directions of consciousness, like left and right, inward and outward. In Twardowski's distinction between act, content, and object, which applies both to judgment and representation (and which builds on the distinction of act and content of Bolzano and Brentano),[139] content and object are related exactly as subject and object are related in this theory. The more content is unified from a certain standpoint, the more it can be considered objective. Thus we can say that the content of ever-shifting immediate experience is objective at every moment. However, viewed as expressing an object, content must be subjective. But if content can be subjective, how does it differ from the act of consciousness itself? As we argued above, when content is viewed as subjective, the act of consciousness is objective. Thus Natorp denies that there is any absolute distinction between content and object, and he sees act as nothing more than the unifying of content.[140] Clearly these distinctions leave much room for further discussion.

We grasp the line on the blackboard as signifying a geometric straight line, although it is utterly impossible for a datum of intuition to realize a mathematical ideal, and although extension in intuition and extension in mathematics have quite different qualities. In addition, the line on the blackboard has utterly non-geometric qualities such as color. Usually a mathematical straight line is thought of as a pure transcendent object which cannot become a phenomenon of consciousness, while such qualities as color are thought of as immanent in subjective consciousness. But this is too simple, for the consciousness of color is consciousness of an object, at least in the sense of Meinong's use of the term "object"[141] or of Husserl's "essence", while mathematical objects are immanent in consciousness in some sense, as long as one is conscious of them. If we analyse the experience of the line on the blackboard into several essences, and say with Husserl that perception and imagination are "a fabric of partial intentions, blended into the unity of a total intention,"[142] then consciousness becomes a contingent union of various objective meanings, in which there is no room to insert subjectivity. If it can be inserted, it must be in connection with the act which brings the object to consciousness, or else in the contingent un-

ion of meanings itself. Or one may say that the notion of subjectivity derives merely from a mixture of various points of view. If we analyse the
conscious acts of seeing and hearing in a natural scientific way, these acts
appear as connections between one thing and another thing, and what un-
dergirds the unity and stability of such connections is grasped as a thing or
as a force. As in psychology, conscious acts are then no more than connections among phenomena unified about the empirical ego as center. They
have been reified, and bear as much resemblance to real subjective acts as
light or electricity does. Real subjectivity is unobjectifiable.

Consider the proposition $2 + 2 = 4$. To the logicists this is an unchanging truth quite unrelated to the activity of thinking, quite indifferent
to whether we think it or not. Yet "activity" thus considered is already objectified as an event arising in time and space. In immediate experience,
conscious acts are always what Husserl calls intentional, always conscious
of meaning. We can distinguish in the meaning, $2 + 2 = 4$, the *content*
which differentiates it from, say, $3 + 5 = 8$, and an *a priori* structure
which it shares with other exemplifications of the same mathematical principle. This principle is not merely subsumptive, but constructive, and constitutive for all such truths as $2 + 2 = 4$ and $3 + 5 = 8$. This constructive
principle can be identified with the non-objectifiable activity of the self. It
is through this activity that our immediate experience is consciousness of
meaning; we do not think by means of the psychological ego, which is only
a product of reflection. But there is a problem here: if this activity of the
subject cannot be objectified, and ceases to be the genuine article as soon as
it becomes an object of reflection, being then only relatively distinguishable from the activity of the psychological ego, how is it possible to say
anything at all about it?

The Impossibility of Reflection

Geibun, VII, Jan. 1916

24

The cognitional world may be seen as transcending the experiential world, or more profoundly, cognitive activity may be seen as itself part of the creative evolution of experience. Various cognitional worlds—the natural scientific, the historical, and the artistic worlds for example—are constituted through the unification of immediate experience from various a priori standpoints. These various worlds are grounded in the synthesizing activity of Kant's transcendental subject, somewhat as in the usual conception that the psychological self is the center of a host of experiences. But if the subject cannot be reflected on, how are we able to make these distinctions between knowledge of the world of objects and knowledge of the synthesizing activity which grounds this world, between ordinary scientific knowledge and knowledge of that knowledge itself, or, in Husserl's case, between ordinary and purely phenomenological cognition?

Husserl, like Twardowski, distinguishes act, content and object, and says we can experience the act and the content, but not the object:

> The sense-aspect of color, e.g., which in outer perception forms a real constituent of my concrete seeing (in the phenomenological sense of a visual perceiving or appearing), is as much an experienced content as

is the character of perceiving, or as the full perceptual appearing of the colored object. As opposed to this, however, this object, though perceived, is not itself experienced or conscious, and the same applies to the coloring perceived on it.[143]

The distinction between content and object is defined as that between the experienced and the non-experienced, and is not, as we have been claiming, a difference in viewpoint. Husserl goes on to distinguish within the "immanent content" between "merely intended or intentional" contents and "truly immanent contents."[144] These last are real but not meaningful, and they cannot be objectified: we can see the color but not the sensation of color. (His recent distinction between *noema* and *noesis* is probably in accord with this.)[145]

Next, Husserl distinguishes within the act of intentional experience between its *quality* and its *material*, "between the general act-character, which stamps an act as merely presentative, judgmental, emotional, desiderative etc., and its 'content' which stamps it as presenting *this*, as judging *that* etc."[146] An identical act can relate to different objects: these variations are variations of material.[147] (What ordinary psychology sees as the act may correspond to what Husserl calls the quality of the act, and so the question what this act is becomes one about the quality of the act, or, about the difference between material and quality.) Let us consider Husserl's discussion of the quality of the act:

> I see a thing, e.g. this box, but I do not see my sensations. I always see *one and the same box*, however *it* may be turned and tilted. I always have the *same* "content of consciousness"—if I care to call the perceived object a content of consciousness. But each turn yields a *new* "content of consciousness," if I call experienced contents "contents of consciousness," in a much more appropriate use of words. Very different contents are therefore experienced, though the same object is perceived. . . .In the flux of experienced content, we imagine ourselves to be in perceptual touch with one and the same object; this itself belongs to the sphere of what we experience. For we experience a "consciousness of identity," i.e. a claim to apprehend identity. On what does this consciousness depend? Must we not reply that different sensational contents are given, but that we apperceive or "take" them "in the same sense," and that *to take them in this sense is an experienced character through which the being of an object for me is first constituted.* Must

75

we not say, further, that the consciousness of identity is framed on the basis of these two sorts of experienced characters, as the immediate consciousness that they *mean the same?* And is this consciousness not again an act in our defined sense, whose objective correlate lies in the identity it refers to?[148]

Every act of perceiving and judging is such a consciousness of identity, and the differentiation of the qualities of the act is based on the differences arising within this consciousness of identity. Criticizing Brentano's view that representation is the basis of all intentional experience, Husserl points out that it is because we cannot judge without representing that we mistakenly see the act of judging as based on the act of representing, and think of representation as the material which together with the quality of the act constitutes the act of judging. Representation has its own material and quality as representation, for every concrete act has these two aspects, but because representation has the same material as judgment the above confusion easily arises.[149] In stating the precise distinction between object and material, Husserl explains that object is wholly transcendent to act, whereas material is a component of act. Since the characteristic of the act of consciousness, the experience of meaning, is that it refers to an object, while the differences in its content concern the way in which it refers to the object, differences in the way of referring to an object, e.g. the difference between "equiangular" and "equilateral," also belong to the material which determines content.

We return to the question of the possibility of reflecting on the act of consciousness itself and the problem that an act upon which we have reflected is no longer act itself. Husserl says we can experience the act through internal evidence, but can the solution be that simple? To Husserl's predecessor, Brentano, every mental phenomenon is not only "consciousness of something" (of its primary object) but consciousness of itself (as its secondary object);[152] every representation is a representation of representation. Brentano deduces that there is

> a peculiar interweaving of the object of inner representation with this representation itself and that both belong to one and the same mental act . . . .The representation of a tone and the representation of the representation of a tone form only one single mental phenomenon, which we conceptually differentiate into two representations only by viewing it in its relation to two different objects, of which one is a physical and the other a mental phenomenon.[151]

Brentano thus thinks it self-evident that the act of consciousness can be an object of reflection, and Husserl's position does not seem to be fundamentally different. Perhaps this is an unavoidable hypothesis, but its necessity needs to be more clearly demonstrated.

25

Postponing further discussion of the possibility of reflecting on the act of consciousness, let us examine the quality of the act. How is it that a perceived object can be identical despite changes in experiential content? What is the quality of the act which combines experienced content and perceived object? We may be helped here by the theory worked out in Section 18, according to which immediate experience is the development of conscious content itself, which as development is a subjective process (marshalling the content as its material), but which in its aspect of self-identity constitutes the objective. Thus in the judgment "A is A" the self-identity of "A" is object, and the development "A is A" is subjective act (while the grammatical subject "A" in isolation represents the content). This judgment is one experience, one concrete act.

Now the perceived identity of the box, in Husserl's example, is an act of the sense of sight, to be differentiated from the act of judgment. Schapp observes that our perception of the crossbars of a window pane as heavy depends on no "accompanying knowledge," but is given as a distinct intuition. Seeing is an "originarily presentive act"[152] which differs from thinking. "The scientist who knows for certain that things are made up of atoms, does not see the atoms in the thing, and one who knows that sugar is sweet does not see the sweetness in the sugar."[153] In ordinary psychology sense perception is distinguished from thought as that which is given, but can we not equally say that such facts of thought as the fact that equilateral triangles are equiangular are intuitively given? As Husserl writes:

> The essential homogeneity of the function of fulfillment, as of all the ideal relationships necessarily bound up with it, obliges us to give the name "perception" to each fulfilling act of confirmatory self-presentation, to each fulfilling act whatever the name of an "intuition," and to its intentional correlate the name of *"object."*[154]

May we not, then, apply all I have said above to the experience of thinking as well?

What I call immediate experience, the development of meaning itself, is the same as Husserl's intentional experience. In pure vision blue requires orange, and the straight line merges with the curve; seeing is the self-development of color or form as such. May not Husserl's "quality" be seen as an aspect of this creative self-development of content? The differences of quality he finds between acts of perception and acts of thought can be seen as differences of the a priori creative instance. From Bolzano to Husserl, philosophers have made an absolute distinction between content and object, but I am inclined to agree with Natorp that the distinction is relative, and that act is nothing more than a way of inserting partial content into the unity of the whole. Husserl and Twardowski argue for the strict distinction of content and object from the fact that an identical object can be apprehended in different contents (the same triangle perceived as equiangular or as equilateral). But may it not be that the object which transcends consciousness is no more than the internal unity of consciousness itself, and that the opposition of content and object is merely one between different ways of determining the same object, different degrees of unity? Thus while the equilateral triangle and the equiangular triangle are contents in relation to a unique object, they can also be viewed as being themselves objects in relation to some more specific contents. Again, the contents corresponding to the various positions of the box can also themselves be thought of as objects.

Lipps presents the distinction between content and object in the following puzzling terms:

> We must distinguish this internal turning to that which at first is only my content and which is to become an object for me, from the object's actually becoming object for me. This internal turning is an *activity*. We designate it the activity of *attentiveness*, or, still more precisely, the activity of *apprehension* . . . .As the object stands over against me, or becomes object for me, *through* this activity of turning my attention to it, this activity must be distinguished from the object's standing over against me or its emergence as object for me . . . .When I think the object I accomplish a "thought-act." Object and act of thinking, or thought-act, are thus correlative notions. This act . . . is the natural end, or the natural conclusion, of that activity [of internal turning]. It is related to the former as the snapping shut of the blade of a pocket knife to the preceding movement which aims at this snapping shut.[155]

For Lipps there are degrees of attentiveness, but one either thinks a thing or one does not.

Just as circle, ellipse, hyperbola, and parabola can be united as maximum and minimum limits in a single continuum by the principle of conic sections, consciousness forms a similar continuum, within which various particular standpoints unify experience within a certain scope, and are themselves in turn united from a more fundamental standpoint. May we not say that the quality of the act is that of a lesser standpoint seen from a greater? Each advance towards the "relative nothingness" at the origin of the continuum of consciousness brings a new stage of reflection, and a new quality of act. When consciousness of a certain scope has been separated from the background of concrete experience, its content is thought of as subjective, because of its particularity, but a further advance provides it with a new foundation, so that it becomes objective; a problem is seen as isolated and subjective, but when the foundation which provides its solution is found, it is seen as objective, because integrated into the whole. (Analogously, specific conic sections in their respective regions are subjective when compared with the concrete universal "conic section," but when unified on the basis of this universal according to the principle of continuity, each region, as founded in this concrete universal, becomes objective. Again, equilateral and equiangular triangles are subjective as differing contents, but in light of the logical necessity of their identity they turn out to be the necessary determinations of the object.)

The act of consciousness connects a certain region of consciousness with the totality of concrete experience. When the secondary qualities (color or sound) are immanent in the act as its content, as components of the act itself, then they have reality as belonging to the totality of concrete experience, whereas Bolzano's "proposition itself" and "representation itself," far from being objective because they transcend the act of consciousness, are for that very reason subjective and unreal. "What has been objectified in the mind" is truly objective when it includes act within itself.

Part Three
How Experiential
Systems are Combined

Various A Priori as Grounded in the Mind's Demand for Objectivity

26

Archimedes is the remote source of differential and integral calculus. Kepler, in his *Stereometry of Tubs*, building on Archimedes, thinks of a circle as constructed from infinitesimal triangles with the center as their apex and the circumference as their base; this seems quite unsophisticated today. The real foundation of differential calculus is Fermat's discovery of the method of maxima and minima and the method of tangents.[156] A polygon remains essentially different from a circle, no matter how short and how many its sides become; yet at its *limit* it coincides with a circle. A set of points at its limit becomes a continuum (a line), by coinciding with the set of the limiting points derived from it. This is possible although polygon and circle, point and line, are concepts constructed according to different a priori and corresponding to different intuitions in immediate experience. What is the nature of this limit whereby one a priori can thus pass over into another?

In contemporary mathematics Dedekind and Cantor have clarified the concept of the continuum, thus securing the foundation of analysis. Underlying the concept of the continuum is the intuition of a given totality, a totality which is not an extrinsic assemblage, but one whose parts are its determinations. Hence Cohen's account of continuity as qualitative unity, which proceeds from whole to parts. Continuity, in the strict sense of Dedekind and Cantor, is not merely infinite divisibility. The infinitesimal, the limit point towards which continuity tends, is not the simple nought towards which intensive quantity tends,[157] but is a point which no matter how often we divide we can never reach, or as Picard puts it, "a point A in whose vicinity, no matter how tiny the area of that vicinity has become, there is always a point of the given set which does not coincide with A."[158] For a set of points to move towards a continuous straight line as its limit, or for a polygon to move towards a circle as its limit, presupposes the intuition of a new standpoint, not unrelated to the former position but containing it completely within itself. A limit point is a point one can approximate indefinitely but never attain. The derivative is the set of a higher standpoint, related to that from which it emerges as Lipps "snapping shut," or Bergson's *élan*.[159] From its own standpoint a set of points, or a polygon, is already a perfect system, and no further position seems necessary. But concrete experience, or life itself, which grounds all abstract thought, can rest content with no abstract system, and always demands a more concrete position, spurring thought to advance infinitely towards the concrete. Indeed it is this advance toward concrete reality which underlies the mathematicians' discovery of analysis. (The transition from logic to mathematics, discussed in Section 11, may be seen as a parallel to this.)

A set of ordered points and Cantor's perfect set (the continuum) have the same foundation in the concept of order, and the former set, as an incomplete state of the ordering action, aspires towards the latter as its completion. We can think in the same way of the relation between polygon and circle. A set of mere points may seem very different from the concept of order, but in concrete experience its elements are no longer simple elements, but possess meaning. The concrete ordering action comprises these elements and a law of combination, and when that ordering action is complete in a perfect set it becomes, in Hegelian terms, *an und für sich*, in and for itself. Bergson says that no matter how many photographs of Paris we assemble we cannot know Paris itself, for no combination of discrete positions can construct movement.[160] Yet just such a transition is made intelligible by the notion of limit, which can relate abstract to concrete and thought to intuition.

In Section 19 we saw that a continuum must be a creative system in which intuitive fact is reflexive act, in other words, a system of self-consciousness. In mathematics only a continuum can have a limit point. In contrast to an irrational number (a Dedekindian section) which is an ideal point we can never attain, the discrete points expressed by rational numbers are attainable by division, and are real points. A continuum which contains the limit point within itself can well be titled "the ideal plus the real," or the *concrete*. Now, the self is an ideal limit point, which we can reflect on infinitely, yet which our reflection can never reach. Though each act of reflection is objectified in a further act of reflection in a never-ending process, each has the continuity of a real act for us, and is comparable to a rational number in this respect. In self-consciousness reflection is the self, though the self can never be attained by reflection; self-consciousness is thus "the ideal plus the real" in a special way, and we may claim that the idea of limit in mathematics is only one particular derivative of this. The limit point constitutive for a continuum is not a mere point, but includes direction, and is self-moving, as in the case of Cohen's productive point of a curve. The self is a productive point in a similar sense. Action is not the mere succession of phenomena, but a development of internal necessity, and if Spinozan substance is "that which exists in itself and is understood by itself,"[161] that which is continuous, that which has a limit is that which includes activity within itself; in limit fact and act coincide.

The uniting of various conic sections as maxima and minima in the formula of quadratic equations is the uniting of the activity of the respective independent internal developments of lines or circles by the action of a more inclusive internal development. Various conic sections do not simply change into one another; each represents an ideal limit for our intuition. Yet all are included in the concrete whole known as the curve of the quadratic equation. The quality of the act of each of these is the meaning-intention it represents: for example, circles, ellipses, and parabolas are distinguished by the distance of their foci (be it infinitely small or finitely or infinitely large), but if we exclude the idea of the distance of the foci, the qualities of the three curves become identical. We can bring each self-conscious productive point of these curves into unity by means of the continuity of the foci, and we can think of the special characteristic of each curve as the limit of one continuous system, as one determination of a certain totality. Analogously, our whole life, throughout its entire course, is not only one self-consciousness; it is moment by moment an independent self-consciousness. Experience in its most immediate concrete totality is a self-conscious system, and each part of it by itself is self-conscious; each is a productive point, a system within a system. Can we not view the acts of intentional experience as also forming such systems within systems? Following the Marburg philosophers, may we not see the various a priori of the experience of thinking as passing over into one another by means of their limits, as the various conic sections do?

Geibun, VII, March 1916

27

It may be objected that I am ignoring the radical difference between the mathematical circle or curve, which are objects of thought, and the intuitively given circle or curve of perception. The former can be united conceptually by means of the notion of limit, but can this provide a frame for thinking the unity of the a priori in intuition?

There are two main reasons for saying that the circle or curve of intuition is totally different from that of mathematics. One is the impossibility of finding perfect mathematical forms in intuition: the perceived line is never without breadth and it is bound to show discontinuities under a sufficiently powerful microscope, and even the most accurate compass cannot draw a circle truly equidistant from the center. The other reason is the difference, underlined by Husserl, between the *representation* and the *thought* of, say, a triangle; though their material basis may be the same, as acts these are totally different mental phenomena.[162]

To deal with the first objection: I do not admit that in immediate perception there is such a thing as discontinuity in the strict sense. Sometimes the apparently continuous turns out to be discontinuous when examined carefully, but no matter how small its parts we must still view them as continuous insofar as they necessarily possess extension. Immediate perception is neither wholly continuous nor wholly discontinuous, but an interpenetration of the two features. (Some may say geometrical continuity and discontinuity are already something conceptual, and that what is really perceived is only color and sound. But color and sound, abstracted from the matrix of concrete experience in which they are pre-contained, are just as conceptual.)

To deal with the second objection: When we think about what we have represented, the contents of the two acts are not immediately identical, though representation, thought, and imagination are unified in some sense as having an identical object. We have seen that for Brentano *representation* is what unites the various mental acts, while Husserl more accurately claims that what unites the various mental acts is the identity of the *material* they share. This identity of material is the identity of *meaning*, a relationship to an identical *object*, and it is based on an unchanging *essence* given in concrete experience. Because the qualities of the acts of perception and thought are quite distinct, it is imagined that in relation to an identical object, the content of the thought of it differs from the content of the perception of it. But in reality there is nothing to prevent the different acts of thinking and perception from sharing the same material. If the essence is the really existent component in our concrete experience, and if the act is founded on it, then two acts can have the same really existent element. Husserl distinguishes sharply between transcendent object and immanent content, but in concrete experience there is nothing either absolutely transcendent or absolutely immanent, and the distinction is simply one between opposite directions of dynamic experience. Knowledge of the object may be imperfect, having as its content only the infinite adumbrations of the thing,"⁷ but the same can be said for the supposedly purely immanent knowledge of mind, and there too the core of developmental experience can probably be described as Husserl's identical material.

It is maintained that the mathematical conception and the perceptual representation of a continuous line are utterly different, just as the representation of the sun does not shine. Yet we have seen that the mathematical conception presupposes an intuitively given totality, and that, conversely, continuity and extension are data of visual experience, in which there is nothing absolutely discontinuous. Our intuition of movement from within, when we simply move our hand from A to B, cannot be dismissed as a merely individual impression bound by time and space. It reveals, at a phenomenological level, an experiential equivalent of the mathematical conceptions of movement or continuity, and suggests that the continuity constitutive of perception is essentially the same as that which is the object of mathematical thinking, and that perception, as Cohen claims, is constituted by means of thought. This is not to deny the difference between a perceptual and a conceptual proof. In geometry, one may use intuitional diagrams as an aid to reflection, but intuition cannot be the basis of proof: ruler measurements cannot prove that the line which divides equally the apex angle of an isosceles triangle also divides its base equally. Yet even the comparison and measurement of the two segments of the base depends on something more than immediate perception, for these procedures already entail a grasp of the significance of the diagram. In analytic geometry, geometric qualities are grasped quite independently of perception, and when a continuous straight line is conceived as a series of real numbers, the straight line of perception is merely a sign of this. But even in this case, is there no relation whatever between the order of the numerical series and the order underlying the straight line? Can we conceive the numerical order except on the basis of a fundamental intuition of order? And does not the same intuition underlie the empirical procedures of measuring and comparing lengths?

The mathematician recognizes the straight line of intuition only insofar as it conforms to the Archimedean axiom. But what is it insofar as it does not conform to this? A collection of muscle movements, which do not possess extension? But this is an unreal construct of psychologists.[164] We should rather understand the difference between empirical and mathematical extension as one of degrees of purity or exactness. Similarly, the difference between the concept of infinity and Fiedler's aesthetic intuition of infinity is one between two derivatives of the self-identical creative system wherein the self reflects the self infinitely. If it is objected that the two kinds of infinity are alike, but have no underlying identity, I suggest that sameness *(Gleichheit)* always has identity as its foundation.

28

I have just argued that the identical essence is the object of thought and the object of intuition or perception. Now I shall discuss their unity in light of the way in which one a priori passes into another by means of a limit concept.

Until Gauss discovered how to express complex numbers by means of a plane, they were thought, even by Cauchy, the great theorist of these numbers, to be incapable of being intuited. Mathematically considered, Gauss's discovery may be only a matter of practical application, but epistemologically it throws light on the status of these numbers, forcing us to ask what his invocation of spatial intuition adds to the view, defended by Hankel, that the assumption of complex numbers into the numerical system is a purely numerical affair. Or in Cohen's terminology, what does consciousness add to thought?[165] (Descartes' invention of analytic geometry already raises these issues.)

In discussing the "judgment of allness," Cohen considers the "allness" as the "unity of plurality" and claims that space is its category. In space finitude and infinity, interior and exterior, are united, and the flux of things is apprehended in a state of rest. The objection that perceptual space, constructed about the fact that "I see," cannot function as such an intellectual object, does not affect concrete space, which must be thought of as a dynamic unity of finitude and infinity.[166] If the homogeneity of space is based on self-consciousness, as argued in Section 6, then so must the straight line of actual perception. We do not see rectilinearity, but something rectilinear, and indeed seeing is always the self-deployment of some such concrete content. Similarly, the concept of mathematical continuity depends on the intuition of some such concrete "allness" as its foundation.

What, then, does mathematical continuity, an object of pure thought, gain by association with intuitive space? Mathematically, it is self-sufficient and the association can add nothing essential, nor does contemporary mathematics require the aid of spatial intuition to deal with complex numbers. (It is evident that, if thought gains something by an association with intuition, "intuition" must refer to something more than the sensory qualities that are the product of psychological analysis.) When a numerical series is correlated with an intuited line, or complex numbers are associated with the intuition of a plane, it is not that the intuition adds anything to the numbers, but rather that, in accord with the axiom of the anticipation of perception, our intuition is constructed by means of thought. The intuition and the numbers have an identical basis; mathematical continuity is nothing more than the purified form of an intuited straight line.

When several mathematical formulas are unified by a more universal formula, or when several physical laws are unified by a more fundamental law, things independent until then are now subsumed under one and the same universal, but there is no change in the fundamental a priori defining the separate items, which rather advance to their completion. The case differs with the relationship between arithmetic and analysis, considered in contemporary mathematics to have different foundations (analysis presupposing the axiom of continuity). Both deal with systems of real numbers, including both rational and irrational, but arithmetic grasps the numbers as discrete points, while analysis groups them in "sections." When one speaks of rational numbers being included in the system of real numbers, dealing with them as elements of an analytic, not a mathematical, totality, this gives them a quite different meaning. Though neo-realists think the part independent of the whole, to think of 1, 2, 3 . . . arithmetically is not the same as to think of them analytically, and unless the totality is presupposed in some sense, no part of it can be conceived. Thus though arithmetic and analysis are based on different a priori, one is unified as a part within the other. How does this occur? One can see the basis of quantity common to the a priori of both as completing these a priori; or one can see continuity as completing the numerical series. (This may be questionable to mathematicians, but I am speaking epistemologically.) The axiom of continuity is not brought to bear on quantity contingently, but is demanded intrinsically by quantity; it is the manifestation of what was implicit in the concept of quantity.

Or if one continues to insist, with the mathematicians, on the difference between the bases of the two systems, one may conceive their relationship in terms of the characteristics of a system of knowledge. If the ideal of knowledge is the *adaequatio rei et intellectus*, this ideal is perfectly realized, not by a formal, abstract knowledge, but only by that which is concrete and objective. A continuous whole is more perfect than a discontinuous whole; in contrast to the continuous system of self-consciousness which expresses reality itself within itself, what is discontinuous is dependent and subjective; in the latter subject and object are divided, but they are united in the former, which is a unity containing separation within itself.

29

If the relationship between arithmetic and analysis is as I have stated above, a numerical system can express continuity by taking in irrational numbers together with rational numbers, thus permitting a mathematical treatment of the real. In addition to the purely mathematical differences between the two, an epistemologist may note that analysis is more concrete than arithmetic. Thinking back to the foundations of both, we recall that Rickert's homogeneous medium is the basis of number, and that this in turn is grounded in self-consciousness. The system of real numbers, as a positive and concrete expression of self-consciousness, is more perfect than a system comprising only rational numbers, which can express self-consciousness only abstractly and negatively. Or instead of saying that number expresses reality, we can say, more radically, that reality itself is number, and that reality in the sense of rational numbers is one abstract aspect of reality in the sense of real numbers. Might we not be able to grasp the union of thought and intuition along the lines of this understanding of the purely intellectual relationships between rational and real numbers?

Thought is usually seen as abstract, and experience as concrete, and it is assumed that thought becomes truly objective by uniting with experience. What is produced when a concept of pure understanding unites with transcendental intuition, as in mathematical knowledge, is not yet objective knowledge; only when it unites with empirical intuition is experience, in Kant's sense, or objective knowledge, produced. It would appear, then, that sensory knowledge is what gives concreteness to thought. But how can sensory content of itself confer objectivity on thought? Mere sensory content, which is similar to Bolzano's representation itself, can claim no rights in a system of objective knowledge, except by conforming to the principle of intensive quantity (as Cohen taught us). But if it is thought which gives knowledge its objectivity, we must face the objection that thought separated from sensory content is subjective: "thoughts without content are empty."[167] This contradiction can be fully resolved only by advancing to the Hegelian position (which is also that of the Marburg school): thought equals being, being equals thinking.[168] But here I should like to take a different approach, starting from given experience, not, like the rationalists, from thought. If what is given in experience is what has been required by thought, perhaps this is due not to thought itself, but to the fact that thought is identical with experience. If one ascribes this requirement of thought to reason alone, it might with equal justification be ascribed to "non-reason." Its true source is neither reason nor non-reason, but pure activity, reason-*qua*-non-reason, being-*qua*-relative-non-being, experience-*qua*-thought, and our thinking always takes place against the background of this concrete whole, so that we can say with Jacob Boehme that wherever we stand, and wherever we go, there is God.

In discussing the relation between logic and mathematics, I remarked that it is not so much a question of logic requiring mathematics, as that in the background from which logic arises there lurks also that which gives rise to mathematics. In other words, when the fundamental condition of possibility of thinking "A is A" is brought to light, it turns out to be that same homogeneous medium which is the basis of mathematics. It is in this sense that logic demands mathematics. One might rather say that the whole of logic-and-mathematics, or the objectivity of knowledge as such, is the source of the demand. Mathematics demands to be thought of as co-originary with logic, and logic to become objective, has to include mathematics. This demand arises from the whole of logic-and-mathematics. When empiricists claim that number has an external, experiential source, they are confusing an issue of value with one of fact. Again, it is easy to see that abstract logic merely as such does not demand mathematics, but this logic never exists apart from the activity of thinking; the reflection of logic is summoned by its concrete context, which demands a suspension of the purely logical attitude (as Husserl might say). While logic does not presuppose mathematics, it requires it in order to provide knowledge of the real.

In this sense, mathematics is the limit of logic. Knowledge is such that it demands a relation to reality (*pace* the logicists who deny this), not in the sense of a transcendent reality, but in the sense of Kantian objectivity, which, in our view, is attained when knowledge is a system of self-consciousness.

Value is within being and being is within value. The two require one another, and their union is objectivity. This requirement is more than a sensation or feeling, and cannot be expressed by these psychological terms. It is a concrete, philosophical reality, and "sensation" (a product of abstract reflection) or "feeling" (the abstract state of pain or pleasure) are merely abstracted aspects of it. Nor is it will in the ordinary sense; it is rather the foundation of will. It is true that Cohen's "demand" always takes the form of a sensation or feeling, or an unconscious following us like a shadow from behind. Yet these terms are highly misleading in the case of this transcendental, or, we should rather say, truly concrete, sensation, feeling, or unconsciousness. It is in fact something akin to religious feeling, something anterior to feeling and sensation in the ordinary sense. This demand is the point of contact between knowledge and reality, the apex of the *élan vital*, the point from which all progress in knowing proceeds. (When psychologists claim that every noetic content is accompanied by a different quality of feeling, they are in fact taking the same content at one time as knowledge and at another as feeling, abstracting both from the one living reality of consciousness. The psychologist may deal with this reality under the heading of the unconscious, but it is an unconscious with concrete content, and scientific psychology can handle only abstractions.)

For the mathematician the correspondence of numerical series and intuited line is purely accidental, but is it really without epistemological significance that mathematics conforms to intuition? The correspondence is not extrinsic, like that of a map to geographical features, but reveals that mathematical thought has a constructive significance in regard to intuitive space. In Cohen's terms, the application of mathematics to intuition is demanded by thought; intuition is anticipated by thought. The intuition of a straight line is a transcendental sensation in which this demand is perceived. It can be seen either as a demand of thought or a demand of experiential content, and we may say that our concrete consciousness is this demand itself. Psychological and mathematical notions of rectilinearity are abstractions from this transcendental sensation of which we are conscious when we perceive a straight line (a consciousness of which the actual seeing or feeling of a line is merely the perceptual content.)

The application of mathematics to geometry which founds analytic geometry is a return to the foundation of this transcendental sensation; it is not that two independent things are contingently combined, but that we return to and become aware of the underlying concrete system. In this system, at the same time that rectilinearity as a content of consciousness acquires objective reality, the mathematical straight line acquires what may be called subjective reality. As one acquires flesh the other acquires spirit, and concrete life is created; spatial perception is the result of this *élan vital*. The application of mathematics to geometry is not of the same order as its application to engineering. In the latter case we are dealing with a use of mathematics for a quite extrinsic purpose, rather than with the intrinsic teleology of knowledge, which impels mathematics to geometry, just as it impels arithmetic to analysis. The goal of knowledge is objectivity, and to become objective is to move close to concrete experience. Thus the transition from mathematics to geometry is demanded by the purpose inherent in knowing. Whereas what impels arithmetic to analysis is the contentless self-consciousness underlying the establishment of discrete numbers, in the application of number to geometry it is a more substantive and concrete self-consciousness which is the source of the demand. Here, in accord with Cohen's "anticipation of perception," mathematical continuity anticipates the straight line; or we can say that intellectual continuity demands the intuited line, so that what is given is what thought required. But it is because intuition itself is a system of self-consciousness and a single continuum that it can be thus anticipated by thought. This anticipation of perception should in fact be seen as the self-deployment of transcendental sensation. A system of abstract thought is not self-contained, but acquires meaning only in a system of concrete, immediate experience, and the point of convergence of the two systems is a state of awareness *(Bewusstheit):* thus the awareness of rectilinearity is the point of contact between the mathematical concept and the concrete experience.

The system of concrete experience is the domain of the senses and sensation. But if we give content to Fichte's self-consciousness, it turns out to resemble Bergson's pure duration, suggesting that the anticipation of perception is not the isolated subject's anticipation of its object, but the self-deployment of the concrete system of self-consciousness. When a system of thought combines with a system of experience it returns to its foundation, in accord with Cohen's principle of continuity, and this return generates a great system of knowledge, in obedience to the demand which appears as a transcendental sensation. This development is the core of temporality: "an-

93

ticipation is the distinguishing mark of time."[169] We may suppose that it is because consciousness is the point of contact of systems of thought and systems of experience that the phenomena of consciousness are temporal. Consciousness, says Cohen, is the "modality of possibility."[170]

Leaving further discussion of these points till later, I now proceed to a discussion of the epistemological significance of analytic geometry.

From Number to Space

Tetsugaku Kenkyū, No. 7, Oct. 1916

30

Although the discrete numbers of arithmetic and the continuous numbers which are the basis of analysis are wholly different as objects of thought, one cannot think of continuity without reference to discontinuity, or of discontinuity without reference to continuity; the two posit each other and are mutually correlated as two indissociable aspects of thought. While the mathematician may advert only to their difference, a phenomenological consideration brings to light the necessary relationship between them. May we not conceive a similar relationship between number and geometric space?

We have seen that true spatial intuition is a transcendental sensation. To determine its nature more precisely, we should first try to focus the notion of pure geometric space, strictly excluding not only all empirical features, but also the element of magnitude. In these respects Euclidean geometry, though for more than two thousand years believed to be self-evident truth, was insufficiently strict, as the development of non-Euclidean geometries has revealed. Euclid's postulate of parallel lines is appropriate only in the empirical world, and has no logical inevitability. In ordinary geometry the idea of magnitude is often intermixed. If these impurities are eliminated, there remain as absolute geometrical data merely such things as straight lines, planes, and angles, as in Staudt's projective geometry.[172] It need hardly be added that three-dimensional space is merely a product of experience, and has no special significance in terms of pure space.

Russell, for whom points are the "terms" of spatial relationships and straight lines the relations determined by two terms, sets forth the following axioms of projective geometry: 1. All parts of space are "similar," and they are distinguished only by the fact that "they lie outside one another." 2. Space is continuous, and infinitely divisible; the result of such infinite division, the zero of extension, is the point. 3. Any two points determine a line, and any three points posit another unique figure, a plane. Four points determine a solid, five points determine yet another figure, and thus one can advance to figures of manifold dimensions. This advance, however, cannot be infinite because it is impossible to determine infinite dimensions.[173] These axioms, though perhaps not mathematically strict, indicate the basic elements of projective geometry. Russell posits "the form of externality" as the basic concept underlying these axioms and the basis of all spatial relations. This "pure externality" is wholly abstracted from substantive distinctions, and hence it is a fundamental postulate of pure geometry that position is entirely relative. The relativity of position immediately entails, as its necessary presupposition, the absolute homogeneity of space. Relativity and homogeneity allow us to conceive infinite divisibility, that is, to elaborate within one relationship an infinite series of similar relationships. Finally, the idea of direction arises from the fact that one position can be determined only in relation to another position; direction is this relation. The possibility of determining a position in this way necessarily implies that the number of its relationships is finite, for one position could not be determined from infinite relationships.

Hegel's statement that space is the externality of nature to itself, an abstract "beside-one-another," also implies that space is a static unity, a simultaneous co-existence, in which relationships are reversible.[174] This chimes with Russell's account of pure externality, as does Cohen's deduction of space, which takes the following form: Thought proceeds from unity to plurality, and allness is the synthesis of these two. Plurality constitutes an infinite series which is interminable, whereas allness completes and summates the series, making possible a unified or positive comprehension of infinity. Its unit is the limit, in which is revealed the inexhaustible power of "infinite summation." In this scheme, time is plurality and space is totality. Time creates the cosmos of pure thought from chaos by means of number, but its content is still wholly internal; space, however, expresses the necessary relationship of interior and exterior, and rescues endless, relative time from its vicissitudes.[175]

If such is pure space, we can now proceed to examine its epistemological status and significance, and to ask what the application of number to space in analytic geometry means in the development of knowledge. I maintain that the simultaneous existence which is the basis of spatial intuition derives from the essence of self-consciousness. The fact that in the judgment of identity "A is A" the subject "A" and the predicate "A" can exchange positions implies their simultaneous co-existence, not in a chronological sense, but in the sense of the reversibility of relationships. Thus, just as it provides the basis of pure time, self-consciousness also provides the basis of pure space, the form of externality. It confers on both time and space their a priori quality. Whereas time and number express the infinite progression of self-consciousness, in endless relativity, flux, and indeterminateness, space is the determination of relationships, the positive manifestation of self-consciousness as the internal unity which grounds infinite relationships. The determining of a straight line by two points, or of a plane by three, is the determining of one particular relation from within endless relativity. The reason that the number of the dimensions of space must be finite, as Russell states, is that the determination of the whole is an indispensable quality of space. Self-consciousness is at once the infinite progression of "reflection-qua-action" and an unchanging unity. Thus it demands both infinite transition and infinite determination. Time manifests the contradictoriness of self-consciousness as infinite transition, while space manifests its absolute reality as creative action.

Space is the "determinate integral" (Cohen), and can also be seen as the universal providing the foundation of the syllogism. Thus it does not supervene contingently and extrinsically on number or pure time, but is in fact a positive expression of the unity which must be postulated as the foundation of number and time. This spatial unity is as essential to the constitution of time and number as continuous numbers are to discrete numbers. In both cases, mathematicians may observe only the differences between the objects of thought, failing to see that space functions as concrete subject or substrate in regard to number, as continuity does in regard to discrete numbers, and that the progression from number to space in analytic geometry, like the progression from discrete to continuous numbers, is one from an abstract state to its concrete foundation, a progression towards objectivity.

31

From the standpoint of mathematics, the possibility of correlating a numerical series and a geometrical straight line does not intrinsically affect the numerical series as such. Epistemologically, however, this union of number with space is a progression from abstract to concrete, in accord with the demand of knowledge for objectivity. We have seen that behind a series of changing numbers a unified space must be postulated. It may be objected that the numerical system is independent and complete in itself, and that there is no need to provide this new a priori. But this new category is demanded not by the "being" of number, but by the "being and relative non-being" of knowledge in search of its foundations. The concrete subject operative here is not the mere unity of numbers, but a continuum embracing this unity as an element. Just as behind our thinking of discrete numbers as objects a continuum extends as concrete subject, and is later manifest as the system of real numbers, so too behind our thinking of the unity of numbers as object there is a continuum which is the unity of this unity, and it later appears positively as spatial intuition. As irrational numbers have a higher unity than rational numbers, spatial unity is of a higher order than numerical (temporal) unity, and implies a new kind of intuition, a new *élan vital*. And as irrational numbers are the limit of rational numbers, space is the limit of time. (Mathematical objections to this use of the term "limit" may be countered by recalling that mathematical limit is only a particular instance of a self-conscious system. Since space, or pure externality, is the unity of a series each of whose elements belongs to a self-conscious system, it must itself be a single self-conscious system including pure time, or number, as its element.)

Now let us reconsider the relationship between logic and mathematics. "A is A" is a universal determining itself, a flux stopping and viewing itself, an ideal becoming actual. This judgment is an activity wherein the self reflects on and determines itself. Here the self (as pure thought) is in a state of self-relatedness,[176] and its object is purely qualitative. To posit "A" in this way is to distinguish it from others; and when its content is utterly void, distinguishing and positing are one activity. When the one and the other are wholly contentless objects of pure thought, they are interchangeable, and, as reflected upon from the standpoint of the underlying concrete whole they constitute numerical one. As we stressed in arguing against Rickert's logicism, object and activity are relative to one another; in wholly contentless, purely logical judgment, we cannot conceive its object apart from the judging act itself (whereas a judgment with content, e.g. "red is red," tempts us to divide form from content). The object of the judgment is nothing but the act of affirmation (which implies distinction), the pure self-positing of a content of consciousness in general (which as pure "something" necessarily implies its other). Logical judgment is the dynamic aspect of purely qualitative objects, and they are its static aspect. Similarly, the dynamic aspect of mathematical objects is an activity of idealization, in which logical judgment is reflected on and objectified as number. In these processes thought itself creates its content, in virtue of the "demand" described by Cohen, or, in Hegelian terms, that which is already included within the concept is "posited." (We might apply here Hegel's remark: "The deduction of their unity is completely analytical.")[177] This emergence of numerical one from interchangeability of position derives from the fact that the self, by reflecting on itself and transcending its actuality, conceives within itself the image of its own independence. Here there is a relationship of container and contained, enabling the transition from qualitative to quantitative determination, in which relations of magnitude arise. Where there is no other qualitative determination, container and contained are identical, the self is reproduced within the self, enabling the conception of an infinite numerical series.

In light of this, mathematics appears as the more comprehensive context of "being and relative nothingness" in relation to logic. When "something," which is a purely logical object, is thought of as "what has been objectified in the mind," mathematical continuity is its subject in the sense of substrate (hypokeimenon). The judgment act is this "something" viewed dynamically in-terms of its substrate as a state of self-relatedness, and the psychological self is this act viewed as subject in abstraction from the entire subject, which is objective in relation to it. This entire subject is the goal towards which knowledge advances in its progress towards objectivity. Knowledge consists in this progress, which underlies the demand of logic for mathematics as its concrete goal. New cognitive content is not supplied from without, as empiricists maintain, but emerges from within; it does not enter from the front but appears from the rear.

If we discuss these relationships in terms of the notion of limit, the nu-

99

merical identity of "one" is the limit to which the sameness of something and its other cannot attain. Since identity is its ideal limit, identity must be postulated as what grounds sameness. This is why Windelband considers sameness subjective and identity objective. Whereas for Rickert the qualitative view which distinguishes between something and another as mere objects of thought is more fundamental than the quantitative view, here numerical one appears as the limit of qualitative sameness. My entire line of argument may appear to be psychologistic, but no matter how much we try to confine ourselves to objects of pure thought, we are bound to recognize that behind their distinctions must lie a comprehensive whole.

I maintain that the purely logical distinction between something and another is based on the homogeneous medium, which also provides the basis of mathematics. In the temporal order of cognition one may become conscious of this underlying unity only in later reflection, but in the logical order it precedes the distinction between something and another. This homogeneous medium cannot be immediately identified with the quantitative "one," for it is first of all the qualitative universal, within which something and another are mutually reflected. Just as, after one has advanced from rational numbers to the Dedekindian section of a real number system, real numbers appear as a concrete whole extending behind rational numbers, so, in the present case, when the complete qualities of the homogeneous medium become manifest in it, "something" becomes the quantitative "one." Behind all cognition there is experience; when cognition bears experience but has not yet projected it in front of itself, when it is still "in itself" and not yet "for itself," or, from the other angle, when experience has not yet manifested its entirety, all things are qualitative. But when the unity underlying the qualitative "something" is projected as an object of cognition, it appears as the quantitative "one." If number appears as "being," a more comprehensive "being and relative non-being" must underlie it, and from the vantage point of this more concrete unity even number is qualitative. That may seem the height of absurdity, yet the contentlessness of number is already a quality. Other qualities of number make it possible to distinguish various numerical systems. The law of composition is operative in all treatment of number as such, but it is not reflected upon. When, however, the natural attitude is suspended (to use Husserl's terms) we become conscious of this law. Thus, concretely, there is a qualitative aspect to quantitative objects, and in qualitative objects there is also a quantitative aspect. Quality is the aspect of the development of experiential content for itself, quantity its being by itself. All experience possesses both aspects, and mathematical quantity is simply its most universal case, the developmental aspect of an object of pure thought.

32

As activity, productive imagination is concrete subject vis-à-vis the activity of logical judgment; the purely mathematical object is concrete subject vis-à-vis the purely logical object; the purely quantitative is the limit of the purely qualitative. The limit of (qualitative) sameness is (quantitative) identity. $1 = 1$, which expresses this identity, indicates the permanence of the identity of the object itself, no matter how its relationships with others change. Discrete and continuous numbers are related in the same way as logic and mathematics. Continuous numbers are a set of limit points vis-à-vis discrete numbers, in the same sense as mathematics is the limit of logic. Continuous numbers are concrete subject vis-à vis discrete numbers, in the same sense as mathematics is concrete subject in relation to logic. The move from discrete to continuous is not one to an utterly unrelated position, but to an underlying position which has already been presupposed. It is a move from the abstract to the concrete, to the true self. The mathematician stresses the difference between discrete and continuous as objects of cognition, and the impossibility of relating discrete to continuous as part to whole. However, it is possible to say discrete numbers are part of continuous numbers, in the sense that a conscious act as object of reflection is part of the self which reflects. Rational numbers are "infinite in their own kind," but continuous numbers are their "absolutely infinite" substance.[178]

A purely logical object is thought of as qualitative, while that which has determined itself as "one" is quantitative. When it becomes a Dedekindian section it can be thought of as once again acquiring a qualitative tendency. Continuous numbers, as Cohen's intensive quantity, can be thought of as qualitative. All experiential content "in itself" is qualitative, but "for itself" (as related to another) it is quantitative. In continuity, it returns to the state of being "in itself," and can again be thought of as qualitative. However, this return does not restore its original state, for the new "in itself" includes the "for itself." The object "in itself" always has a concrete subject as its background; this is the goal towards which all knowledge is a constant progress. A cognitive stance always implies opposition between the object and the underlying concrete subject; only in a volitive stance can we identify with this concrete subject.

101

The relationship between space and number also illustrates these patterns. The identification of the elements of geometry varies somewhat from author to author, but we may accept, with Hilbert, that they comprise point, straight line, and plane, whose mutual relationships are described by such words as "to lie," "between," "parallel," "congruent," and "continuous." The simplest, most fundamental geometrical objects are points and straight lines. The point is not defined, but a straight line is defined as the only relationship that is determined by two points. According to Hilbert we may say that a straight line passes through two points or that a straight line combines two points, or that two points lie on a straight line.[179] Coolidge considers point and distance as the fundamental objects of "metrical geometry," and states as axioms the following: "Axiom I. There exists a class of objects, containing at least two members, called points, Axiom II. The existence of any two points implies the existence of a unique object called their distance."[180]

Viewed epistemologically, the most fundamental object of geometry, the point, which for the geometer is indefinable, is an object of cognition grasped independently of its content; it indicates merely the position of our cognition, the "something" which is the object of the purely logical act of positing an object. We might think of the simplest relationship determined between two such "somethings" as a straight line. This entirely abstract relation between "position" and "position" can take any concrete form. It may be a relationship between color and color, or between two persons. In itself it has no specific content. However to the straight line of geometry some quality necessarily attaches, such as Hilbert's axioms of "ordering," for example:

1. When A, B, C are points of a straight line, and B lies between A and C, then B also lies between C and A;
2. When A and C are two points of a straight line, then there is always at least one point B that lies between A and C, and at least one point D such that C lies between A and D;
3. Among any three points of a straight line there is always one and only one that lies between the other two.[181]

How does the straight line, so defined, differ from a numerical series? How does a straight line connecting two points differ from the number two? If we think of the number two as the unity of cognitive objects the positions of which are interchangeable by means of a homogeneous medium, there is no distinction whatever between the number two and two points, and we can say that both are based on Russell's form of externality. Logically,

Hilbert's axiom of ordering is not different from an ordering of numbers; it is only that the former is linked to intuition by such words as "between" and "to lie." Therefore, I wonder whether, in the case of analytic geometry, rather than speak of number being joined to space, we should not say that they are united at their common basis in the homogeneous medium?

The "homogeneous and isotropic" space of the geometer is nothing more than the product of an ideal; the ideal which, on the one hand, creates this kind of space, on the other, creates a system of numbers. Space is simply the point at which the numerical system, a system of pure thought, determines itself through coming in contact with experience. This sheds light on the meaning of Poincaré's statement that the axioms of geometry are neither synthetic judgments a priori nor experiential facts but merely a human convention, and that we are free to select any form of geometry we wish, on the one condition that it be without self-contradiction.[182] Again, the "projection and section" which Cremona considers the "fundamental operations" of projective geometry—which is the science of pure space—can be seen as the determining act of a self-conscious system of pure thought.[183]

When a self-conscious system has determined itself, it is a geometric point; the logical judgment "A is A" is a point. Since a point lies in the state of "immediacy" of a self-conscious system, we can say that a point is qualitative. The point of pure geometry, from which quantitative aspects have been completely eliminated, is produced by abstracting the qualitative aspects of the elements of number. And since in a self-conscious system "ought" is being and being is "ought," the determination of a single position includes its direction of development within itself. The relation of two positions in this direction can be grasped as a straight line determined by two points. The geometrical straight line is simply the abstract reflection of the relationship of two determinations in a self-conscious system. Hilbert's axiom that "Two different points always determine a straight line"[184] expresses this abstract relationship, which is further determined in the axioms of ordering quoted above. These axioms also express abstractly the order of number (larger or smaller), and Hilbert goes beyond rational numbers in the axiom of continuity, the Archimedean axiom, in which a system of self-consciousness is perfectly expressed and a union with the system of real numbers reached.[185] The relationship between two points in one direction seems to be no different from the number two, but when it is seen as a combination of determination and determination it acquires the quality of a geometric straight line. If we grasp the self-consciousness whereby we move from one determination to another as a concrete whole it appears as a quantitative (metric) straight line. (In pure geometry a plane is a relationship determined by three points which are not co-linear: "Three points which do not lie in one straight line always determine one plane."[186] In determining this relationship we must distinguish directions of determination rather than merely relate two determinations of a self-conscious system as above.)

From purely logical cognitive objects number is developed, and the geometric straight line brings out the qualitative aspect of number. However, while self-consciousness can develop infinitely in one direction it can also be infinite in its transformations of direction; it can be infinite both vertically (quantitatively) and horizontally (qualitatively). While our selves are all self-conscious systems, they are unified by means of an even greater self-consciousness. Herein lies the basis of geometric dimension in self-consciousness, which is precisely the a priori of geometry. Since a self-conscious system in a state of immediacy is qualitative, pure geometry is qualitative. The unity underlying the geometric a priori is qualitative unity.

As (quantitative) mathematical objects are the limits of (qualitative) logical objects, may not purely geometric objects in turn be purely qualitative relationships transcending all quantitative relationship? And if geometric space is thus the qualitative limit of number, may not the object of analytic geometry be a limit which unifies continuous numbers as a concrete subject?

Consciousness of Rectilinearity

Tetsugaku Kenkyū, No. 8, Nov. 1916

33

The term "qualitative" usually suggests such experiential contents as red or blue, but it properly refers to all instances in systems of experience which are in a state of immediacy. Thus, not only sensation, but also the self which has returned to itself in reflection, can be called qualitative. Conversely, such contents as red or blue need not be only qualitative; insofar as these are grasped as concepts, they can also signify the *relations* between various experiences. In a comparison of a system of pure thought and a system of color-perception, on the subjective side thinking is correlated with seeing, and on the objective side Bolzano's proposition itself, as the object of thought, corresponds to the representation itself of the color which is the object of sight. In terms of the categories of objective existence, the proposition itself corresponds to truth, and the representation itself corresponds to natural scientific reality. There is thus a one-to-one correspondence between the two systems. Their distinction is not, however, one between independent realities, but merely one between differing aspects of one self-conscious system. These reflections may help us in our search for the point of contact between thought and experience.

A given experience, as a concrete universal developing through and in itself, is neither subjective nor objective. When this experience is viewed in terms of its continuity with the underlying comprehensive subject, its self-development now appears as subjective activity (whether thinking or seeing), and the point of origin of this activity, that is, the point of contact between the experienced activity and the underlying concrete subject, is the *psychological self*. In contrast, when this experience is unified as an object, that is, when it is viewed as part of the object world of the comprehensive subject, it is *objective existence*. To use our geometrical analogy, circle, ellipse, and parabola are each a single continuous subject, when in a state of immediacy, but when unified by a limit concept as particular instances of the more comprehensive subject defined by the formula for quadratic equations, they appear as objective. Circle and ellipse in a state of immediacy are qualitative, but grasped in terms of the comprehensive subject, the curved line of a quadratic equation, as its limits, they are quantitative. (Continuous numbers enable us to think the qualitative quantitatively: continuity is the internal unity of quality and quantity; it is the quality wherein quality is quantified; the subject wherein the subject is objectified.)

When self-consciousness has determined only itself, and is in the state of "self-relatedness," it is logical judgment, which is purely qualitative. Self-consciousness, however, contains the motivation for development within itself; its self-reflection is immediately development and vice versa. Self-consciousness is the unity of relation with itself and relation with another, as Hegel states.[187] Since it includes relation with another within relation with itself, the move from the standpoint of logic to that of mathematics is possible, and the qualitative "something" can become the quantitative "one," the concrete object which exhibits both self-relatedness and relation with others. If we were to add qualitative distinctions of content as between red and blue, this unity could not emerge; but in the absence of such distinctions between the objects of thought, this unity is an internal necessity. The quantitative "one" unifying both aspects internally, a Hegelian being-for-itself, is both numerical one and the geometric point. These elementary mathematical objects are thus manifestations of self-consciousness.

Whence arises the distinction between numerical one and the geometric point? In each of these mathematical elements, a self-conscious individual is thought of formally and as wholly without content. But self-consciousness, as introspection shows, develops in two directions. On the one hand, there is the chronological and vertical development seen in our individual history, while, on the other hand, one develops horizontally toward the center of a greater self; the former is individual development, and the latter is universal development. I believe that we may already detect both lines of development in contentless, formal mathematical development, which thus exhibits the basic structure of self-conscious unity. While for each of us our self-consciousness is an independent, free personality, it is also part of a greater self-consciousness; indeed, our personality is a part of the personality of God. Individual development is the basis of time, characterized by Cohen's "anticipation," and of number. Universal development, the union of person and person, is the basis of space, and of geometric relationships. These two aspects represent progression and reflection respectively, and their inner unity is self-consciousness. One might also say that the former is our mind and the latter our body, and that our action is the self-conscious unity of both. Reflection becomes space, extra-mental nature: ordinarily thought of as returning to the past, it in fact moves from a limited position to a more comprehensive underlying one. Self-consciousness, mapping the self within itself, grounds the infinite series of natural numbers, and the outcome of a return to the source of this series in reflection thereon is a straight line. The definition of a straight line as the relationship determined by two points indicates this reflection. The form of a certain individual's self-consciousness is one straight line. The straight line of pure geometry is the extremely abstract self-consciousness of an individual. But the self-consciousness of one individual implies the infinite self-consciousness of other individuals; to recognize one's own personality one must recognize its relationship with others (just as one cannot apprehend a rectilinear relationship in one direction without apprehending the same relationship in other directions). The relationship of two free personalities is two-dimensional, the relationship of three personalities is three-dimensional, and so on, but the union of an infinite number of personalities is again nothing other than a return to the original, reflectionless, infinite series. (One might claim that ethical society and pure space have the same foundation: the union of two or three directions figures the greater single personality joining two or three personalities.)

A geometer, to define a straight line, employs such terms as "segment" and "extension" and uses the equation $\overline{AB} \equiv \overline{AC} + \overline{CB}$, wherein C stands for a "segment of A and B," and B defines an "extension of (AC) beyond C." A straight line is then "the assemblage of all points of a segment and its extension" (Coolidge). Segment and extension figure the reflective and progressive, inward and outward, directions of self-conscious development.

The numerical series is the objectification of this development and geometric relationships express its subjective activity. Thus, when a self-conscious system has been expressed perfectly, it is, objectively, a system of real numbers, and, subjectively, a continuous straight line. Our intuition of rectilinearity derives from our awareness of this infinitely developing self-conscious system. When this system has effectively constituted itself as self-conscious, it negates itself and demands another independent self-consciousness. This is the basis of the geometric axiom that "All points do not lie in one line." When a self-conscious system has completed itself as a series of real numbers, as a continuous straight line, wherein its "in itself" or qualitative aspect attains a positive manifestation, the idea of the qualitative distinctions within a purely intellectual system of self-consciousness, relating one "in itself" to another, must then emerge, founding the various functional relationships between variable and variable. Moreover, when various qualitative relationships have been unified quantitatively through their limits, we can say that a self-conscious system appears concretely in its perfect form. Thus analytical geometry, far from being a non-essential application of mathematics to geometry, corresponds to the developmental demand of self-consciousness for objective knowledge and is the concrete manifestation of a self-conscious system, including within itself the intuition of space as transcendental sensation.

34

What is an objective straight line (an experiential straight line as distinguished from a geometric one) as a content of consciousness? To the psychologist a straight line which we see by moving our eyes from point A to point B, or which we sense by moving our hands in the same way, depends on the muscular perception of movement. Thus Wundt describes the spatial representation of a blind person as "the product of a fusion of external tactile sensations and their qualitatively graded local signs with intensively graded internal tactile sensations of the inner world."[188] Awareness of a straight line is constituted, in this view, from sensations graded qualitatively and intensively. But if we must think of consciousness of rectilinearity as one sensation, on the same level as other graded sensations, how can it be a synthesizing function which unifies other sensations? Conversely, if we consider it as consciousness of a higher order than other sensations, then we are bound to admit that there is a higher order of consciousness than sensation, interpreting in this sense Wundt's statement that, as a special feature of the psychological law of causality, a unique characteristic not included within the elements themselves is created by their union. For us to be aware of graded sensations as one spatial perception, the consciousness of meaning must be added to them; from the mere arithmetical sum of graded sensations no higher order consciousness can emerge. What is it, then, that unifies graded sensations and constitutes the consciousness of a straight line? I think that it is precisely the developmental aspect of a self-conscious system. Introspection reveals the infinite possibilities of the development of the self, and this is the origin of the consciousness of rectilinearity; the notion of straightness reveals the being-in-itself, the state of immediacy, of self-conscious development. (Usually we class straightness with red and blue as a subjective quality of mental phenomena, but these qualities, Bolzano's representations themselves, are not necessarily either mental or physical. Immediate concrete reality is transcendental sensation, which can be either physical or mental depending on one's point of view. Psychology takes the being-in-itself of self-consciousness as the concretely real, and thus grasps straightness as a mere sensory quality.) The emergence of a spatial image possessing a special feature not included in the graded sensations which are its elements means that we have become conscious of these sensations in the form of a self-conscious system which is their concrete state. To grasp the unity of the minutely graded sensations is to be conscious of the continuum which underlies these grades. Graded sensation is an abstract fabrication of psychology; concrete reality in itself is a continuous self-conscious system. In the combination of mental elements, their union is not effected from without, but consists in their return to their concrete source.

When reflecting on a self-conscious system, we can view it either from its own center in its concrete original form, or as an object from the standpoint of a still more comprehensive system. In terms of natural science, the latter is the mechanistic viewpoint, and the former is the teleological one. The psychological viewpoint is still closer to the former. Each of these viewpoints bears on the same reality. The progress from the physical to the psychological viewpoint is not a shift from one set of phenomena to another but an increase in concreteness in our grasp of reality. Wundt divides the content of immediate experience into extensive syntheses which are repeatable and other contents, and says that the system of the latter is subjectivity, a system of concrete immediacy.[189] If we see the self-conscious system as a syllogism, its hypothetical major premise is the underlying comprehensive standpoint of objective, universal physical knowledge, its categorical minor premise is the core of immediate psychological fact, and in the conclusion these two are joined to form the totality of the system. Neither Husserlian essences nor simple factual data are either physical or psychological; the distinction of fact and essence depends on whether one emphasizes the universal or the particular. Consciousness does not add something to a pre-given content, but merely reflects the extent of the development of the content. Every content is essentially an independent reality like Bolzano's representation itself or proposition itself, so that even such "secondary qualities" as color and sound are not subjective, but transcend the act of consciousness. Ordinarily we start from the idea of an organism, and think that secondary qualities arise from its relationship with the external world, but we should rather think that the qualities themselves are fundamental, and that organisms too are established by their union. Content and its transformations are the immediately given and "matter," "organism," or even "spirit" itself, are merely various centers that unify this content.

These reflections have brought us close to the insights of Bergson, according to whom the material world results from the mind's transformation of pure duration, which is vertical rectilinear progress, into the plane of simultaneous existence, our body being the point of contact between the two:

> Everything, then, must happen as if an independent memory gathered images as they successively occur along the course of time; and as if our body, together with its surroundings, was never more than one among these images, the last, that which we obtain at any moment by making an instantaneous section in the general stream of becoming. In this section our body occupies the center....We may speak of the body as an ever advancing boundary between the future and the past, as a pointed end, which our past is continually driving forward into our future.[190]

Rather than imagine that the potential for sensation is lodged in the brain, ready to be activated by external stimuli, we should think of consciousness as emerging when the spearhead of pure duration pushes the plane of simultaneous existence on. The body is merely the organ of movement and the brain is merely the pivot of movement; our body is the shadow of memory cast on the material world, which is the transverse section of duration. The reverse side of tension is relaxation, and the former is the side of pure memory, i.e., spirit, whereas the latter is the side of matter. The former is time and the latter is space:

> Let us seek, in the depths of our experience, the point where we feel ourselves most intimately within our own life. It is into pure duration that we then plunge back, a duration in which the past, always moving on, is swelling unceasingly with a present that is absolutely new. But, at the same time, we feel the spring of our will strained to its utmost limit. . . .Now let us relax the strain, let us interrupt the effort to crowd as much as possible of the past into the present. If the relaxation were complete, there would no longer be either memory or will . . . .Behind "spirituality" on the one hand, and "materiality" with intellectuality on the other, there are then two processes opposite in their direction, and we pass from the first to the second by way of inversion. . . No doubt we make only the first steps in the direction of the extended, even when we let ourselves go as much as we can. But suppose for a moment that matter consists in this very movement pushed further, and that physics is simply psychics inverted.[191]

The body expresses duration in the material world. Consciousness does not emerge by adding something to matter, but rather we arrive at matter by subtracting something from consciousness.

I believe that the notion of a self-conscious system allows us to give an even more profound and universal meaning to these views of Bergson. His internal or pure duration is the self-conscious system of self-generation and self-development, wherein meaning equals being and act equals fact. Time is thought of as something real, but if we refine Bergson's concept of "the flux of time" (le temps qui s'écoule),[192] it is self-conscious in our sense. (Or we may also say that it is syllogistic.) Conversely, the aspect of static unity of a self-conscious system, the major premise of the syllogism considered in isolation, is space, and the self-conscious system isolated from the determining act is the material world of simultaneous existence. If, as Bergson says, pure time is unrepeatable, the reason must be that there is something at its foundation which transcends time. Bergson's excessive attachment to the idea of time causes him to overlook this aspect of unity which transcends movement. At the vanguard of the élan vital, there is neither space nor time; as Faust declares, "In the beginning was the Act." This act is not a temporal act, but something more immediate and fundamental than space and time; it is the development of reason itself. With Hegel we may say that all reality is syllogistic, and that its major premise expressing universal

111

law is the material world, or space, while its minor premise expressing fact is the world of consciousness, or actuality; here is the point of contact between mind and matter, i.e., our body. If the major premise indicates the scope of objective matter, the minor premise indicates the scope of the subjective self. Bergson's inner duration is the a priori linking the syllogism together, or Cohen's principle of continuity. Thus we can think of mental activity as the process whereby the universal which is the foundation of the syllogism determines itself, while the specific difference of the major and the minor premises corresponds to the quality of that activity.

Spirit and Matter

35

I have shown how in consciousness of rectilinearity a self-conscious system reflectively apprehends its infinite capacity of development. I should now like to extend this discussion to experiences with content, such as color-sensation. Sensory qualities are often thought of as phenomena of consciousness which, in response to external stimuli, arise in the brain center, as if by magic, bearing no resemblance to the purely mechanical movements, vibrations of ether or air, which occasioned them. If, however, we proceed from our awareness of red or blue as immediately given experiences, it appears that what we term material phenomena are simply abstract concepts whereby we have unified the relationships of these experiences. Moreover, these immediately given experiences resemble less the unambiguous, unidimensional sensations which psychology attempts to construct than those which are the material of artistic expression, as analyzed by Max Raphael (lines which are a tension between rectilinear and curvilinear; colors which intrinsically call forth their complements, and which are always embedded in three-dimensional continuity).

In terms of Meinong's *Sosein*,[193] in immediate experience such qualities as color and sound can be thought of as constituting one system, apart from the relationships of space, time, and causation, by means of their own content. Meinong's "object theory" and Husserl's "science of essence" refer to such a system, of which the contents are thought of as wholly unreal, or hypothetical. Only when it is recognized to be inherently developmental can the system of immediate experience be grasped as real, and it is this unification of experiential content under the aspect of development which constitutes what we call visual and aural acts. These mental phenomena may be regarded as what is most concretely real, in line with Bergson's thesis that material phenomena are conceived through the subtraction of something from the phenomena of consciousness. Physiology and psychology derive immediate experience from what is latent in the nervous system, but we prefer the Bergsonian view that the body is merely the representative of the spirit in the material world, the projection of pure duration in the plane of simultaneous existence. The eye, for instance, is thought of as the cause of color sensation, but it should rather be grasped as a projection in the material world corresponding to that sensation, as the point of contact between the experience of color and the material world, or, more accurately, as the point at which the self-conscious system which is color determines itself.

Psychologists claim that our distinctions of sensory qualities have developed by differentiation from original "universal sensations." If mankind has evolved from the lower animals in whom, apart from the tactile sense, there are no special sensations, this is a plausible view. It is said that we can clearly trace this evolution in the construction of the internal ear. Thus sense distinctions have developed from something latent in the nervous system, just as various living species evolve from a germ-plasm.[194] Yet we cannot admit that the sensory qualities of immediate experience are derived from physical and physiological stimuli. The incontrovertible facts of immediate experience are the alterations and mutual relationships of sensory content, and these must be more fundamental than external stimuli. (It is said that Fresnel's mirror experiment proves that light rays are vibrations of ether, but its only incontrovertible result is the differential equation expressing the quantitative relationships of the alternations of light and darkness and their distances. These are the fundamental data, and the explanations a Fresnel or a Maxwell provide have only the status of hypothesis.)[195]

Immediate experience, as developmental, is a movement from universal to particular, the process of self-determination of a universal, simultaneous existence. The universal concept of color is a reality of immediate experience. Physically color may be defined as the vibration of ether, but experientially it is a concrete universal operating on itself; it is one inner continuum. (In Fresnel's experiment too, the act of minute discrimination of light and darkness must be given first, for the act of discrimination, which is a judgment, to be possible.) Behind immediate experience creative evolution is always operating; the development of the experience of color is a creative evolution. In this process of self-determination of a universal, we can distinguish two directions: the *specifying* direction, from universal to particular, and the direction of *horizontal expansion*, from particular to particular. The first involves creation of new contents and passage to new standpoints, while the second is a development within one standpoint. The first corresponds to Bergson's vertical development of pure duration and the second is development in a plane of simultaneous existence. The single continuum wherein various conic sections can pass over into one another by means of a limit concept can be thought of either as specifying itself in the various positions of straight line, circle, ellipse, parabola, and hyperbola, or as resulting from their synthesis in light of the quadratic equation they instantiate. Differentiation is the law of development of mental phenomena, synthesis that of material phenomena. When animals first acquired eyes, their vision was probably an extremely blurred consciousness of light and darkness, which gradually developed by differentiation to become the minute color discrimination we have today. Such differentiation is the specification of an a priori; behind it, in each instance, an *élan vital* is at work. Psychology attempts to sight this "leaping-point" through qualitative analysis of mental phenomena. As moments within a system of self-consciousness these qualitatively differentiated phenomena reveal a mutual disparity, for they are each a trace of where the *élan vital*, which is the life of the universe, has leapt. From another angle, these simple qualities, the separate positions of a self-conscious system, are each a distinct self, the center of a distinct self-conscious system, and we can also think of each as a distinct act. Mental acts present a process of differentiation similar to that which we have reconstructed in the case of sensory qualities: in relation to acts of sensation, acts of representation or of thought are centers of the leap to a higher order of *élan vital*.

These notions prompt various questions: Whence did consciousness arise? Did the world not exist prior to the emergence of consciousness? Is the scientific theory of the evolution of the universe wholly false? I venture to assert that the order of the development of the universe as grasped by natural science is only one way of thinking of the world of experience. The order grasped in terms of physical time and physical a priori is not necessarily the order of inner creation of the *élan vital*. This inner order, or what Husserl calls phenomenological time, is more basic than physical time, which is founded on it. The true beginnings of the universe lie, not in the distant past of the nebulas, but in the center of inner creation. As relativity theory shows, absolute time is an ideal without a secure basis in actuality, and the selection of the coordinates of physical phenomena, as we arrange experiential content in the form of space, is what determines the order of time.

If we attempt to grasp the order of experience as it is found prior to all such processing, there are various possible approaches. In the case of spatial experience we can begin by thinking of the developmental order of our individual history, and extend this way of thinking to the history of mankind as a whole or even of life as a whole. But we can also adopt a purely logical viewpoint, and conceive all relationships as relationships of reasons and conclusions. Or we can proceed to an epistemological discussion of the grounds of knowledge and, with Fichte, Hegel, and Cohen, grasp spatial categories in terms of the creative development of thought. Psychological and biological approaches are more fundamental than the physical one, since in them experiential content develops in accord with value. While the order of value cannot be identified with that of time, nonetheless, temporal order, as one possible way of viewing experience, is preceded by various orders of value and of the qualitative differentiation of experience, so that we can say that the order of time is in fact based on the order of value.

36

Without the eye there cannot be a sensation of light, and it is by the development of this sense organ that the worlds of light and color open to us. If we lose the eye, we lose the sensation of light, and the worlds of light and color instantly disappear. What is the condition of possibility of this function of the eye as the cause of light perception?

The eye, as a part of the material world, must be thought of as a combination of a few chemical elements. Chemical elements can be scientifically defined only in terms of such things as atomic weights, or, in other words, by reducing the qualitative to the quantitative. (It is true that, because chemical elements are not purely homogeneous, they cannot yet be thought of purely quantitatively. If today's electron theory develops, and the various atoms can be explained, as in the theory of Thomson, by the number of electrons and their combination, then for the first time the distinctions of matter may become quantitative distinctions of homogeneous things.) This cannot explain how sensory characteristics are produced from the quantitative relationships of homogeneous things, as when stimuli to the eye retina caused by long-wave light rays are felt as the color red or those caused by short-wave rays as the color violet. We must say, with Du Bois-Raymond, that here we are at "the limits of natural science." Since the energy of light existed long before the emergence of life, science locates the power to transform light energy into the sensations of light and color in the optic nerves and their nuclei. But one cannot explain the relationship between physical and psychological by simply asserting that the nervous system has this power. All we know is that mental phenomena such as color or sound always accompany the chemical phenomenon termed a nerve stimulus. If physiological phenomena can be explained physically or chemically, as mechanists maintain, then the fact that the same physical or chemical phenomenon is accompanied in certain circumstances by mental phenomena, but in others not, depends on the way these physical phenomena are combined. This does not explain why mental phenomena accompany only certain material combinations.

Physics understands heat as a species of energy, which can be transformed into mechanical energy, as mechanical energy can be transformed into heat. This does not mean that mechanical movement is transformed into our *sensation* of heat, but concerns merely an unchanging quantitative relationship between the two forms of energy. The question of how living beings sense it is indifferent to the scientific account of the energy of heat, nor does it explain why we do not feel as light that which we feel as heat or vice versa. If we take the material world as our starting point we cannot explain the correspondence between mental and material phenomena. If, however, we begin from consciousness, our body appears as simply one phenomenon of the world of consciousness, and the eye, which senses light and color, itself belongs to the world of light and color. From one angle, consciousness appears as simply an adjunct of material phenomena, but, from another, what we call objective phenomena are simply an interpretation of phenomena of consciousness. Thus, to say that if there is no eye there are no sensations of color and light, means no more than that there is an unchanging correlation between the eye and these sensations, or, in terms of the entire world of consciousness (in which the eye which is the cause of sensation for one person is only part of the object world of another person), that the extinction of a certain sense spells the extinction of the group of phenomena constituting the light perceptions of a certain individual. If the eyes of all living things (which are one phenomenon in the world of light perception) were to disappear, the world of light perception as a whole would be simultaneously extinguished. Since our body too belongs to the world of consciousness, the assertion that sense organs or nervous systems are the cause of sensation means only that together with the emergence and destruction of certain phenomena of consciousness certain other phenomena of consciousness emerge and are destroyed. If the eye belonged only to the world of light and color and were utterly without relationship to the other sensory worlds, there would be no such thing as the eye to be considered the cause of light perception. No matter how we consider the problem, since both our sense organs themselves and the external stimuli inevitably belong to our sensory world, we ultimately cannot escape from the sphere of consciousness. We must say that the sense organs which give rise to sensation belong within sensation. If we abstract from sensory content, we cannot think of anything whatever other than the functional relationships between phenomenon and phenomenon. To say that spirit is born from matter is a complete inversion of their true relationship.

We tend to think of the sense of touch as the sense organ of reality, but there is no reason why touch should come closer to the qualities of objects themselves than light or sound perception. The matter discerned by the interpretation of tactile phenomena is the same as that revealed in auditory phenomena. But this identity means only that the same laws of energy apply. Since the phenomena of light perception could not be explained by the same laws, it was necessary to postulate an extra-material ether. If we were able to explain all physical phenomena in terms of electromagnetic energy, matter would be identical with electricity and objects would no longer be defined primarily in tactile terms, but in terms of the phenomena of light perception. In the evolution of living things, it is clear that the sense of touch developed first and perception of light and sound came later. However we cannot say that the past sense of touch is the cause of present light and sound perception. Just as Herbart's "reals" correspond to sensation,[196] common sense makes tactile content the real, and thence conceives the permanent, unchanging, objective world. However, if matter is electricity, we can no longer say that the material world constructed from the sense of touch is the real material world, for the phenomena of light and magnetism reveal the inner structure of matter and its delicate properties in a way touch cannot. Light perception comes late in the development of consciousness, but from the standpoint of Herbart's "reals" we may say that it is fundamental.

Tetsugaku Kenkyū, No. 9, Dec. 1916

37

Consider the case of a ball moving in a fixed direction with a fixed speed, which collides with a ball of identical mass and stops, while the second ball now moves ahead in almost the same direction and with almost the same speed. In this case we say the momentum of the first ball has been transmitted to the second. When two forces act on a particle, causing it to move along the diagonal of the parallelogram they form, we say the two forces have combined to become one. Similarly, though they are intuitively utterly different phenomena, we say that heat is transformed into movement and movement is transformed into heat, and, to give a less precise illustration, when phosphorus melts at 44 degrees centigrade, we say that 44-degree heat has melted phosphorus.

Contemporary science does not speak of forces behind phenomena, but like Kirchhoff, who reduces dynamics to the description of movement,[197] it confines itself to the description of empirical events, seeing the causal relationship as a merely functional one between the changes in two kinds of phenomena and the laws of nature as signifying only that there is a fixed relationship between the appearance, disappearance, or transformation of certain phenomena and the appearance, disappearance, or transformation of other phenomena. Can we use this model of causality to understand how the brain and sense organs can cause the phenomena of consciousness? For this to be possible, sensory experience would first have to be given, and to be projected as object. While the sense organs appear as sensory experience, they are also its condition, and thus have a unique, double status among material phenomena, at once sharing their common causal relationships and eluding treatment in terms of these relationships. An unchanging relationship between two optical phenomena suggests a physical causal relationship between them, yet what makes this optical relationship possible is a sense organ. What establishes relationships must lie outside them; thus the sense organ lies outside the relationships of sense experience at the same time as it is sighted within them. On this contradiction the attempt to explain the mind-body relationship founders.

As the condition of sense experience the sense organs must be more than material combinations, for all organic functions are intelligible only in teleological terms. Analysis of the digestive process, the circulation of the blood, or respiration, reveals only physical or chemical phenomena, and even the vitalist tenet of a force within cells which cannot be explained in terms of chemical functions merely points to an unknown quantity. Only a teleological conception permits us to think of our bodies as different from natural objects and as individual entities possessing a special significance. The mechanistic view, which analyzes phenomena into individual elements and reduces each series to a universal law, only apparently contradicts the teleological view, which finds an overall significance in the totality constructed by these mechanical causal series. There is no conflict between viewing a certain piece of marble as a work of art and viewing it as material for chemical experiment. If body is to be intimately linked with spirit, it must be a teleological unity, the unity we call "life" and to which we think of consciousness as an accompaniment. What links body and spirit in this way, is, I suggest, *the activity of the will,* and this must be analyzed in depth if we wish to gain further insight into the mysteries of the mind-body relationship. Without consciousness of volition we could not distinguish our body from other material objects, and would have no reason to believe it to have a special relationship to spirit.

However much we try to view our body in the same way as other material things, we cannot gainsay our sense of a special relationship between the cognitive acts of the self and the one material thing we call our body. We are aware that with the appearance and disappearance of the sense organs, eye and ear, the sensations of color and sound also appear and disappear (not that the eye itself produces the sensation of light, without the stimuli of the light rays which cause a chemical change in the rhodopsin of the eye, but that our light perception accompanies this chemical phenomenon). But how can the spiritual activity of the self combine with natural scientific phenomena? To answer that question we must view a physical organism as a single functional unity. Certain physical processes are an absolutely necessary condition of the perception of light, yet the rhodopsin on its own does not produce that perception, and can do so only in collaboration with the entire body, particularly the nerve centers. Our body is not merely a mechanical unit, but a teleological unity. The difference between inorganic and organic matter is not one of substance but of the form of combination; it is a functional difference. It is because our spirit combines with the body, which must be viewed as a unity of teleological function,

120

that the eye feels the light rays. Without this vital unity the eye could not see light nor the ear hear sound.

What is this vital unity? How does it differ from the unity of inanimate things? Biological phenomena are not of a higher order than material phenomena, for like them they are natural phenomena and belong to the world of things. They do not necessarily entail a spiritual dimension. Only when it can be ascertained that spiritual phenomena accompany the phenomenon of life is it correct to say that the eye sees light and the ear hears sound. What is it that joins the objective phenomenon of life with the subjective phenomenon of spirit? When two things combine there must be a common factor, in this case, something joining subject and object. Our voluntary activity, which is the consciousness of self-consciousness, inwardly attests the unity of subject and object, and it is as a projection of this that we conceive the unity of spirit and body.

The spirit of the self which we think of as joined with our body is objectified spirit, based on a reflection on consciousness and projection of it on the natural world. This self is the abstraction of the psychologists, which Wundt describes as the feeling of activity, or the apperception, that accompanies our will or attention.[198] He sees this as the core with which bodily sensations and representations are joined. But what is this activity of apperception? Viewed introspectively or immediately, it is the internal development of consciousness content itself, a basic fact of consciousness, which cannot be further explained. At a deeper level, it is the consciousness of the self-conscious system which is the basic form of reality, and denotes the self-generative, self-developmental aspect of reality. One's consciousness need not be termed particularly "mine," for all content of which one is conscious is universal, and only the consciousness which accompanies the developmental activity of a certain content can be called the self.

Can we derive the body from the conjunction of the psychological self with a purely material world? Behind the psychological self is the logical or transcendental ego, which constitutes the material world as its object. This universal ego is the condition of possibility of our cognition of the external world and our self-realization through willed activity in that world. It grounds our unity with the natural world. It is by extracting from the world of pure experience that which conforms to the will of the self that we conceive of the self's body, which can thus be seen as a creation of the will. Yet it could also be said that this body is the reason for the creation of the

121

self. When I stretch out my hand, this is a matter of will if looked at from within, but from without it is a movement of the body. The will is the body of the spiritual world, and the body is the will of the material world; our body, as the fusion of mind and matter, is a work of art. In the same sense that Fiedler states that speech, as the last development of the advance of thought, is its expression and that art, as the last development of the advance of sight, is its expression, we may say that the body is the expression of the will, and that that which combines mind and body is the internal creative act.

To know external objects is to view the self's experience from the position of the universal ego. From one angle, it is the universalization of the experience of the self, and from another, it is a universal realizing itself. The synthesis effected by the universal ego combines into one the centers of various self-conscious systems, just as various conic sections are united in the formula of one continuum by a limit concept. In the unity created by such a formula the circle or ellipse which was a single self-conscious system when considered by itself now loses its separate individuality. If the circle or ellipse represents individual consciousness, the formula represents the standpoint of materialism. (A self-conscious system develops both qualitatively and quantitatively; projective geometry expresses only its qualitative relationships whereas analytical geometry expresses its concrete totality. In this vein, we can think that individual consciousness corresponds to the geometric dimension and that the material world corresponds to a system of mere numbers. This is the reason the material world is thought of merely as a hypothetical, possible world. We can think that the combination of mind and matter has the same foundation as the basic combination of number and geometric bodies in analytic geometry, namely the self's reflection on itself.)

In the judgment of the law of self-identity, "A is A," that which combines the subject "A" with the predicate "A" is the dynamic unity of judgment itself; as phenomena of consciousness they are different representations, but in their object they are one. Abstractly, representation, object, and the dynamic unity of these two are thought of separately, but concretely they are one self-conscious system, in which meaning presupposes judgment, and judgment presupposes meaning. If we separate for a moment the series of objects from the series of acts, we can see each object as separate, but when we view them all as manifestations of a single objective self, this objective self is a teleological unity vis-à-vis the series of separate objects. Each act is a separate spiritual phenomenon, but that which unifies the series is the consciousness of one individual. The teleological unity in the realm of objects corresponds to the unity of consciousness in the realm of acts. This is the key to the fusion of spirit and material objects, linking mind and body within one self-conscious system. Meaning postulates act, act postulates meaning, and their union is Act, *Tathandlung*. In the same way, the body, a teleological unity, postulates spirit, a unity of consciousness, and the latter postulates the former. Their union is the will, expressed as self-conscious development in art and religion.

When one ball hits another and moves it, we say that it acts on it, but this is a reciprocal action *(Wechselwirkung)*. Behind it lies a mechanical force which establishes this relationship and of which this movement is the phenomenon. In contrast to this, when a movement is governed by a single purpose, as in the impulses of living things, we suppose that a "vital force"[199] underlies it. Even if a chain of continuous movements of a living being is also governed by mechanical causality, what unites and orders them is this force. If, with Lotze, we say that reality is the underlying unity of things which founds their reciprocal action,[200] then the vital force is more real than the mechanical force. Organic bodies, however, are not yet true reality in the sense of Lotze's "unity of things," for true reality must be self-conscious. If the force which causes the operation of things is their goal, the relationship between spirit and material objects is not a parallelism as is usually thought but a teleological union. As the concrete whole is the goal of what is abstract, spirit is the goal of material objects.

38

Lotze's absolute which grounds reciprocal action must be self-conscious, for reality demands to be self-conscious, and matter requires spirit. Natural laws of the type "If A occurs, then B follows" are simply hypothetical propositions expressing potentiality, and the system they combine to constitute is the material world. But this world can be concretely real only as a single system of self-consciousness, possessing its own motive and direction of development. Objectively, its center is material force; subjectively, it is the unity of thought. The purpose of the material world is accidental with respect to matter itself, which would not be intrinsically affected by any change in the direction of the teleological development of the world. The material world can achieve full determinate reality only by combining with immediate experience. That the physical world-view does not express concrete reality is clear from the antinomies it constantly generates. The infinity of time, space, and causation indicates that they are intrinsically incomplete. Even if they were finite they would be self-contradictory. Their infinity needs to be grounded in self-consciousness. Time, space, and causation are merely the "represented," but concrete reality must be the "representing." The true reality of space is the activity wherein subjectivity represents itself. Thus, for Lotze, space is phenomenal as a quality of the external world, but real as a fact of the internal world.[201] Space is not the form of the reproduction of things, but together with them constitutes one flowing reality.

Since true reality must be determinate, if the material world or material force do not have a determining direction within themselves they cannot be fully real, and are merely potential. Some may claim that the material world is a complete and self-contained system, in which all events can be explained by mathematical necessity à la Laplace; but such necessity belongs to an external order, which is accidental to matter and has no relation to its internal qualities. In organic bodies, in contrast, the principle of order is an inner governing instance, and the chain of mechanical causation is only its means. Because they are self-determined, organisms are more fully real than matter. Those who see the material world as a reality to be taken for granted are likely to suppose that organic order is accidental. In fact the material world is an *interpretation* of reality, which we accept because it is without internal contradiction and because it is warranted by experience.

Our idea of reality is centered on the actuality of the present. The present is the center of gravity of reality (not merely its central point). The past belongs to memory, the future is no more than expectation, and it is only in the present that I and reality come in contact, that I can lose myself in the real, becoming one with it. The present is the place where reality is in a state of absolute activity. If true self-consciousness, as Fichte tells us, is absolute activity,[202] then the present is the precise locus of self-consciousness. The present of a living being is the vanguard of the process of self-determination of a self-conscious system. Only life, which has an inherent order that cannot be overturned, knows a unique present. In the material world, where present events are grasped merely as exemplifying universal laws, there is no such thing as the present in the strict sense. The present is the consummation of determination, an absolutely unique point. In living things this unique point resides within the phenomena themselves, but in the material world the present is determined as a given position, accidental to matter itself. If we were to think of life as a finite and unrepeatable unity, it would not differ at all from the system of material forces; but in fact life as actually lived is in contact with the flow of infinite reality, infinite self-consciousness, and bears its stamp.

It is true that there are no completely undetermined systems, and that even systems of pure thought move in the direction of determination, but the material world is like the plane plan of a solid which depends wholly on the solid for its determination. The teleological disposition of the material world, which permits a one-to-one correspondence between the material and spiritual, comparable to that between plane and solid, is what conjoins mind and body. To develop our simile, each surface of the solid may be taken to correspond to one psychological individual, and each facet of each surface to various spiritual acts. The line uniting the solid with the plane can, from one angle, express psychological activity, and from another, physiological activity—in short, it expresses psycho-physical parallelism. The plane, viewed in isolation, is only a set of lines or figures—thus in materialism all phenomena are reduced to mechanistic relationships. Teleology adds the lines of union with the solid to the plane, allowing us to see material phenomena in relation to original concrete experience. The basis of teleology is our volitional activity, and life is the shadow of our will in the material world. Teleology overturns the mechanist law, "If A occurs, then B must follow," and replaces it with "In order for there to be B, A must precede it." It has the power to do this, because it stands outside mechanistic relationships. Material force is the plane, life the solid: both are simply interpretations of the real, but one interpretation approaches nearer to concrete reality.

Though teleology comes closer to concrete reality than mechanism, it does not immediately follow that life is more real than physical force. The latter is, after all, indestructible, and does not know death. Lotze, discussing the relationship between life and nature, says that if a certain impulse can attain its ends unaided there is no problem, but if not, it must use already given reality as a means, and is obliged to follow the laws of the means. Thus its force is finite. As long as a system can react in a purposeful way to the influences of the external world it is alive, but when these influences exceed its capacity for reaction it faces death. What we call life is simply the teleological interpretation of one part of experience. The life of all nature, the purposeful thrust of evolution, *can* attain its ends unaided, and cannot be destroyed by material force, which it includes as one of its aspects. In individual experience, I think of my self as the center of reality and my body as acting with "my life," which is its projection, as the center. But Lotze proposes a plausible alternative vision of the life of the self:

> If the soul in a perfectly dreamless sleep thinks, feels, and wills nothing, is the soul then at all, and what is it? . . . Why have we not had the courage to say that, *as often as* this happens, the soul is not? . . . Why should not its life be a melody with pauses, while the primal, eternal source still acts, of which the existence and activity of the soul are a single deed, and from which that existence and activity arose.[203]

If life is nearer to reality than matter, consciousness is still nearer. These are not different realities, but different interpretations of the same reality. If we do think of them as independent, we can say that they meet in the present, which is the point of junction of several object worlds. We usually think of the present as one point in the infinite flow of time, and we think of time as a continuum of presents. Yet just as a continuum cannot be made intelligible as a collection of discrete points, neither is time a collection of isolated presents. The real present is a *section* of the temporal continuum and captures the meaning of the entire continuum in a single point. It is an arbitrary point, like one chosen at random on a straight line, but it is determined from the totality of a self-conscious system in both its qualitative and its quantitative aspects, and is thus the focal point wherein the totality of the real is reflected. In the present we touch the core of the universe. As gravity is present in every part of an object, but all forces converge at the center of gravity, which is determined by quantitative relationships, so the present is specified by the qualitative relationships of various worlds, and is the point towards which the totality of immediate experience, self-conscious development, converges. The relation between the present and the physical center of gravity is that between ideal and real. The reason that the present is given to us as absolutely determined, yet in such a way that we cannot grasp it in reflection, is that it lies on the line of absolute, infinite unity, of pure activity in which existence and value are one, or of creative evolution.

Here too lies the union of the form and content of knowledge. New knowledge always enters from the vanguard of the *élan vital*, not only empirical knowledge, but also that which is added in the progression from logic to mathematics, or from arithmetic to analysis. Scientific knowledge, which casts aside conjecture as much as possible in order to approach fact, centers on this actuality. The progress traced by Hertz from the dynamics of distant forces to the dynamics of energy to his own dynamics,[204] or even

126

better, the theory of relativity, show this urge to approach actuality itself, without recourse to a world view. To center one's thinking on actuality is to approach that which is at once utterly concrete reality and utterly universal principle. Even if this infinite unity is, strictly speaking, inconceivable, the very notion of it lends dynamism to thought.

We can clarify the meaning of the center of gravity of a self-conscious system from the analogy with the syllogism, another directional process whereby a universal determines itself. This process can advance infinitely, or in the terms of Cohen's thinking of the origin, it can infinitely return to its past and lay foundations. If the major premise is the ideal, and the minor premise the factual, the conclusion is the totality of a self-conscious system combining both. If the major is the material world, the minor is psychological subjectivity, and spirit and body are joined in the conclusion. To science, individual spiritual phenomena are only exemplifications of universal law, in which true reality consists. But the objectivity of the syllogism is not the abstract universality of its major, but comes from a concrete universal, a creative thing in itself. The syllogism is the creative action of a self-determining concrete universal, an action governed not by a cause behind it, but by a goal towards which it advances. The abstract universal is not the goal of reality, but the means of its development.

Reality is the boundless self-conscious continuum through which one system is internally transformed into another. The moment in which this transformation occurs, and in which subject and object are one action and one flow, is the real present. When we conceive a material thing teleologically, directionally, it must have a center, and this center is the point of transformation of a self-conscious system, the point at which the system of matter meets that of spirit. This "seat of the soul"[205] we may identify as the point of contact between the motor nerves and the perception nerves. Thus with Bergson we can say that spirit and body are united at the vanguard of the *élan vital*, and that spirit is the "origin" of body in Cohen's sense, the goal to which the body is the means, the concrete reality of the body, in the same sense as mathematics is the concrete basis of logic, or life the concrete basis of matter. Each of these pairs can be divided in abstraction, but concretely the merely objective member of the pair relies on the underlying subjective act for its reality, and the pairs are self-contradictory until this higher, concrete position is reached. The abstract member of the pair is the means not the goal, logic the means of the development of mathematics, discrete numbers the means of the development of serial numbers, matter the means of spiritual development. One might figure this as a syllogism in

127

which spirit and matter combine as goal and means, and whose minor premise is the seat of the soul, the spearhead of the *élan vital,* the center of gravity of reality, our concrete actuality. As Lotze observes, our sense organs do not exist to reproduce the external world, for a gleam of beautiful light or an exquisite melodic phrase are ends in themselves, which their material embodiment subserves.[206]

Tetsugaku Kenkyū, No. 10, Jan. 1917

39

Fiedler corrects the common notion that the experience of thinking is merely subjective by his insistence that it possesses independent reality and has both an internal and an external side. Indeed, one cannot divide spirit from matter; they are two aspects of concrete self-consciousness, the major and the minor of the syllogism which according to Hegel constitutes reality. The major is the material world, the world of potentiality, in which immediate experience is expressed in its most universal aspect; the minor is the world of consciousness, the world of actuality, in which experience is specified or determined. Concrete experience, progressing from moment to moment, is first universalized within the scope of individual consciousness, then developed in inter-individual experience, and finally purified rationally to form the trans-individual physical world. The physical world is not reality itself, but only an aspect thereof. Concrete reality is here and now actuality, and it is this actuality which gives its objectivity to physical knowledge, and conjoins the material and spiritual worlds. This actuality is found only in the present of the self, the point where the self is reflecting on the self.

We tend to imagine that there is an underlying unchanging self from which the present activity of the self arises, and that this underlying self is more real than its activity. But in reality there is no self apart from the Act whereby the self reflects on the self, and this Act is the totality of the self. Nor can either the past self or the future self claim to be the true self, which can be found only in the present. From the present center the past self is recalled and the future self is imagined; their only reality, then, is as representations of the present self. Although there is a contact with the past self through the continuity of our activity, we cannot return to it, for "the past is past"[207] and no longer exists. Only the present active "I" is real. The objectified, determined self of our thoughts lacks this active character and cannot be conceived as creative freedom. Determinism has its roots in this abstraction.

The present is the center of gravity of the real because it is the point where our experience is in motion, and only that which is in motion is real. If we imagine a given system of experience as a circle, and the combination of an infinite series of such systems as innumerable circles touching internally at one point, then the straight line which is perpendicular to the tangent at this point, and which passes through the centers of all these circles, is the direction in which experience is moving, the direction of concrete duration, Bergson's flux of time. Experience develops in two directions, either within a single a priori, or from one a priori to a more comprehensive underlying one. The first direction may be thought of as a straight line and the second as the transition from one curve to another by means of a limit. The first direction we think of as one experience, comparable to an infinitely extending straight line, or the numerical series, while the second unifies an infinite series of such systems, and the limit whereby it does so is the complete unification of experience, or the absolutely real. This infinite, absolute reality, the limit to which all less concrete systems tend, must be self-moving, for what is stationary is always finite. It must be the actuality of self-consciousness. In the present we connect with and move into this infinite reality. The present is not only the point of unification of one system of experience, but it is also the point where this system transcends itself and passes over into other systems, or returns to its own foundation. It is the point at which the various systems are unified in absolute reality.

The present is both the apex of creative evolution and the point from which we look back to the past in reflection; it is the point of fusion between the will's advance to the future and reflection's return to the past. But here we are contradicted by the fact, insisted on by Bergson, that we cannot return to the past of even one moment earlier. How can we square reflection with the unrepeatability of the past? Maeterlinck suggests that the past has not passed away, but exists perpetually, not as something immobile, but "depending entirely on our present and changing perpetually with it."[208] Only in that which is morally dead is the past entirely fixed. We can take this to mean that in teleological causality the past is a means to the present and the future, and its meaning changes in accord with the path on which it advances to the future (whereas mechanical causality supposes an immobile past). Thus the meaning of Augustine's previous life was changed by his conversion.

129

> The moment of repentance is the means by which one alters one's past. The Greeks thought that impossible. They often say in their Gnomic aphorisms, "Even the Gods cannot alter the past." Christ showed that even the commonest sinner could do it . . . .Christ, had he been asked, would have said—I feel quite certain about it—that the moment the prodigal son fell on his knees and wept, he made his having wasted his substance with harlots, his swine-herding and hungering for the husks they ate, beautiful and holy moments in his life.[209]

This is not a moral possibility only, but is true of all teleological relationships. In absolute time the past is unrepeatable, but absolute time is only a requirement of thought. It is not even a necessary postulate of mechanism, since the physicist's time is only a coordinate, and in fact, insofar as substance is concerned, mechanism works on the understanding that the identical phenomenon is repeatable. Absolute time is a product of reflection which spatializes the temporal and grasps it as a strictly determined, closed system. Since real duration eludes our reflective grasp, while it cannot be thought of as repeatable, neither can it be thought of as unrepeatable. Absolute time stems from the illusory objectification of the unity of all experience. This cannot be objectified since it is nothing other than an ideal demand of thought. Even if the totality of experience were finite, and we could be fully conscious of it, our reflection on it would already constitute a new experience, and thus the series of new experiences could never be closed. (The unattainability of this ideal limit does not mean that experience has no unity, for no experience can be constituted without the anticipation of such unity. Here, too, what is given in experience is what is demanded by thought. The unity of experience is a unity of demand, a unity of action, to be sought not in knowledge, but in the will.)

Self-consciousness includes consciousness of emotion and will as well as consciousness of self as object of knowledge. In ordinary cognition will is no longer will when it becomes an object of knowledge, but this is not true of self-consciousness, in which knowledge and will are one and can only be abstractly distinguished, and in which to know is to act and to act is to know. (Though this may sound absurd, the fact that we know that we cannot reflect on the self is precisely what proves we know the self.) Such consciousness of act or will is also found within the consciousness of rectilinearity as that movement of the *élan vital*, Lipps's "snapping shut," whereby we move from representational consciousness to mathematical insight. Will is consciousness of the limit whereby we thus move from one a priori to another. Its locus is the point of contact between our consciousness and the *élan vital*.

Brentano discusses consciousness in terms of the relationship between self and object. But this relationship need not be the cognitive one in which self and object are opposed. In will and emotion we meet a quite different form of consciousness, in which self and object coincide and merge. In introspection we can distinguish clearly between "I know," "I want," and "I feel." Clearly, when I know that "I want," will is an object of knowledge, and when we know a past will, we know it as will, as "I wanted." The object of immediate awareness and the object of reflection are of the same order. We suppose a past will which is reflected on to be merely an object of cognition and no longer will, because we think objects of consciousness must always be objects of cognition. But this is too rigid a conception. The artist senses his special "knack" as a kind of force, but is not cognitively aware of it—such awareness would destroy it. What the artist senses may elude conceptual grasp and verbal expression, but it is not therefore less clear and distinct than what the thinker thinks. Now, if there is an intrinsically clear consciousness of will, it can also be clearly distinguished from the cognitive when it is recollected. As we distinguish the dimensions of space according to the transcendental form of space, we distinguish knowledge, will, and emotion, whether past or present, according to the forms of transcendental knowledge, will, and emotion, and these preside equally over present perception and recollection of the past. We touch will as will, and feel emotion as emotion, without having to transform them into cognitional objects. If the addition of the idea of pastness makes it impossible for the recollected will to be will, why should not the idea of the present make it equally impossible for the will of present consciousness to be will? If will ceases to be will when we are conscious of it, there is no such thing as will, for anything corresponding to that description has quite disappeared from our ken. But if will is a datum of consciousness, past will and present will are equally so. In will there is no temporal distinction; like thought it is a consciousness which transcends time. Its unity is deeper than that of thought, and it lies at the foundation of thought. The universal which orders concrete experience is not a concept but a motive, not thought but will. Will is the form of every autonomous, self-developing experiential system. Intuition of the will underlies intellectual unity and the order of time.

Past and present acts of thought may be generated by the same meaning. To recall the past act in the present we must adopt the vantage point of this meaning. The situation may be compared to that of habitants of a two-dimensional world who, in order to understand a map as projection of three dimensions, must step outside their world. So, when we recall past thought, we step into a trans-temporal position. The meaning of which we are conscious is identical in past and present, unaffected by our changing acts of thought. We think phenomena of consciousness can occur only once, because we imagine our consciousness of them is their essence and that they occur in time. But consciousness of meaning and consciousness of will transcend this order. Indeed, if one confined oneself strictly to such a view, it would be impossible to conceive any unity among phenomena of consciousness, and one could not go beyond the pure factuality of consciousness, which can just as well be interpreted in physical as in psychological terms.

The will, in which self and object merge, is the fundamental unity of consciousness, whereas in knowledge the self cannot coincide with the self or return to the past of even a moment ago. Through the will we can transcend time and return to the absolute free self which creates time. In will the objective world is no longer object, but means; the self, having returned to itself, controls the objective world. The will is a cause teleologically superior to temporal relationships, which are grounded on it. Thus Kant sees the categorical imperative as beyond natural causation, and Fichte regards the practical ego as the foundation of the intellectual world.[210] In will all object worlds, past, present, and future, are the present, and the past belongs wholly to, and changes with, the present. Though pure duration is unrepeatable, in creative evolution the entire past acts as present, and the more we attain the deep foundation of the self, attaining a state of pure creative evolution, the more we are able to transform the past into the present. Bergson compares memory to a cone, with the past as its base and the present as its apex; this cone continually advances at its apex.[211] Developing this image, we can say that the farther back we go toward the broad base of the cone, and the more concentratedly we assume the movement from base to apex, the more the entire past becomes the present, so that the present becomes the center of gravity of the totality. In the will we can make the entire past present, uniting the entire content of experience in a dynamic state. Or rather, in this dynamic state, past, present and future are abolished and time is transcended. As Lotze tells us, time is not the form of dynamic reality, but only of phenomena.[212]

It is the will which makes the past present in memory. We imagine the recollected self and the present self differ, because we are confusing the entire self with the self as object of cognition, and fail to realize that even in present cognition the self as object differs from the self which cannot be grasped in reflection. Again, we imagine we cannot return to the past, because we are thinking of time as an infinite straight line, and of the self as a point advancing along it. But to think thus is already to view the one-dimensional line from a two-dimensional position which transcends it. As object of cognition the self cannot return to the past, but as unobjectifiable will, as true subject, the self can make the past the present. The true sense of the unrepeatability of time is the impossibility of our going behind the self as active subject, the impossibility for self-consciousness of making the entire self its object. The self recalled, just as much as the self of present reflection, differs from the true self, because the true self is unfathomable, no matter what plumb-line we use.

Memory makes the past present; it thus transcends time, and is immediately identical with the action which anticipates the future. Memory transcends the present self, returns to the base of the cone, and unifies thence the entirety of the individual self; thought transcends the individual self and unifies the entirety of the transcendental self; will transcends the worlds of cognition and unifies the whole of reality. Memory allows us to act from the depth of our individual personality, by thought we act from the foundation of the objective world, and by will we transcend the various objective worlds and become creative evolution itself. Thus, the movement from memory to thought, and from thought to will, is one from a lesser position to a greater and deeper one. To memory corresponds the world of imagination, to thought the world of scientific hypotheses, to will the world in which we can freely create reality. The unrepeatability of time holds only in the determined object world, the world of "being," but each of these worlds is both "being" and "relative non-being." They are grounded in the moral will, which Maeterlinck tells us is able to change the past, and from the position of this categorical imperative which transcends all worlds we are free to choose any world.

One can take the activities of the will, one by one, as temporal facts and construct their inalterable sequence, the order of real duration. But the will does not move in a straight line from past to future; its progression is undulatory, spreading out in a circular way from the present as its center. If we try to connect the tracks of the will's activity in a straight line, we can construct the order of the will, but of a fossilized will. We fail to grasp the free movement from one a priori to another which characterizes the living will. The will overturns the past and makes it present. Order cannot be imposed on it, for it is what imposes order. In Fichtean terms it is "utterly active."[213] Knowledge takes a certain a priori as its standpoint and advances thence, but will transcends all such standpoints; it is absolute reflection, the unifying point of infinite possibilities. The position of knowledge is negative infinity (endlessly advancing from being to relative nothingness), but will is the positive infinity uniting being and relative nothingness. In the developmental progression of the Hegelian idea, will is the final sublation of the abstract in the concrete.[214] Since it is always concrete, will, in contrast to knowledge, is creative.

Nonetheless, is there some order to will, or is it absolutely free at every point? If there is an internal order to experience, it may be the logical order of ground and consequence, or the order of Husserl's phenomenological time. Might the activity of will not be conditioned by such an order? In accord with Hegel's statement that "If all the conditions are at hand, the fact (event) *must* be actual; and the fact itself is one of the conditions,"[215] we note that relations of ground and consequence in logic, geometry, and natural science are mutual; ground controls consequence, but consequence also controls ground; cause and effect, like left and right, are one in their foundation and are a static unity internally. No matter where we begin in geometry we must fall into line with the identical pattern of reason, which cannot be altered. Thus there is nothing in common between the fixity of thought and the free activity of will. Husserl's system of essences cannot do justice to will for the same reason. Scientists seek to ground the will in physiological traits or physico-chemical causal relationships, but this is to put the cart before the horse. The cause of the will remains an incomprehensible mystery. At the end of his famous work, The Ego and His Own, Max Stirner declares that of the ego as much as of God it can be said: "Names do not name Thee!"[216] No concept can capture and no quality can exhaust the self, which comes from, and returns to, creative nothingness.

I have argued the independence of the act of will from the object of thought, but the act of thought enjoys the same independence in regard to this object. The object is commonly thought of as becoming part of the act as its content, but as not intrinsically affected by the act. But there is an active and a passive side to the consciousness of anything. As active, thought is a kind of will. When an object becomes a content of thought, the act of thought is a self-development of the object, but since a thing can act only by entering into relation with other things, the act of thought can also be seen as that wherein the object becomes involved in mutual relationships with other objects of thought. True, no matter how close the mutual relationships of ideal entities, they cannot become real by their own power. Just as no matter how often a given rational number is divided it cannot reach the limit point, so if we set out from the ideal we cannot rejoin actuality, and from the relationships of objects of thought we cannot construct the act of thought. Actuality is at an unattainable infinite distance, yet without it there is no ideal; without act there is no object. As the unity of infinite objects and the limit of infinite thought systems it is, negatively, the unattainable, and positively, the actual here and now, the present which is consciousness, and which alone is consciousness. (Of course our habitual objectified notions of present and consciousness cannot be thought of as containing such abundant content.)

Just as Cohen's productive point is not determined by the curve but generates the curve, so consciousness is not produced by natural causation but itself generates nature. Psychology substantializes something abstracted from concrete experience and tries to explain the actual thereby, but the consciousness which discriminates among a number of stimuli transcends them all. Actuality is thus revealed to be an abyss, Boehme's *Ungrund*,[217] whose bottom we can never reach, and the mark of actuality is this infinite unattainability. If we could not know it in any sense at all, it would be nothingness, but if we could know it completely, it would not be the real. Reality, like Kant's thing in itself, is the limit of thought. This unattainable depth, the limit of the unity of thought systems, is positively the self-moving, never resting present, which is precisely the will. If we try to think of the will rationally, it appears as accidental in relation to any thought; for any system of thought the will is an unfathomable infinity. The will eludes reflection, yet it is that which grounds reflection, and reflection is itself a kind of will. Like the God of Pseudo-Dionysius, the will is in everything but it is not anything.[218] It embraces infinite order, but is not itself characterized by any order. Since it grounds causation, it cannot be governed by causal law. The reason the will, or the act of knowledge, adds nothing to the content of knowledge, is that will transcends everything at the same time that it grounds everything. The will adds nothing to content, only in the sense that "is" predicates nothing of a subject, for it is that which gives all content its reality.

The moment we think of order we are thinking in objectified terms and cannot grasp creative actuality, just as, according to Rickert, historical presentations of individuality already proceed from a concept and are objectifying constructions.[219] The infinite development of the "ought" which is one with being in a self-conscious system is what constitutes a single personal history; but this already belongs to the object world, and we must think of an absolute will behind it, which transcends and grounds this historical development. In other words, we must move from the merely philosophical viewpoint to the religious one, from self-consciousness as a theme of conscious reflection to the world of mystery that lies behind it.

Bergson says that we can predict in general terms the outcome of a painter's work, if we are sufficiently well-informed, but its particular qualities remain unpredictable even to the painter.[220] This applies too to the art of living. And just as artistic talent is formed by its exercise, so is our situation perpetually changing and the self ceaselessly creates the self. Mechanism misses this, seeing all as pre-determined, but teleology misses it too,[221] for in the creative moment in which the self is submerged in itself, "time" and even "pure duration" have become meaningless terms. Faced ineluctably with this unknowable self we can only say with Epictetus: "Use me henceforward for whatever Thou wilt; I am of one mind with Thee; . . . where Thou wilt, lead me;"[222] or in Christian language, "Do unto me as Thou wilt." From the point of view of knowledge, absolute unity is disunity, infinity is mere endlessness, but from the standpoint of absolute will we can experience the unity underlying this contradiction. As Eriugena teaches us, when we deny all categories to the super-essential divine nature, we can then become conscious of it.[223] Eriugena had great problems in reconciling God's infinity with God's self-consciousness,[224] yet the truly infinite has to be self-conscious, for self-consciousness is the positive experience of infinity.

Part Four
Conclusion

Absolute Free Will

Tetsugaku Kenkyū, No. 11, Feb. 1917

40

We have finally come to something beyond intellectual knowledge, which obliges us to recognize, with Kant, that there is a limit to such knowledge. Whereas Bergson's pure duration, by the very fact of being called duration, shows itself to be merely relative (his stress on its unrepeatability already suggesting the possibility that it can be repeated), Pseudo-Dionysius and Eriugena evoke an absolute, truly creative reality which is both everything and nothing, both motion and rest, "motion at rest and rest in motion"[225] (in a sense deeper than Bergson's view that relaxation is the other side of tension). Even to call it absolute will is misleading: "the moment one tries to explain it, one misses the target."[226]

What contemporary philosophers call the pre-conceptual can be thought of as an unbroken process like pure duration, or as still unformed material, or as an abstract world of Ideas. Yet each of these notions is merely relative, and must be numbered among the objects of knowledge, rather than identified with the immediate pre-cognitive absolute. Pseudo-Dionysius and Eriugena are far more searching in their designation of the absolute when they deny that it is correct to say that God is being, or that God is non-being, or that God is motion, or that God is rest. "Thirty blows

if you can speak, thirty blows if you can't."[227] (In a similar profound paradox Eriugena identifies the God who "creates and is not created" and the
God who "neither creates nor is created.")[228]

Since this language cannot be applied to ordinary things, the absolute
may seem a wholly unnecessary hypothesis. Yet the ground of the proposition "A is A" can be found neither in its subject nor its predicate, nor in
something apart from them, but only in an underlying pre-cognitive concrete totality. To think of a continuum we must proceed from the same pre-
cognitive ground, for we cannot derive it from the activity of dividing
endlessly. The pre-cognitive totality is not a simple whole but includes dis-
junction. Though we cannot define it as an object of cognition, it is the
foundation of cognition and of the relationships of the various elements
whose unity analysis cannot bring to light. (Neo-realists divide the elements and their relationships as different entities, but this is impossible.) It
is not correct to say that the totality of elements is one, or that it is many,
or that it changes, or that it does not change. As the eye cannot see the eye,
nor the camera photograph itself, so it is impossible to capture this totality
within the lens of the camera of cognition, yet it is immediately tangible as
the freedom of the will, or as Kant's moral consciousness which declares:
"Thou shalt act thus," and which is not only a deeper and more immediate
fact than cognition, but comprehends cognition within itself. Wide as is
the world that we know, and still more that of possible knowledge, the
world of desire is still wider, for even fantasy and dreams provide volition
with its objects, and even what knowledge sees through as delusion can be
real for the will. Against the rationalists who dismiss free will as a
fantasy—because they have objectified it and projected it into the world of
natural causation—I agree with the teleological critical school that knowing is part of will and will is at the foundation of cognition. To hypothesize
causation of any kind behind the will is already to deny its reality. The
world of necessity, which is the privileged domain of knowledge, is
grounded on the infinitely broader world of will. This truth is reflected in
Eriugena's claim that in God there is neither necessity nor determinism and
that predestination is nothing more than a decision of God's will.[229] Just as
the will cannot be subject to external, causal necessity, neither is it con-
strained by internal necessity, as in Spinoza's notion of necessary freedom.

To say that the will comes from, and returns to, creative nothingness,
or that the world comes to be by the will of God, seems to be in serious
contradiction with the law of causality. However, there is no fact more immediate and indubitable than the birth of being from non-being, which oc-

curs constantly in the actuality of our experience. To satisfy the demands of logical reason we think of this as the manifestation of what was latent, or find some other equally vacuous explanation. But when we penetrate to the immediacy of that creative act which produces being from nothingness, letting no such explanations overlay it, we find absolute free will, and come in contact with infinite reality, with the will of God. The present, as the point of contact of infinite worlds, can be identified with will, which thus appears as what unites these worlds. When we say that nothing can emerge from empty will, we are substantializing the abstract notion of will. But even from being, conceived thus abstractly, nothing could emerge. The transcendental ego of Kant, the notion of transcendental meaning or value, or Descartes' idea of perfection as it functions in his ontological proof of God, can help us grasp more concretely the possibility of the world's being grounded in the form of will. (Descartes' argument that a perfect being must exist is childish, and confuses the conceptual with the real, if we take existence in the sense of natural science; but if we remember that there is no existence before meaning, that being is based on a prior "ought," then it becomes indubitable that the idea of perfection implies the existence of an absolute exemplary consciousness.)[230]

Science explains things in terms of quality, force, or energy. But these are abstractions, and when we substantialize them and project them behind the alterations of phenomena, as their explanation, we are reversing primary and secondary. If we focus these alterations in immediate experience, however, we find that they are not discrete, but constitute a continuous process, which is the self-realization of a concrete universal. Again, when we unite fragmentary sensations to form "red things" or "blue things," and call these things objective reality, the intellectual satisfaction we find in this is really based on a return to the core of the self, an advance to more immediate, concrete thinking. If thought thus creates natural reality, it is itself in turn created by will, the immediate, absolute process of creation. Beneath these apparently solid cognitive activities, being is constantly being produced from nothingness. (Fichte seems to confuse logical and causal necessity when he claims that the ego gives birth to non-ego,[231] but he is speaking of absolute, not relative, ego, which is the absolute creative will.)

"Settle down nowhere, yet will the ultimate."[232] The absolute annuls all thought and distinction, but the best approximation to the truth of it is absolute free will. Concrete, immediate reality is both infinite development and infinite return; both *egressus* and *regressus*; both infinite progression as "ought"-*qua*-actuality and the eternal now of reflection returning to its source; both the quantitative basis of number and the qualitative basis of geometry; uniting apparent contradictories, like the God of Eriugena, in a way that baffles explanation, yet at the same time providing the basis of logical thought. (Lotze's unity of reciprocal action anticipates this characterization of reality as absolute free will.) Up to this point I have grasped reality as self-consciousness, but behind all self-conscious systems lies this absolute will. The practical ego underlies the cognitive ego, and the world of hope is broader than the world of cognition, which is only one part of the possible world. To the cognitive ego the practical ego appears irrational, but it has its own unity, which is what we call conscience. Logic is only a part of conscience, and the categorical imperative is incomprehensible to it. Reality begins with the imperative, and the biblical "Let there be light" shows that moral freedom is at the foundation of the world, a truth defended by Origen when he contradicted the Neo-Platonist view that matter was the last emanation from God, and made it a world of punishment.[233] It seems irrational to speak of God creating from nothing, but God transcends causation, and can be conceived neither as being nor as nothingness. Moral causation is more fundamental than the natural causation our minds can apprehend, as Augustine recognizes when he teaches that God created the world out of love.[234] If, as Lotze thinks, reality is activity, its internal relationships must be relationships of will and will, or moral ones. Natural causation derives from a superficial, extrinsic apprehension of these relationships.

If will grounds knowledge, the immediately given object of knowledge must have the form of will, must be dynamic reality. Bergson grasped this as pure duration and Rickert found it in the infinitely heterogeneous which history comes nearer to than natural science.[235] We commonly think of the object of knowledge as standing over against us, but what gives objectivity to cognition is the concrete background to the act of knowledge, the subject in the sense of *subjectum*. Objective knowledge is a return to the foundation of the self and a looking back behind the self. Thus the ultimate object of cognition is absolute free will. Of course absolute free will as it is in itself is inaccessible to cognition, but it presents the aspect of absolute activity to cognition as its first object. One might claim this role for Rickert's transcendent meaning and value, dividing experience into activity and the meaning which transcends and founds it. But before this meaning comes the experience of the concrete totality (as even Rickert admits). Though the world of fact is established from the world of meaning (or from Husserlian essences), there is a world of experience which is yet more fundamental, as

142

the Plotinian One is more fundamental than the Platonic Ideas—except that the true One is not the source of emanation, but creative will, as Origen insists.[236]

When absolute free will turns and views itself, or, in Boehme's terms, when the objectless will looks back on itself, the infinite creative development of this world is set up. That is why history is the first, immediate object of cognition. How is this reflective moment of absolute will possible? Absolute will, as both "creating and uncreated" and "neither created nor creating," includes the possibility of retreating as well as advancing. To reflect is to move from a lesser to a greater standpoint, while to act is to progress in a single standpoint. The self returns to its foundation in reflection, while it develops itself in action. But reflection is itself action, self-return is itself self-development, retreat is itself advance. Thus cognition can be seen as a kind of will, so that everything appears as a development of will. The notion of simple reflection is the result of viewing a greater standpoint from a lesser; from the absolutely comprehensive standpoint of will, everything appears as one will. Since we cannot think of absolute will in terms of the objective world, we cannot adequately describe its absolute unity as either unity or disunity. Augustine's statement that "God does not know creatures because they are, but they are because He knows them,"[237] well expresses this absolute unity of will and knowledge. When science moves in the realm of trans-individual consciousness and constructs the physical world, this is both the development of knowledge and the constructive act of a greater ego. Our thinking and acting is, viewed from within consciousness, a striving forward of the subject, whereas viewed externally this subjective will is but an association of ideas, and intellectualist psychology reduces everything to knowledge. The choice of standpoint thus determines whether everything is seen as will or as knowledge, but this choice depends on the faculty of abstraction which is the aspect of disorder of absolute free will.

41

Just as various thoughts are under our command, so too are various contents of experience. Seeing, hearing, thinking, acting—the will is the synthesis of all these abilities. The formal, contentless notion of freedom that assures us of the possibility of moving this arm from left to right is grounded in the concrete freedom which is the self itself present in every such activity. Discussions of the freedom and necessity of the will proceed from the notion that the will is determined by the competition of two given impulses, just as when two straight lines are given, their point of intersection is determined. This is a misleading objectification, for the will is not a point of intersection between motives, but rather that which lies at the basis of their competition. Here too what is given is what has been sought. The unity established among our actions by the will is the unity of personality. Our most immediate experience is personal, and when the arm moves, or the foot walks, our entire personality is involved. As the Hegelian concept is "the presupposing of the immediate,"[243] the will, or personality, is not a controlling instance outside each conscious activity, but the internal creative power at the basis of each activity, present in it as a great artist's creative power is manifest in each stroke of the brush. The will, or the self, as what grounds and unifies all activities, is free, and in this it is made in the image of God.

Perception is not passive, for, as Fiedler shows, total absorption in vision is an infinite development, leading to artistic creation, and the same may be said, I think, for all other sensations. Perception, thought, or any other activity developing itself from one a priori, is in itself infinite self-development, and the unity of all of them is our will or personality. In this connection we may extend to the whole of experience the relationship between logic and mathematics, which our analysis showed to be a generative one, like that of seed to plant. We traced several such relationships in the world of pure thought, but when it came to the transition from thought to experience we faced a great chasm. Now it has become clear that what bridges this chasm is the unity of the will. It may well seem impossible to move from a system of pure thought, if we think of it abstractly as object of cognition, to a system of experience possessing concrete content, and we inevitably imagine that content is given contingently and extrinsically to the form of thought. But if we return to the concrete subject of both thought and experience we discover the unity of the will, the unity of the personality. Both activities belong to one concrete self. The unity of this self is above logic, and cannot be grasped within any of the a priori of pure thought which are its partial aspects. Yet without the experience of this unity it would be impossible to conceive in any way the relationship between the form and content of knowledge. The demand for objectivity which impels knowledge manifests this concrete unity, and the unity of thought and experience corresponds to the will's demand for unity, a demand of the whole self. Only through this can knowledge return to its concrete foundation and satisfy its demand for objectivity. (The transcendental sensation earlier discerned at the heart of spatial perception can now be identified with the consciousness of the will arising from the unity of the whole of experience. Spatial consciousness is given in the form of the will, dynamic in itself, and this underlies the "anticipation of perception." Just as, according to Bergson, we grasp movement, and confute Zeno, by simply moving our hand, so, we recall both psychological sensation and mathematical continuity to their concrete foundation in transcendental sensation by simply moving our hand, that is, through the immediacy of willing.)

The passage from the world of cognition to the world of will implies Lipps's "snapping shut," and a leap of the *élan vital*. It brings us to the unity of the self, which is the ground of all its activities, and which cannot be grasped by cognition, for it is the limit of cognition. This unity may seem irrational, yet if one defines the rational too narrowly, one reaches the position of Rickert for whom even mathematics appears irrational and accidental in relation to logic. Neither does the impossibility of clarifying this unity conceptually imply that it is an empty form. Each self has a determinate, inalienable individuality. One could not say that the painter's or the novelist's study of such unique personality is unclear or contentless in comparison with the scientist's knowledge of electricity, for the artist's consciousness is no less determinate than the scientist's, and may be superior in terms of its grasp of the real. When an object moves from one point to another, we think of a force behind it, but we can neither hear nor see it, and sensationalists conclude that it is an empty term. But if force is an empty concept, so is elemental sensation. If it is real, because self-moving, the force of personality is real for the same reason. I would maintain that it is the most basic reality, conferring reality on all realities.

I should now like to reflect on the relationship between absolute free will, which is the creative activity of the universe, and individual free will. The phenomena of consciousness are unified by a single self, yet each of them is at the same time a free activity. The totality which grounds these phenomena does not negate its parts but allows each autonomy and freedom, so that they form a "kingdom of ends" like Kant's moral society and are governed by a moral "ought" which is not a mere imperative but a force: "You can, because you ought to." As artistic talent develops through the creation of works of art, so, while the entire self creates its parts, they also create it; according to Bergson, the self's acts belong to the self, and are the self.[239] In the same way our individual will remains free within the will of absolute freedom. Indeed, it is through allowing the independence of individual wills that the absolute will can itself be truly free, much as the white man can be said to have set himself free in freeing the Negro slaves. When we objectify the will and the relationship between will and will, we can no longer grasp the will as free and we fall into the notion of a conflict between absolute will and individual will. Even when we call God infinite potency we are already objectifying Him. Defenders of the freedom of the will who simply appeal to the deliveries of introspection are objectifying phenomena of consciousness, and have not reached the unobjectifiable will at the foundation of consciousness, which differs from the world of objects as radically as the world of solids differs from a world of planes. The freedom of each of our voluntary acts is attested by moral conscience, as Kant saw, and those who appeal to physical causation to deny this forget that physical causation too is founded on an "ought." In this present moment I am free to move either left or right, or if this is physically impossible, to consciously mark my decision. Only the will moves the will.

But in saying that absolute will does not conflict with the freedom of the individual will, I do not suggest that our will can break the laws of nature and act with utter freedom, for as objectified in the natural world, the will is evidently subject to its laws. But at root our will belongs to a world of deeper, truly concrete experience, Kant's intelligible world.[240] In this world, as in Hegel's concept, each part is the whole. Concrete reality is individual, possessing rationality within irrationality, necessity within contingency. We have declared the superior reality of the continuous as against the discontinuous, but the merely continuous is not yet the absolutely real, for it does not yet unify within itself discontinuous acts, does not yet include the aspect of contingent actualization; it is not will. It still belongs to the world of cognitive objects, and cannot include concrete actuality, which is foreign to that world. An artist's work, like the merely continuous, may unite the actual and the ideal, but it does not contain the creative act within itself. True reality must be creative in itself, and Lotze's notion of reality as reciprocal action is still incomplete. In concrete reality contingency cannot be lacking; if everything is rationalized, everything is unreal. To rationalize everything is impossible, for at least that which knows everything is rational must be irrational. Even if we can explain contingent determination rationally, only what unites rationality and contingency, the will, is truly real.

As the entire life of an artist is present in every stroke of the brush, so the entire reality of the self is present in every contingent determination.

We must not ask how the determination arises, but realize that the determination itself, as will, is immediately the concrete totality. We objectify this when we think of an infinite behind the finite or of substance behind actuality. In immediate experience of will the finite is immediately infinite, actuality is immediately substance, and there is no room for conceptual division of the single actuality of acts of will. People frequently say that knowledge is but one phenomenal aspect of the infinitely abundant content of immediate experience, but to speak thus is already to objectify that content, putting it on the same level as conceptual knowledge, and however abundant the content thus conceived its infinity remains relative. Real immediate experience belongs to a different dimension from conceptual knowledge and comparisons of amount between them are not in order. The true background of consciousness is not this objectified infinity, or a substance (which belongs to the same dimension as the actuality with which it is paired), but opens onto the world of infinite mystery, as Eriugena shows. Like a point on a straight line which while lying in one dimension can connect with others, each consciousness is the point of contact of many dimensions.

SECTION 42
Thought and Experience

Tetsugaku Kenkyū, No. 13, April 1917

42

From the vantage point we have attained, let us reconsider the relationship between thought and experience, and between spirit and matter.

Absolute free will, like the Kantian thing in itself, cannot be encompassed by our thinking and its discriminations, yet this does not mean it has no connection with knowledge, for it includes knowledge within itself as one of its aspects. Knowledge expresses the will's self-return, its *regressus*, and the world of the objects of knowledge is as a mirror in which the will's form is reflected. Thus knowledge gives an image, not the substance of the thing in itself, which is unknowable. Will both casts the image of itself within itself, and views this image; it is both infinite development and infinite reflection. The union of reflection and what is reflected in self-consciousness (which is impossible to doubt, since one enacts it in the very act of doubting) throws light on this union of contradictories. Every activity of consciousness at the same time that it is "reflection in itself" is "reflection in another,"[241] and when a certain moment of consciousness has been determined it immediately includes the negation of itself, and is ripe for sublation. Thus act is immediately reflection; self-development is identical with self-return. When the infinity of the relationships of consciousness in its developmental aspect is conceived abstractly it loses all determination and becomes meaningless, like the figure with an infinite number of sides of which Russell speaks. One should rather grasp the infinite relationships to the other, which each moment of consciousness possesses, as concretely determined by the living activity of consciousness. We objectify this if we think of each moment as having infinite latent force, for each is free subjectivity, and its infinite relationships to the other constitute infinite freedom. These relationships include, of necessity, infinite error and infinite evil. Evil comes from the power of free subjectivity to negate the self within the self. Absolute reality is inherently moral, and its concrete starting point is the actuality of each moment of consciousness. Thus we touch the true reality of God in each act and we can also touch the devil, as Augustine realized in stressing the freedom God gave to the first humans.[242]

The moment of negation in absolute free will, its aspect of "neither created nor creating," lies in the abstractive activity of reflection. Pure thought is simply the limit to which this activity tends, and the objects of pure thought are its experiential content. When we are conscious of the self itself, we become intellectual subjects, and our thinking is a negative synthesis whose negation bears on the self itself. The experience in which the self was unreflectively absorbed, for instance the experience of intuiting a straight line which is neither that of the mathematician nor that of the psychologist, is sublated into a more comprehensive reflection. In reflection the self is able to move from any one of its various activities to another, and thus reflection is the discovery of the other in the self. The other is in the self and the self is in the other. Thus the self has within itself that which impels it to negate itself in reflection. Just as when we concentrate on one line or one color, they turn out to be a complex of several continuums, so any single activity of the self, such as pure vision, turns out to be a complex of various activities. This necessary inclusion of the other in self-consciousness does not mean a confusion of self and other. Rather, in order for the self to grasp its position lucidly and penetratingly, it must necessarily bring the other into view. Thus in the case of visual and aural perception consciousness of them is their negation, or their assumption into a greater unity. To reflect on the experience of the color red and say "This is red" is to transcend and negate the standpoint of that pure perception. The act of reflection may appear to supervene extrinsically, but from the viewpoint of absolute free will the unity it fashions is already anticipated in the original givenness of the perceptual acts it assumes. What we call empirical

149

knowledge consists in a reflection on perception, whereby the perceived line or color is cognized as an object of perception. Cognition depends on pure perception for its objectivity, and makes it its goal, according to Cohen's principle of the "anticipation of perception." But it is a goal it can never reach. The intrinsically dynamic pure experience, which is the developmental aspect of absolute will, and which we should rather think of as Fiedler's pure perception than as Cohen's mere awareness, remains precognitive, and can never be caught in the form of reflection.

Since, as Brentano observes, the same essence can be the object of both perception and thought, the essence can be seen as the point of intersection of various acts. The developmental aspect of the essence is what is grasped in intuition, while its reflective, or negative, aspect is what we know conceptually. What the psychologist calls perception, perception in its reflected form, is the plane of contact between pure perception and cognition, pure perception reconstructed with a view to its transference to another system. The reconstructed perception is not the same as the original pure perception, yet the essence is the same—red does not become blue when reflected on—and that is why it can be grasped as linking one act with another. The unattainability of pure perception by cognition does not mean the two are utterly different in quality, for cognition is included within pure perception, not as a quantitatively distinct part of it, but as a partial dimension like one line of a triangle (Windelband). Pure perception is of a higher order than cognition and has the form of absolute will.

But thought is itself an act, and is just as much pure experience as the pure perception of the artist. The limit of infinite reflection is itself a development having its own center (as one can say that a straight line is a circle having a center at an infinite distance). The God who creates is at the same time the God who does not create; affirmative will and negative will are ultimately identical. Pure perception includes its reflected form as an aspect of the experience. Where Rickert focuses narrowly on reflection and cannot recombine it with intuition, from which he distinguished it so sharply, Cohen sees thought as the foundation of the intuition given to it, and is thus able to grasp the constitution of knowledge from a higher position as the infinite development and progression of an idea. Thought is the reflective aspect of absolute free will, which both negates and unifies various systems of experience (as the function which unifies various a priori). As the content of these systems belongs to their respective a priori, thought itself, reflective subjectivity, is purely formal and lacks any specific content—just as the straight line of intuition is always finite, while an infinite line is merely an object of thought. But true infinity is autonomous self-reflection, not the mere absence of limits. As mere negative unity thought is the merely formal "A is A," but when this reflective aspect of absolute will assumes its autonomy it appears as a creative a priori, no less than pure perception.

Since the unity of thought is the unity of all a priori and the limit of relationships with others, we think of it as common to all experience and as constituting a world of unchanging and universal forms, most evident in the objects of pure thought, that is, in mathematics. Yet since we can grasp thought as a single a priori, it is revealed to be one particular aspect of absolute will, not absolute will itself. Creative absolute will is not mere negation, and indeed cannot be determined in any way. It is the unity of affirmation and negation, form and content, both infinitely poor and infinitely rich. In this personal unity lies the conjunction of thought and experience, and the objectivity of knowledge. We can never reach this pure unity, but we continually approach it, and depending on its quality and degree various worlds appear. The experience of absolute will unfolds both as the universalizing reflection of the unity of the various a priori and as the particular development of each of them individually. Though the form of this experience is fundamentally one, it unfolds in different stages, as pure perception (which can be seen as absolute affirmation), as pure thought (or mere negation), and in the various intervening standpoints. If art (pure perception) is the absolute affirmation of a content, thought is its negation, and the negation of this negation, or the absolute affirmation of the whole, is the standpoint of religion. The various partial affirmations of perception are unified by the negation of knowledge, but knowledge does not advance to the negation of this negation. The first stage of knowledge is sighted by Rickert as the "category of givenness,"[243] the form unifying the data of perception from the standpoint of reflective negativity. Here the perceptual datum grasped reflectively as "this color" or "this sound" represents the turning point where absolute will passes from affirmation to negation, the border one crosses in passing from the world of perception to that of thought.

Consciousness at every moment includes the possibility of reflection and opens onto the world of knowledge. Pure thought, the self-reflecting self, creates the world of number, and originates time and space (the former being its quantitative, the latter its qualitative aspect). As it returns to its foundation in absolute creative will, it unifies pure experience, the entirety of absolute will, and the actual world, the world of experience in the

Kantian sense, is constituted according to the categories of time, space, causation, thing, and quality. Time is formed from the development of the self, space from the distinction of the directions of this development, and thinghood from the unity of both. (What Poincaré calls a "crude law"[244] is in fact less a law than a derivative of the categories of thing and quality, or thing and function.) Thus is produced the objective world, governed by the unity of the transcendental ego and common to all persons. Yet from the viewpoint of thought as thought this world appears subjective and relative, and philosophers have always sought the world of essences beyond it. That demand is an intrinsic requirément of thought. It is the intellectual demand for unity, which, according to Kant, obliges the mind to see all things as the reciprocal action of substances.[245] Nor can this demand, being an aspect of absolute will, stop at merely conceptual unity—it demands concrete content, the unification of all experience. This is the foundation of natural science, whose "empirical world" is experience unified from the position of absolute reflection, and whose "witness of the senses" is immediate perception as focused in reflection (not the true immediate perception of the artist). The development of scientific knowledge by means of hypotheses, or Poincaré's principles, has this profound demand as its motor.

But this standpoint of absolute reflection cannot completely unify concrete, personal experience. Such experiences as hearing and seeing elude its framework. Thus the hypotheses of science can be seen as only a subjective, extrinsic unification of experiential content, and the essence it seeks behind phenomena as a subjective projection. We can effectually unify the whole of experience only by rejoining the inner freedom in the depths of the self, or rather by returning to that original unity which precedes the emergence of anything we can call self. In this regard the artist's pure perception is a more concrete consciousness than that of science, more interior, freer, and more immediate. The standpoint of art is not mere affirmation, just as that of thought is not mere negation, for as a creative "formative activity" (Gestaltungstätigkeit) it also encompasses negation. Only the abstract perception of the psychologist is merely affirmative; therein color and sound are mere phenomena, whereas in art they have a more profound and immediate reality than their physical form.

In all its dimensions consciousness is both affirmation and negation; thus art is not merely intuition, while thought in one of its aspects is intuition. Hildebrand, in a discussion of form as perceived (Wirkungsform) says that when we look at a finger we gain an impression of its size and shape, but when we look at the entire hand we form a new impression by relating the part to the whole, and this process is repeated when we look at the arm.[246] So, too, each pure perception immediately subverts itself to be sighted in terms of another. This pattern of will within will is the stamp of will on every moment of consciousness. If pure thought in this sense, which we may call the pure perception of the universe, is the aspect of negation of absolute will, moral will is its affirmative aspect, and religion is the unity of both. Religion may be called the artistic standpoint of transcendental consciousness, while art is the religious standpoint within partial experience. Though quantitatively partial in comparison with pure cognition, art qualitatively expresses the concrete whole, while the world constituted by the "forms of reality," time, space, and causation, though objective for cognition, is but an abstract aspect of absolute will. Should we attempt to insert the concrete whole of will within these cognitive forms, we would immediately fall into antinomies. Cognition is quantitatively objective but qualitatively it can be classed as subjective, while art is qualitatively objective and in immediate contact with the inner absolute will. For absolute will to return to its own concrete totality it must transcend cognition, and enter the sphere of art and religion. Thus the turning-point where absolute will passes from negation to affirmation is the moral will.

Various Worlds

Tetsugaku Kenkyū, No. 14, May 1917

43

The true core of our immediate experience is absolute free will, which holds activities of various kinds together in unity, and which provides the internal bond of various systems of experience. If we compare systems of experience to circles, the line joining their centers is absolute free will, so that what unites them is not a static cognition, but infinitely dynamic autonomous will. Reflection, the negative aspect of absolute will, may in contrast be seen as a circle of infinite radius. The world of time, space, and causation, founded by reflection, is the first object of our cognition, our first step from will to knowledge, and thus the boundary of two worlds. Immediate experience as sighted negatively in scientific reflection, which in its "liberation from anthropomorphism" reduces every activity to physical terms, belongs to the material world. But as the obverse of the same medal, immediate experience, as partial will, maintains constant connection with the affirmative aspect of absolute will, and abides within one great personal unity. Thus while the experience of color is classed in reflection among material phenomena, it maintains the autonomy of its own a priori which is utterly non-rational. Experience, as qualitative, insists on its autonomy, and on an originality no less than that of thought, so much so that we can say with the nominalists that it is thought that is subjective and experience that is objective.

Experience grasped in reflection is the material world; but in its obverse affirmative aspect it is a spiritual phenomenon. Introspection shows that the autonomous identity of immediate experience, in artistic intuition for example, transcends the cognitive. This autonomy is negated in reflection, and the center of unity shifts to thought, which unifies the original experience from outside. But infinite affirmation is the obverse of this negation, and in the negation of negation, the reflection of reflection, the spiritual world comes into view. This is still not the true negation of negation, and the affirmation it effects is only relative; it is a case of turning from absolute unity to view a single system of experience. True affirmation is reflection-*qua*-development, negation-*qua*-affirmation, and thus something which entirely eludes reflection.

In relation to seeing, hearing, and thinking, intending to see, intending to hear, and intending to think are a standpoint of will from which we can view these acts as objects. If we view thinking from this standpoint, it too appears as an affirmative position, which can be reflected on, and thus negated. This shows that the cognitive world is not the only one. But there is no standpoint from which we can reflect on will itself. When we think we are reflecting on will, on personal unity, we are dealing only with a relative affirmation, which belongs not to the true self but to the external world. The world of absolute will is essentially one of mystery, inaccessible to cognition, but approached in art and religion. The object world of cognition is thought of as fixed and immovable, while it seems impossible to reflect on the act of cognition without its ceasing to be the act itself. Yet from the standpoint of absolute will all other acts, even the act of reflection, appear as objects. The object world for will is the world of possibility, in which all acts are objects of choice. The fixed and abstract world of cognition is overcome in this concrete whole, so that while knowledge cannot make will its object, will can make knowledge its object. This standpoint of absolute will is that of Natorp's reconstructive method,[247] and what comes into view from this standpoint is the world of spiritual phenomena. Such phenomena are a combination of various acts united in Lipps's "consciousness ego,"[248] as various curves are united in the quadratic equation. From within an act we cannot grasp it as object, but from the standpoint of absolute will we can, by transcending it. An object of free will differs, of course, from an object of cognition, and only free will can comprehend spiritual phenomena.

In terms of a theory of stages of reality, Plotinus, Pseudo-Dionysius, and Eriugena show that God transcends all categories, that absolute free will which entirely eludes reflection is the most concrete, primary reality.

Then comes the world of the voluntary relationships, the pure activities of spirit, which are the objects of this absolute free will. We may call this the symbolic world. It is a world in which there is neither time, space, nor causation and in which, as the Symbolist poets rhapsodically declare, everything one sees and hears is a symbol, and even science and mathematics become song at the feast in the realm of the Blue Flower.[249] In the world prior to the a priori that founds knowledge, the object world of absolute will, each object is the symbol of an infinite spiritual act. It can be seen as a world of infinite numbers, such as only autonomous self-consciousness generates. In contrast, our world of knowledge can be seen as a system of finite numbers, which at its limit transcends itself to enter this world of infinite number. If we try to grasp this world in terms of time, space, and causation, we become entangled in antinomies. The world of the thing in itself is the world of will, and can be reached only by will. We cannot write off as obsolete fantasy the Gnostic speculations on the relation of this universe to primordial spirit, and their mythology of the "abyss" (Valentinus) and the "not yet existent God" (Basilides), figures of what first emerges from absolute will.[250] This we identify as our true self, which even now lives in the world of mystery which the Symbolists see as underlying all phenomena.

The first object world from the standpoint of absolute will is the world of art or religion, from which we are able to objectify the world of cognition as one act. Now this reflection on reflection takes the form of a phenomenon of consciousness, and we may therefore say that the point of contact between the cognitive and the symbolic is a phenomenon of consciousness. Earlier we saw that the world of space, time, and causation is the boundary where the spiritual and the material worlds meet. The material world is a precipitate of the cognitive effort to unify all experience. In absolute will each act, as *élan vital*, demands equal independence with thought. The historical world is the world of time, space, and causation as reflected on from absolute free will. If the scientific world is based on will as objective negation, the historical world is based on relative affirmation, and art and religion are the standpoints of affirmation-*qua*-negation. The historical world is still part of the cognitive world, but art and religion utterly transcend cognitive categories. Art, we say, is subjective and imaginary, yet here it appears as the truly objective viewpoint, wherein the universal contains the specific and the individual is immediately the whole. The historical world provides the scientific world with its concrete, objective foundation, but art and religion are even more concrete, for in history pure thought is still attempting to unify the whole of experience, whereas art and religion can turn and view it from the more concrete standpoint of complete personality, the a priori underlying all a priori, whose universality is not that of an abstract concept but of creative power. If the material world grasped in negative reflection is the major of a syllogism, and the psychological self is its affirmative minor, then its conclusion is the world of history, in which phenomena of consciousness are viewed from the standpoint of the whole, and the syllogism itself as a concrete whole is unobjectifiable absolute will.

Phenomena of consciousness come into view when we reflect on the object world based on a certain a priori from the standpoint of absolute will which is the unity of all a priori. The a priori of pure thought founds mathematics, and when all experience is unified in accord with this the natural scientific world emerges. This in turn can be divided hierarchically into the worlds of physics, chemistry and biology, according to their respective a priori. If we reflect on the a priori of pure thought, we may find it to be the unifying activity of pure ego, the model consciousness which is the object of Rickert's transcendental psychology. If we reflect on the a priori of the natural scientific world, we discover phenomena of consciousness, for instance, the visual faculty as the a priori of the experiential world of color. Phenomenologically the experience of color is more fundamental than the eye, and unless color is first given the eye has no special physiological significance. At this level of immediate experience causal thinking has no place; being is born from nothingness. Only when this experience has been reflected on from the standpoint of absolute will, and when instead of the juxtaposition of reflection it is related with other experiential content, can we conceive of the eye.

The a priori of color, as grasped in reflection, is the psychological act, and our personal self is nothing more than a bundle of such acts. Our conscious ego is the unity of various a priori as grasped in reflection from the standpoint of absolute will, and our body is the projection of this unity upon the object world of reflection (just as a sense organ is the objective projection of a certain sense experience). An organism is the material world as viewed in light of the immediate object world of absolute will, and it is the junction between matter and spirit. The same a priori which is spiritual act as belonging to the affirmative aspect of absolute will is organism as belonging to its negative aspect. The teleological view of nature, which grasps it concretely from its origin, contrasts with the mechanistic view based on mere negative unity. To seek to replace teleology with mechanistic explanation is to commit an error like that of the ancient analysts who tried to find the limit point by dividing infinitely; the goal is not to be constructed, but is given from the start, and advance to it is no more than its means. The teleological goal is the concrete foundation of the object world, and as Lotze says, organism is the goal of nature, and spirit is the goal of organism. Matter viewed in relation to the acts which are the immediate object of absolute will becomes teleological, and the point of junction between the two can be thought of as the center of life or as the point of union between spirit and body. Through this point absolute will moves from affirmation to negation and from negation to affirmation; thus it is that, as I claimed earlier, spirit and matter are united by voluntary acts. When, as in artistic activity (in Fiedler's account), all behavior has become expressive movement, the negative world of reflection is negated, and we return to absolute will itself; the material world loses its reality as material world and becomes symbolic through and through.

To summarize: When a specific content of experience is grasped in reflection, it enters the object world of negative unity, the world of space, time, and causation. This world is the boundary line between the universalizing and the individualizing directions of thought distinguished by Rickert as natural science and history.[251] Science unifies this world from the standpoint of pure thought, and history views it in relation to the immediate object world of absolute will. History is the biography of the spirit of the universe. Finally, when we leave the standpoint of reflection and the world of fact behind, and return to personal unity, we enter the realm of art. History can be seen as the standpoint of art in the factual world. The psychologist's world of consciousness lies between natural science and history.[252] This psychological world is viewed by the historian as a spiritual phenomenon, while the scientist views it as a biological phenomenon. Psycho-physical parallelism is merely a postulate. Psychological phenomena are immediate experience grasped in relation to the body, and the body is matter grasped in relation to the psychological. In physiological psychology, if it is thoroughly consistent, spirit is reduced to matter. But if psychology tries to record faithfully immediate experience it finds itself drawn in the opposite direction and becomes biography. Wundt's invocation of creative synthesis, consistently followed through, leads to Bergsonian creative evolution, subverting scientific psychological law. Psychology focuses a bundle of acts called the conscious ego in correspondence to a bodily unity, and calls the resultant object world, which lies somewhere between that of science and that of history, the world of consciousness. This we can think of in material terms to the extent, and only to the extent, that it is based on the negativity of will as reflection; then we can construct universal laws and see this world as corresponding to physiological phenomena.

Mental and physical phenomena result from the negation of partial will (a given system of immediate experience) by absolute will. The body is the product of this negation in the object world of reflection, and mental phenomena are the same reality viewed in relation to its original state. (Bergson means the same thing when he says that matter is simultaneous existence, spirit pure duration, and that the point at which they touch is our body and consciousness.) Does this help us to rethink the relationship between consciousness and unconsciousness? In Section 17 we saw this as the relationship between a certain content of consciousness and its concrete background, between what has been determined and the process of self-determination which is its matrix. To say that there is unconscious activity cannot mean that it exists as an object or functions as a cause in the sense of natural science. Such an objectification of unconsciousness would equate it with a material force, and make it nothing more than a hypothetical unity between the physiological activities of the organism and the conscious activity of the ego. To see this as the cause of consciousness would then be as topsy-turvy as to see matter as the cause of spirit. If it is the foundation of consciousness, unconsciousness can be thought of only as something like Cohen's origin, which exists in the same way as a Platonic Idea does, as an object of absolute will, a thought of God before the creation of the world. It cannot exist apart from consciousness, for there cannot be an Idea lacking any determination whatever; yet it may exist in itself apart from any given, individual determined consciousness. Thus if mankind, or living matter, as a whole did not exist, ideas themselves would not exist.

Meaning and Fact

44

The above discussion of the relationship between material and spiritual phenomena may seem in contradiction with science and common sense. For common sense, body is the cause of spirit, sight is produced by the eye, and hearing by the ear. For science, the world of time, space, and causation is the incontrovertible reality in terms of which all phenomena are to be explained, and spiritual phenomena can only be conceived as adjuncts to the nervous system of living things at a certain stage in evolution. Yet the ego who thinks thus, and whose unity founds the world of time, space, and causation, does not itself belong to this world. Thus the effort to apprehend all reality in terms of this world immediately runs into contradictions. As we transcend the world of planes toward that of solids, so the world of scientific cognition can be transcended toward that of free will. In this world even dreams are incontrovertibly real, and the act of looking at a woman with lust already constitutes adultery. Before physical time is the time of value, which we may also call phenomenological time. (Science may find mechanical explanations for artistic creation, but it can never grasp its inner, immediate meaning. Moreover, even these mechanistic explanations depend on the recognition of a meaning in art.)

Spirit can be seen as depending on the body and belonging to the material world, but it is also immediately part of the personal history of universal spirit. (Bergson says that body is not the repository of spirit, but a transverse section of spirit.) The road to the kingdom of God is always open before us, and in our present self the kingdom of God touches the kingdom of Satan, for, as Augustine teaches, we belong to both.[253] It is not the nebulae, but the history of personality, that is the origin of the world. My world begins with my life, and the human object world begins with human history. The world of personal history is a more concrete reality than the material world which is the object of pure thought. Spiritual phenomena are not ephemeral, as is commonly thought, and Bergson has demonstrated the tenacity of memory.[254] Historical reality as surely exists within as the material world, we deduce, exists outside, and is in fact more immediately real than the material world. As a human act is the sum of its effect and its motive, so all concrete reality is matter plus spirit. In historical reality phenomena arise in accordance with teleological, not mechanical, causation. It may be impossible for our little personalities to grasp all reality teleologically, but the greater the personality, the more it approximates to such a comprehension, and to one who has attained the godlike intellectual love described by Spinoza,[255] all appears as at once necessary and teleological. Such a person lives in an eternal now, for though to the scientist time is that which passes, spiritually it simply revolves on the plane of simultaneous existence, and though scientific time is unrepeatable, like a straight line running on infinitely, one who has transcended this unidimensional horizon can return to the past at will. Physical time is only the most abstract way of viewing reality.

The fact that spiritual phenomena must be accompanied by physical ones does not mean that physical phenomena exist before spiritual phenomena without any connection with them, spiritual phenomena being added later as mere accessories. The distinction between the two orders is one between interpretations of reality, and their parallelism is simply a demand of thought. The fact that visual experience depends on the eye does not mean that it arises from matter, but only that in the material world, the object world of absolute will in its negative, reflective position, there is no system of experience which does not have the projection called the eye. Thus spiritual phenomena cannot really be attached to the material world. Material phenomena may be thought of as organs depending on teleological unity, and the center of organic unity, the point of junction of the sensory nerves and the motor nerves, may be thought of as the seat of the spirit. Thus sense organs can be seen either as pure matter, or as subjective, as the seat of spiritual phenomena. Nerve activity is nothing more than the first stage in the movement of absolute will from negation to affirmation (from the physical to the physiological, to the psychological, to the historical), or the last stage in the reverse movement. The will, which thus combines the physical, physiological, psychological, and historical realms, is itself an eternal now transcending time and place, centered always on the present and expressed by the word "this." The present will is the point of union of various worlds. Our experience is stamped in all its forms by absolute will, and belongs to its kingdom of ends. Since absolute will unifies all worlds of experience to form a single system, one may hold, with religious people, that the world is a personal manifestation of God, that the material world is the body and history the biography of God, and that the world of truth is the thought of God.

We have argued that reality is one immediate experience, and that oppositions of thought and experience, spirit and body, rational and irrational, necessary and contingent, are but differences of the a priori of experiential unity. When the experience constituted by the a priori of various sensations is unified by pure thought, it naturally appears irrational and contingent in contrast to thought, but Meinong's theory of objects shows that there are transcendental fields of learning based on sensation, for instance the "geometry of color."[256] So what seems irrational and contingent from one position (as even mathematics appears from the still purer viewpoint of logic), can be rational and necessary from another, and the terms "rational" and "irrational" denote only differences in position.

Now, what unifies the various a priori is the a priori of absolute free will, which combines thought and experience, spiritual and material, meaning and fact. Even a certain individual's thinking a certain truth at a certain time and place depends on this a priori of absolute free will. While the objectified psychological ego cannot link up with universal valid truth, the self as free personality, bearing the vestige of absolute will, is the unity of various a priori, the point of contact of various worlds, and is not limited to a given time and place. Through this point of contact, absolute will freely moves from the world of time, space, and causation to other object worlds, from the two-dimensional cognitive world to the three-dimensional symbolic world. Thus psychological phenomena are not confined to natural scientific existence, but are symbols bearing universal meaning. When a certain individual thinks a certain meaning, that individual moves to a higher world, from two to three dimensions. As Hegel shows, even when we are conscious of the here and now we transcend it, and even this time and this place become objects of universal consciousness, the transcendent meaning of the logicists.[257] That which is determined as "this" cannot be conscious of "this"—to be conscious of "this" our subjectivity must rise to transcendental subjectivity. The universal "this" transcends not only the consciousness of others, but the very consciousness which was designated as "this."

In addition to this aspect of the problem of how the individual can grasp universal truth, there is the question how the self, which cannot separate itself from the Heraclitean flux of pure duration, is able to look back on the past. Can the position of transcendental subjectivity arise within pure duration? Though this position transcends natural scientific time, can it transcend Bergsonian duration? Even though the free moral act transcends natural scientific time, it is a fact of a deeper personal history, and the traces of the past inscribed in this history cannot be erased. But Bergson's duration, too, belongs to the world of objects, and is based on an a priori. In absolute free will, which moves freely from one a priori to another, no fact can leave any trace whatever. As an infinite number is everywhere infinite, absolute free will can never be passive in any sense: "Sitting in meditation in any place whatever, as the moon allows itself to be reflected in all waters, one practices all deeds in emptiness."[258] If we speak of absolute will as determining itself in an act, we have already objectified it. Our ego in its innermost depths is in contact with absolute will. Here lies our intelligible character, where we are free to take any a priori, and which is not to be confused with the empirical character of which we are conscious. It is the subjective, free act of this intelligible self which makes error a possibility, for in a purely objective world no error could arise, which is why science has to explain error by necessary causal laws. Error, or evil, arises from a confusion of the different positions which the intelligible self freely assumes. While error shows the incompleteness of things, it also indicates their concreteness, for only abundant and profound reality can fall into error, and light is emitted only from that which burns: *"Unde ardet inde lucet."*[259]

Postface

Tetsugaku Zasshi, No. 364, June 1917

I shall conclude by relating the ideas of this work to Kantian philosophy. The significance of Kant's contribution to epistemology is that he effected a radical change in our idea of truth, moving from the dogmatist idea of truth as union with the real to the critical idea that knowledge is constructed by a priori subjective forms and that universal valid truth is a function of our inability to think apart from these forms. Such seems the chief intent of Kant's philosophy, even if he himself never expressed it in exactly these terms. Rickert expresses the radical significance of Kant's thought in the phrase: "Before being there is meaning."

Kant forces us to abandon the common sense view of the mind as a mirror reflecting objects and the more "scientific" view that the mind possesses some special quality which allows it to sense the reality of the external world while transforming it. Both views ground knowledge in a causal relationship between the mind and things, but Kant makes it impossible to think of a law of causation prior to the construction of knowledge, for the law of causation is nothing more than one of the categories of thought which make the empirical world possible. According to critical philosophy, to know things is to unify the given experiential content: "It is only when we have thus produced synthetic unity in the manifold of intuition that we are in a position to say that we know the object."[260] An object is nothing more than the unity of manifold experiential content: "An object is that in the concept of which the manifold of a given intuition is united."[261] This is what Rickert has in mind when he describes cognition as an "ought" or value.

What, then, of the thing in itself prior to cognition? At some points in the transcendental aesthetic one wonders whether Kant is not thinking of the thing in itself as the cause of sensation, but in strict Kantian principle it is clear that the thing in itself must be utterly unknowable, at least in the normal sense of categorical knowledge. How, then, is it related to the world of cognition? If it is not related to it at all, it would be better to eliminate it from Kantian philosophy. However, if knowledge is construction from a certain standpoint, there must be something which has been given as its cause. This is not the thing in itself, but immediate pre-conceptual experience, and it seems that contemporary Kantians are interpreting the thing in itself in this sense. Knowledge is the unification of the concrete abundance of this experience from a certain standpoint. Windelband and Rickert are those who have best expressed this reinterpretation of the thing in itself. Windelband says that it was a mistake for us to have thought until now of the thing in itself and the phenomenal world as differing qualitatively, and that we should rather think of this difference as quantitative.[262]

The notions of subjectivity and objectivity must also be brought into accord with these refinements of the notions of truth and of the thing in itself. We commonly think of the mind as subjectivity and the contrasting external world as objectivity, but what we call the self as the object of introspection is grasped by the cognitive subject in the same way as external objects are, as simply one object among others in the world of cognition, located in a causal relationship with external objects and belonging to the same rank as a phenomenon of the natural world, deserving no less than they do to be called "object." The true epistemological subject is not the self known in introspection, but the unifying activity which constructs a certain objective world. This self cannot become an object of reflection. It is the process of construction of the objective world, and it now appears that subjectivity and objectivity are to be defined as the two inseparable extremes of a single reality.

In light of this, we note how different object worlds arise according to different subjective positions—the worlds of the mathematician, the artist, the historian. The world of natural science, commonly thought to be the only one, is thus seen to be only one world among others. Let us examine

165

these worlds and their mutual relationships. We may ask what the world would be like if none of these positions were adopted, or if we eliminated them all, the true, given world of immediate experience, Kant's thing in itself. Well, such a world inevitably transcends our speech and thought, and even to call it a world of unthinkable mystery may already be an error. To address this world directly is the task of religion, not philosophy. But in a tentative attempt to discuss it from the standpoint of philosophy, I should like to think of it as the world of absolute free will. Our experience of personal unity, which, synthesizing and unifying our various abilities, is able to use them freely, is an experience of absolute free will which can provide some insight into this world. It would be a mistake to think of it, as is often done, as a world of pure sensation, for sensation is a mediated construction. Bergson's pure duration catches well the immediacy of this world, but it, too, is objectified when he insists on its unrepeatability. A truly immediate world is, in Eriugena's terms, one of stationary flux and mobile rest, utterly transcending all categories of thought like the God of Pseudo-Dionysius, who may not be described even as Being without missing the mark. Like our will, which is nothingness while it is being, and being while it is nothingness, this world transcends even the categories of being and nothingness (not to speak of space, time, and causation), for here being is born out of nothingness. In this respect, I find a profound significance in the shift from the emanation theory of Neo-Platonism to the creation theory of the Church Fathers at the end of the Hellenistic period. The deepest interpretation of reality is to be sought not in reason, but in creative will.

How then do the various object worlds emerge from this immediate reality of absolute will? Introspection shows that our will, while free at every point, is subsumed within one great free will. While it is free in each moment, our self is free in its entirety, as the Kantian kingdom of ends, or the Hegelian concept. Each will is independently free, but all are included within absolute will. Freedom includes negation within affirmation, and affirmation within negation, and our self, being free in every circumstance, can negate and reflect upon the self, and can unite all experience as the object world of negative unity of absolute will. Despite the fact that individual selves are each independent and free, the world of reality is constructed by the attempt to unite all experience from a standpoint of trans-individual consciousness, the standpoint of thought as the negative aspect of absolute will. But since thought is only one act of absolute will, the object world based on it is relatively subjective and abstract, and thought must complete itself by advancing to the unity of the entire personality. Rickert says immediate experience first conforms to the category of givenness and then to the categories of time, space, and causation. Thus arises the world of reality, which is most thoroughly developed in the world of science, in Planck's "unity of the physical world-picture." As long as we stand in a certain position we cannot objectify that position itself, and so the physical world appears as incontrovertible reality. But if thought is nothing more than one activity of absolute will, then if we move to the position of absolute will itself, the a priori underlying all a priori, the activity underlying all activities, we can reflect on thought as an object for the first time, as Kant, for example, does.

When we restructure the world of reality in the form of the original experience, it becomes the world of history, which is the inversion of science; for science advances by universalizing, history by individualizing. Taking history and science as two extremes, we can distinguish several intervening worlds of reality, the psychological, the chemical, or the biological worlds for example. To approach history from the physical world is to approach the concrete experience of will in which everything is teleological. The present self is the point of contact of these various worlds, and through it we can freely enter or leave any of them. This hierarchical world of reality is transcended by absolute will, which, by negating negation, makes itself independent of all positions and has other worlds beyond the world of reality. "To those who are awake, there is one ordered universe common to all, whereas in sleep each man turns away to a world of his own."[263] So, too, absolute will transcends the common real world to open up the world of infinite possibility, the world of imagination. The immediate world of absolute will is one in which all things are individual independent acts, in which even the natural world, which we think of as the only real one, becomes a symbol, and in which there is no time, space, or causation. The man who lifted the veil of the goddess of Sais, strange to say, saw only himself;[264] so at the foundation of the world of nature we find free personality. The Gnostic Valentinus, in his mythological scheme of the realm between the primordial abyss and the creation of this world, was close to this depth.

The primary world of the immediate objects of absolute will, which eludes reflection, is the world of art and religion. In these worlds each phenomenon is a symbol and a free personality. There our thought is but one act among many, and the world and the truth based on it are only one world, one truth, among others. Number is the reality of the world of pure thought, but if we consider mathematics as immediate object of the will it reveals its symbolic meaning; hence Dirichlet could draw mathematical inspiration from Easter music he heard in Rome.[265] The unity of absolute will thus advances in two directions, each position growing in depth on its own terms, and at the same time, as an act of the personality, advancing to the unity of the total personality, in accord with the demand of knowledge for the most concrete objectivity.

On the same grounds that we think the physical world exists independently of the subjective ego, or on even stronger ones, we can say that the historical world exists objectively. As Bergson says: just as we believe this door leads into the neighboring room, we can believe that past events have incontrovertible reality.[266] Physicists think psychological phenomena are ephemeral chimerae, and even psychologists see them as confined to the unrepeatable moment in which they come to be and pass away. But the unchangingness of material phenomena means no more than the repeatability of certain spiritual phenomena, or what Mill calls "the permanent possibility of sensations."[267] If spiritual phenomena were indeed an unrepeatable, perpetual flux, the permanence of material phenomena would be lost. We think of reality as the merely unchanging, the perpetually present; but this is an abstraction, and concrete reality must contain the dimension of the past. Any human being, when dead and turned to ashes, differs from no other in the same state, yet as a historical reality each was a unique individual. When a man falls on hard times and becomes a beggar, it may be because of his sins or because of inevitable fate; but without taking the past into account this distinction is illusory. We can make no sense of such realities if we confine ourselves to the physical present. Immediate concrete reality is historical. The historical world is more concrete than the material one, but the worlds of art and religion are still more so. We belong, thus, to various worlds, which we enter and leave at will. We belong to the City of God and the City of the Devil, and this is the root of all human progress and decline, tragedy and comedy.

Let us try to link all these ideas with the problem of human life. All things aspire to the concrete reality which is their foundation. Various worlds are created by various a priori—the world of rational numbers by the a priori of arithmetic, that of real numbers by the a priori of analysis, that of geometric figures by the a priori of geometry, the mechanical world by the a priori of dynamics, the biological world by the life force. These worlds arise in linked order, from the most abstract (logic and mathematics) to the most concrete (history and art), the more concrete position always figuring as the goal of the more abstract one, and containing it within itself. The goal of all positions, and the foundation of all, is absolute free will. Knowledge advances in objectivity with each acquisition of new content, but it reaches its ultimate point in will or action.

The fulfillment our life aspires to lies in moving from abstract positions to their concrete source. The *élan vital* is continually leaping towards this concrete source. The word "life" is an objectification of this teleological unity, in which our will is projected into the object world, and the meaning of this word differs according to the content of the different goals toward which it strives. One who understands only material desire will grasp the meaning of life within the limits of physical life, while one who lives a profound ideal will be able to say with Paul, "it is no longer I that live, but Christ who lives in me."[268] The truly self-sufficient and autonomous is the truly living, and true life is the concrete totality of the real, towards which all the development of life advances. Physical life is an abstract position, not the end itself. When Christ says that "he who finds his life will lose it, and he who loses his life for my sake will find it,"[269] his words have more than a moral meaning. I should like to observe, further, that we cannot think of true life apart from a "cultural sense", the "will to live" must be "will to culture," as Fichte so rightly insists.[270] Absolute will is trans-intellectual, not anti-intellectual; indeed, it includes intellect as one of its aspects. If it negated intellect it would decay, for it would be reduced to the heteronomy of brute nature.

From all we have seen, it is clear that the material world is merely the world of mediate experience, and that our most concrete immediate experience is that of a return to the concrete life of actuality, which is to the material world as a world of solids to the world of planes it projects, a return to the immediate totality of absolute free will, which is both "creating and not created" and "neither created nor creating," and at every point includes the negation of itself. The significance of physical life lies in spiritual life, to which it is no more than a means. The development of a culture tending unilaterally toward the material life is certainly not the true goal of human existence.

Notes

Translator's notes are between square brackets. Masao Yamashita's list of Nishida's books (*Nishida Kitarō zenzōsho mokuroku*, Kyoto University Institute for Cultural Sciences) has been consulted. An inspection of some of these books in Kyoto University revealed that several of them had been marked in pencil, presumably by Nishida himself, and that occasionally a piece of paper, still in place after seventy years, had been inserted at the point at which the markings ceased. Generally the passages underlined dealt with topics of special interest to Nishida. In the following notes the editions used by Nishida are indicated where possible.

1. [*Hekiganroku*, Case 33, in *Two Zen Classics*, trans. Katsuki Sekida, New York, Tokyo: Weatherhill, 1977, 152.]
2. [Henri Bergson, *Essai sur les données immédiates de la conscience* (1889), 8th ed., Paris: Alcan, 1911; *Time and Free Will: An Essay on the Immediate Data of Consciousness*, trans. F. L. Pogson, New York: Harper and Row, 1960, 90, 128: "Our projection of our psychic states into space in order to form a discrete multiplicity is likely to influence the states themselves and to give them in reflective consciousness a

new form, which immediate perception does not attribute to them." "Below homogeneous duration, which is the extensive symbol of true duration, a close psychological analysis distinguishes a duration whose heterogeneous moments permeate one another; below the numerical multiplicity of conscious states, a qualitative multiplicity; below the self with well-defined states, a self in which *succeeding each other* means *melting into one another* and forming an organic whole. But we are generally content with the first, i.e. with the shadow of the self projected into homogeneous space" (*Oeuvres*, ed. Henri Gouhier, Presses universitaires de France, 1963, 61, 85).]

3. [Johann Gottlieb Fichte, "Versuch einer neuen Darstellung der Wissenschaftslehre," *Fichtes Werke*, ed. Immanuel Hermann Fichte, repr. Berlin: De Gruyter, 1971, I, 527: "How did you come to this consciousness of your thinking? You will answer: I was immediately aware of it. The consciousness of my thinking is not something accidental, added to it after the event, but is inseparable from my thinking." Nishida's text: *Erste und zweite Einleitung in die Wissenschaftslehre und Versuch einer neuen Darstellung der Wissenschaftslehre*, ed. Fritz Medicus, Leipzig: Eckardt (Meiner), 1910 (rev. ed. Peter Baumanns, Hamburg: Meiner, 1975).]

4. *Fichtes Werke* I, 522-23 [Two words are missing from this quotation as it appears here, but it is quoted correctly in *Nishida Kitarō zenshū*, Tokyo: Iwanami, 1978, I, 338.]

5. Josiah Royce, *The World and the Individual: First Series*, New York: Macmillan, 1899 (repr. Dover Publications, 1959), 5025-07.

6. [William James, *The Principles of Psychology*, New York: Holt, 1890 (repr. Dover Publications, 1950), I, 333-34 and 337-38.]

7. [Cf. Immanuel Kant, *Kritik der reinen Vernunft*, ed. Raymund Schmidt, Hamburg: Meiner (1926), 1976; *Critique of Pure Reason*, trans. Norman Kemp Smith, New York: St. Martin's Press, 1965, 152-57 (B 131-39).]

8. [Kant used the term *Sollen* in an ethical context, but Wilhelm Windelband and Heinrich Rickert extended it to logic and aesthetics. Cf. Rickert, *Der Gegenstand der Erkenntnis: Einführung in die Tranzendenzphilosophie*, 6th ed., Tübingen: Mohr, 1928, 202-45. (Nishida uses the 2nd ed., 1913.) Rickert's "ought," like Hermann Cohen's "demand," recalls Kant's "regulative principle of pure reason," described in *Critique of Pure Reason*, 450 (B 536-37), as "a *problem* for the understanding, and therefore for the subject, leading it to undertake and

to carry on, in accord with the completeness prescribed by the idea, the regress in the series of conditions of any given condition . . . a principle of reason which serves as a *rule*, postulating what we ought to do in the regress. . . ." This line of thinking brought a revival of interest in Fichte, as is noted in *Friedrich Ueberwegs Grundriss der Geschichte der Philosophie*, IV, ed. Traugott Konstantin Oesterreich, 12th ed., Basle: Benno Schwabe, 1951, 449-67]

9. [The non-objectifiability of the subject is discussed in Paul Natorp, *Allgemeine Psychologi nach kritischer Methode*, Tübingen: Mohr, 1912 (repr. Amsterdam: Bonset, 1965), 29-31. In Nishida's copy pages 22-131, 154-162, 189-200 are marked, indicating that he skipped Natorp's historical excurses.]

10. [Rickert argues against "every theory of knowledge which presumes that there is a reality outside the contents of consciousness and independent of them, and that representations are a knowing of this reality which somehow reproduces it or 'corresponds' to it," and which leads to "a doubling of the world, a splitting of the real into self-subsisting real things common to all, on the one hand, and a world of perception or representation known only to the individual, on the other" (*Gegenstand der Erkenntnis*, 122, 119).]

11. [This phrase, as Nishida explains in *Zenshū* I, 223, refers chiefly to Windelband's theory of "normative consciousness." Cf. Windelband, *Präludien*, 9th ed., Tübingen: Mohr, 1924: "The validity of the axioms is always conditioned by an end, which must be presupposed as an ideal for our thinking, willing, and feeling." "The system of logic is the collection of all those basic principles, to be developed teleologically, without which there can be no universally valid thought." "All axioms, all norms show themselves to be the means to the end of universal validity" (II, 111-12, 125, 126).]

12. [*Fichtes Werke* I, 524: "The concept of a thinking which returns within itself and the concept of a self are mutually exhaustive. The self is that which posits itself and nothing else. From the act above described emerges nothing other than the self and the self can emerge from no other act."]

13. [*Ibid.*, 525: "You know of this existence which must be presupposed, only insofar as you think it, and thus this existence of the self is nothing more than your being posited by yourself."]

14. [Rickert, "Zwei Wege der Erkenntnistheorie. Transcendentalpsychologie und Transcendentallogik," *Kantstudien* 14 (1909) 169-228; here,

203. This article is substantially reproduced in *Gegenstand der Erkenntnis,* chapter four.]

15. [Rickert, *Gegenstand der Erkenntnis,* 213: "If 'object' denotes only that which stands *over against* the subject, and by which it must be *directed* in order to know, then only in the 'ought' which is recognized in judging can we find the factor which confers objectivity in cognition, and so, too, the 'object' of knowledge, insofar as it does not coincide with its 'material,' must be sought in the 'ought,' and not in the real existent. . . . No other object can be found, for a transcendent reality has become inconceivable: we can never understand how something beyond consciousness can be *known* as real."]

16. [*Ibid.,* 188: "Cognition, in its intrinsic logical meaning, is recognition of values, or rejection of disvalues."]

17. [*Ibid.,* 184: "All knowledge begins with judging, proceeds by judging, and can end only with judging. As 'actual' knowledge, then, it consists entirely in acts of judgment." Cf. *Zenshū* I, 219.]

18. [Rickert, *ibid.,* 47: "As immanent realities there are only psycho-physical or psychological subjects, and whatever is real in these subjects can be thought only as object. Indeed my entire inner self is, as a matter of fact, an object for every other self, just as other selves are objects for me. The non-objectifiable has no reality in time or in space. . . . As the limit-concept of the series of psycho-physical subjects, we found a subject which was no longer physical, and similarly the limit-concept of the series of psychological subjects can be thought of as no longer a psychological subject. This will be denied only by those who refuse to entertain the idea of a subject which is not a reality. If, however, one allows one's thinking to include the non-real, then the last member of the series is a subject which is. . . only an 'empty' *form.*" Cf. *Zenshū* I, 222.]

19. [Windelband, *Präludien:* "It belongs to the concept of the axioms to be unprovable." "The critical method presupposes belief in the universally valid goals and in their capacity to be known in empirical consciousness. . . . With this presupposition the critical method finds itself in a circle from the very start. . . . Hence Lotze well says that since this circle is unavoidable we should embark on it as purely as possible" (II, 108, 122-23).]

20. [Rudolf Hermann Lotze, *Logik* (1874), Leipzig: Meiner, 1912, 525: "The testing of the truth of our knowledge as a whole is impossible without presupposing the basic principles to be tested as the basis of

decision in every doubt.... Since this circle is unavoidable, one must embark on it purely" (*Logic*, trans. Bernard Bosanquet, Oxford: Clarendon Press, 1884).]

21. [Rickert, *Gegenstand der Erkenntnis*: "Is it possible to doubt that the 'ought' which we recognize in judging has a real, transcendent theoretical validity, independent of the subject...*without at the same time denying altogether the possibility of judgment*?" "One may alter the judgments as one wishes, in order to rule out every apparent connection to a transcendent reality, but one will nonetheless always recognize their truth as a timelessly valid transcendent *value*" (237, 239-40). These references to Windelband, Lotze and Rickert appear also in *Zenshū* I, 211.]

22. [Leonard Nelson, founder of the Neo-Friesian School, differed from the Neo-Kantians in adopting an empirical and psychological interpretation of Kant's critique, inspired by Jakob Friedrich Fries. He borrowed from Fries and Lotze (*Logik*, 489) the "principle of reason's trust in itself." Nishida possessed his *Die Unmöglichkeit der Erkenntnistheorie*, Göttingen: Vandenhoeck und Ruprecht, 1911 (17: "The possibility of knowledge is not a problem, but a fact").]

23. [*Fichtes Werke* I, 526-27, 530: "To be conscious of your thinking you must be conscious of yourself. *You* are conscious of *yourself*, you say; so you must have distinguished your *thinking* self from the self which is *thought* in the thinking thereof. But for this to be possible, what thinks in this thinking must itself be the *object* of a higher thinking ...and once we have begun to draw conclusions in this way, you can never point to a place where we should stop; thus we shall constantly need to supply a new consciousness, for which each successive consciousness figures as object.... In this way consciousness becomes simply inexplicable... [because] in each consciousness subject and object are separated from one another, and each seen as something particular.... But since consciousness in fact exists, this assertion must be false. If it is false, its opposite must be valid; thus the following proposition holds: there is a consciousness in which subjective and objective are quite indissociable, and absolutely one and the same.... The consciousness of our own thinking is this consciousness.... The intelligence beholds itself, merely as intelligence or as pure intelligence, and its essence consists in just this self-beholding. This intuition can thus rightly be called...*intellectual* intuition" (*Werke* I, 106-07, 110).]

24. Fichte, "Zweite Einleitung in die Wissenschaftslehre," par. 4 [*Werke* I, 458-63; *Science of Knowledge (Wissenschaftslehre), with First and Second Introductions*, trans. Peter Heath and John Lachs, New York: Appleton-Century-Crofts, 1970, 34-38.]

25. Windelband, *Präludien* II, 126 ["Fichte clearly discerned the teleological character of the critical method, and defined the task of philosophy as the working out of the system of the (teleologically) necessary operations of reason....He deduced normative consciousness as a teleological system"].

26. Rickert, "Urteil und Urteilen," *Logos* 3 (1912) 230-45 [233: "Every event in the psyche has a temporal course, that is, it begins to be at a certain point, and either goes on continuously, or is interrupted, and must eventually come to an end at some moment in time.... Accordingly the psychology of judgment can speak of judging only as a temporal process in individual consciousness....Should it appear that logic is not concerned with formations whose reality consists in temporal happenings in this or that psyche, then it already follows that the apparently self-evident assertion that the psychology of judgment has the same material as the logic of judgment is false." For a later version of this essay see *Gegenstand der Erkenntnis*, 156-65.]

27. [Rickert, "Urteil und Urteilen," 233: "What we think or understand when we say $2 \times 2 = 4$ is certainly something other than a component of an individual's psychological experience, for all who understand or think it experience it in common. All of them grasp the *same* meaning...and this can be thought or understood, by many individuals by means of different acts, but it cannot appear in many forms in the different individuals as psychological reality, for then it would no longer be the same."]

28. [For the distinction between cause and reason see John Stuart Mill, *A System of Logic* (1843), 10th ed., London: Longmans, 1879, Book VI, chapter 2 (*Collected Works* VIII, Toronto and Buffalo: University of Toronto Press, 1974, 836-843).]

29. [This reference to Laplace may be inspired by Emil du Bois-Raymond, *Über die Grenzen des Naturerkennens und die Sieben Welträtsel*, 2nd ed., Leipzig: Veit, 1903 (*Vorträge über Philosophie und Geschichte*, Hamburg: Meiner, 1974, 56-63).]

30. [Wilhelm Wundt, *Grundriss der Psychologie*, 15th ed., Leipzig: Kröner, 1922, 399: "The principle of creative synthesis has long been recognized in the case of the higher spiritual creations, but its signifi-

cance for all the other processes of the psyche has not, on the whole, been adequately recognized; indeed because it has been mistakenly associated with laws of physical causality, it has been turned into its opposite" (*Outlines of Psychology*, trans. Charles Hubbard Judd, 3rd ed., New York: G. E. Stechert, 1907). Nishida uses the 10th ed., Leipzig: Engelmann, 1911.]

31. [As an example of Rickert's subtlety in siting the realm of value, see *Gegenstand der Erkenntnis*, 296-97: "Only with the *splitting* of value from actuality, non-real meaning from real being, form from content, do we come to the region where there is theoretical *truth*. But for one who has seen this, the unity of the divided 'realms' is in *this* regard no longer a riddle, a problem needing a solution. . . . It is enough to say that there is indeed something 'incomprehensible' here, but not so much *supra*-comprehensible as *pre*-comprehensible, for this unity is immediately experienced before we have yet learnt to divide value and actuality, non-real meaning and real being, transcendent and immanent."]

32. [Cf. Rickert, *Gegenstand der Erkenntnis*, 215, 217: "If, to avoid linguistic awkwardness, one wishes to apply the notion of 'being' to everything that is thinkable, . . . whether real or unreal, form or content, or both together, one may well do so. . . . But by the same token the 'ought' and validity . . . must be carefully separated from existence and real being. . . . The 'ought' and real being are never identical."]

33. Windelband, *Über Gleichheit und Identität, Sitzungsberichte der Heidelberger Akademie, phil.-hist. Klasse*, Abhandlung 14, Heidelberg: Carl Winter, 1910 [51-52: "Representational contents which are still distinguishable in only a single respect are called the same. . . . From the reciprocal action of sameness and difference are produced all further categories of reflection"].

34. Windelband, *Vom System der Kategorien*, Tübingen: Mohr, 1900 [4-5: "Sameness, the basic category of the reflexive series, develops as the limit case of the function of differentiation. Corresponding to it on the side of objective relations or of constitutive categories is identity, which in this sense denotes nothing other than really existing sameness. . . . A judgment of sameness can be passed only on things which are different from one another"].

35. [Kant sharply distinguishes the "two fundamental sources" of knowledge in *Critique of Pure Reason*, 92, 283, 297-98 (B 74, 327, 350), but he also suggests that they "perhaps spring from a common, but to us

unknown root" (61, B 29, cf. 655, B 863). Heidegger makes much of the latter texts in an interpretation directed against Hermann Cohen's subordination of intuition to thought, and places the"center of gravity" of human knowledge in intuition (Martin Heidegger, *Kant und das Problem der Metaphysik* (1929), Frankfurt: Klostermann, 2nd ed., 1951, 29, 66; *Kant and the Problem of Metaphysics*, trans. James S. Churchill, Bloomington: Indiana University Press, 1962, 30, 70).]

36. Rickert, "Das Eine, die Einheit und die Eins," *Logos* 2 (1911-12) 26-78. [61: "The purely logical medium gave *only* the distinction of one from another. It must therefore be called a purely heterogeneous medium.... That an object can occupy different places without any change of content can be expressed by calling space and time *homogeneous* mediums.... Homogeneity is a general expression, independent of the specific characters of time and space, for one of the alogical factors in number. Numerical 'one,' whatever else it may be, is a single or identical object in general, occupying one place in the homogeneous medium... and therefore it is possible to equate it with another, but not a different, object, occupying another place in this medium. Objects *equal* to one another are found only in a *homogeneous* medium." See Ernst Cassirer, *The Philosophy of Symbolic Forms* III, New Haven and London: Yale University Press, 1973, 346-79.]

37. See my discussion of this in "Logical Understanding and Mathematical Understanding" [*Zenshū* I, 250-267].

38. G. W. F. Hegel, *Enzyklopädie der philosophischen Wissenschaften (1830)*, ed. Friedhelm Nicolin and Otto Pöggeler, Leipzig: Meiner, 1975, 155-56, par. 166 (*The Logic of Hegel*, trans. William Wallace, Oxford: Clarendon, 1892, 297). [Hegel, unlike Fichte, does not have a high estimate of the speculative status of "A is A": *Enzyklopädie*, 125-26, par. 115 (*The Logic of Hegel*, 212-14); *Wissenschaft der Logik*, ed. Georg Lasson, Hamburg: Meiner (1934), 1975, II, 23-26 (*Hegel's Science of Logic*, trans. A. V. Miller, New York: Humanities Press, 1969). Nishida's edition of the *Enzyklopädie* is that of Leopold von Henning, C. A. Michelet, and Ludwig Boumann, Berlin: Duncker und Humboldt, 1841, 1842, 1845, which contains "Zusätze" omitted in the Meiner edition.]

39. [Kant, *Critique of Pure Reason*, 69-70 (B 39-40).]

40. Henri Poincaré, *Science and Hypothesis*, trans. George Bruce Halsted, New York: The Science Press, 1905, 48 (*La science et l'hypothèse*, Paris: Flammarion, 1901).

41. [Kant, *Critique of Pure Reason*, 198-99, 203 (B 203-04, 210).]
42. Paul Natorp, *Die logischen Grundlagen der exakten Wissenschaften*, Leipzig and Berlin: Teubner, 1910, 52-54.
43. [Lotze, *Logik*, 148-86.]
44. [Bernard Bosanquet, *The Essentials of Logic*, London and New York: Macmillan, 1895: "Ultimately the condition of inference is always a system.... Wherever there is inference at all, there is at least an identity of content which may be more or less developed into a precise relation of parts." "In induction you are finding out the system piecemeal, but the system, and the system only, is the ground of inference in both [induction and deduction]" (140, 162). Cf. Bosanquet, *The Distinction between Mind and its Objects*, Manchester University Press, 1913, 35: "I cannot understand any attempt to explain a *universal* which does not recognize that *it absolutely consists in the effort of a content to complete itself a system.*"]
45. [On Oct. 16, 1913 (*Zenshū* XVII, 324), Nishida was reading "Husserl's *Phänomenologie*," a reference to *Ideen zu einer reinen Phänomenologie und phänomenologischen Philosophie*, Halle: Niemeyer, 1913 (ed. Karl Schuhmann, *Husserliana* III, 1, Hague: Nijhoff, 1976; *Ideas pertaining to a pure Phenomenology and phenomenological Philosophy*, trans. F. Kersten, Hague, Boston, and London: Nijhoff, 1982). Eiichi Shimomissé writes: "It is generally accepted that Nishida was the first Japanese philosopher who made reference to Husserl in his article entitled "On the thesis of the Pure Logic schools of Epistemology" (1911) [*Zenshū* I, 209-34]. Nishida saw Husserl holding an almost identical position with Rickert's, although they belonged to different 'trends' of thought.... The object of Husserl's philosophy is, according to Nishida, a concrete phenomenon of consciousness, and the realm of phenomenology is that of pure experience, which phenomenology intends to investigate by sustaining all possible attitudes" (*Japanese Phenomenology*, ed. Yoshihiro Nitta and Hirotaka Tatematsu, *Analecta Husserliana* VIII, Dordrecht and Boston: Reidel, 1979, 8).]
46. [Wilhelm Dilthey, "Ideen über eine beschreibende und zergliedernde Psychologie" (1894), *Gesammelte Schriften* V, 3rd ed., Stuttgart: Teubner, 3rd ed., 1961, 139-240; 200: "Every psychical condition emerges within me at a given time, and vanishes again at a given time. It runs its course: beginning, middle, and end. It is a process."]
47. [*The Logic of Hegel*, 297 (slightly modified); *Enzyklopädie*, 155-56, par. 166.]

48. [Rickert, *Gegenstand der Erkenntnis*, 274: "The 'ought' is not pure value. It signifies the non-actual as an imperative over against the ego-subject, from which it demands obedience, recognition, submission. That is a secondary, indeed misleading, circumstance. . . . Only the value which abides in itself, and which is valid as value independently not only of every real demand and recognition, but of every *connection* with a subject to which it addresses itself, or *for* which it is valid, is the formally *transcendent* object."]

49. [Natorp, *Die logischen Grundlagen*, 47: "Thinking is unification, we said; then, however, at the same time, division; for where there is not a many, hence the possibility of division, unification is not a possibility either. But this need not be understood to mean that the manifold as such is first given, and the unity of the manifold only subsequently brought about by thinking; rather, in every essential act of thought, as an act of determination, an *X* determines itself as one and yet manifold, the unity of a manifold, the manifold of a unity."]

50. [Kant, *Critique of Pure Reason*, 135 (A 105).]

51. [Natorp, *Allgemeine Psychologie*, 67-68; the correlativity of subject and object, described as a "correlative monism," is the main theme of Natorp's book.]

52. Fichte, *Grundlage der gesamten Wissenschaftslehre*, par. 1, *Werke* I, 91; *Fichte's Science of Knowledge*, 94. [Nishida uses the edition of Fritz Medicus, Leipzig: Eckardt, 1911 (3rd ed. Wilhelm G. Jacobs, Hamburg: Meiner, 1979).]

53. [Natorp, *Die logischen Grundlagen*, 59.]

54. *Fichtes Werke* I, 93; *Science of Knowledge*, 94.

55. [*Fichtes Werke* I, 95; *Science of Knowledge*, 96: "the proposition 'I am I' has a meaning wholly different from that of 'A is A.' For the latter has content only under a certain condition. . . . The proposition 'I am I' is unconditionally and absolutely valid, . . . valid not merely in form but also in content. In it the I is posited, not conditionally, but absolutely, with the predicate of equivalence to itself; hence it really *is* posited, and the proposition can also be expressed as 'I am.' "]

56. [For the distinction between presentative consciousness (immediate present perception) and representative consciousness, see Natorp, *Allgemeine Psychologie*, 53-58.]

57. [Hegel, *Wissenschaft der Logik* II, 27.]

58. [Bergson, *Matière et mémoire* (1896), 9th ed., Paris: Alcan, 1913; *Matter and Memory*, trans. Nancy M. Paul and W. Scott Palmer,

New York: Macmillan, 1913, 178: "In that continuity of becoming which is reality itself, the present moment is constituted by the quasi-instantaneous section effected by our perception in the flowing mass; and this section is precisely that which we call the material world." (*Oeuvres*, 281).]

59. [Bergson, *L' évolution créatrice* (1907), 6th ed., Paris: Alcan, 1910; *Creative Evolution*, trans. Arthur Mitchell, New York: The Modern Library, 1944, 7 (*Oeuvres*, 498): "Memory, as we have tried to prove (*Matter and Memory*, chaps. ii and iii) is not a faculty of putting away recollections in a drawer.... In reality, the past is preserved by itself, automatically. In its entirety, probably, it follows us at every instant."]

60. *Enzyklopädie*, 311, par. 377 (*Hegel's Philosophy of Mind*, trans. William Wallace and A. V. Miller, Oxford: Clarendon, 1971, 1).

61. *Enzyklopädie*, 200, par. 247 (*Hegel's Philosophy of Nature*, trans. A. V. Miller, Oxford: Clarendon, 1970).

62. [Kant, *Prolegomena*, parr. 20, 22 (*Werke*, ed. Wilhelm Weischedel, Darmstadt: Wissenschaftliche Buchgesellschaft, 1975, III, 166, 171).]

63. [Fichte expresses a different view in *Science of Knowledge*, 103: "the form of counter-positing is so far from being contained in that of positing, that in fact it is flatly opposed to this" (*Werke* I, 102). But see Hegel, *Enzyklopädie*, par. 116.]

64. [Hegel, *Wissenschaft der Logik* II, 308; *Enzyklopädie*, 162, par. 181 (*The Logic of Hegel*, 314).]

65. [*The Logic of Hegel*, 314.]

66. [Richard Dedekind, *Was sind und was sollen die Zahlen?*, 3rd ed., Brunswick: Vieweg, 1911 (*Essays on the Theory of Numbers*, trans. Wooster Woodruff Beman, Chicago: Open Court, 1901; repr. 1963).]

67. [Correcting Kant, Hermann Cohen constructs time and space as logical categories (*Logik der reinen Erkenntnis*, Berlin: Cassirer, 1902; repr. of 1922 ed., *Werke* VI, Hildesheim and New York: Olms, 1977, 149-55 and 188-98.)]

68. Henri Poincaré, *The Value of Science*, trans. George Bruce Halsted, New York: The Science Press, 1907, 118 (*La valeur de la science*, Paris: Flammarion, 1970, 158). [The context is a refutation of Edouard LeRoy's claim that "the scientist creates the fact."]

69. [Poincaré, *Science and Hypothesis*, 13 (also referred to by Natorp, *Die logischen Grundlagen*, 14, as an illustration of the process-character of knowledge).]

70. Rickert, "Das Eine," 62-65 [here the + sign is seen as an additional alogical factor in mathematics.]

71. *Ibid.*, 78.

72. Thus Bolzano, opposing the separation of form and matter, argues that form is simply that which can be understood by itself: "If I may make a somewhat daring suggestion, I should say that one calls *formal* those propositions and representations which can be determined merely from certain of their component parts, while the other parts, consequently named material or matter, are to remain arbitrary" (Bernard Bolzano, *Wissenschaftslehre* I, Leipzig: Meiner, 1914; repr. Aalen: Scientia, 1981, 51; *Bolzano's Theory of Science*, trans. Rolf George, Berkeley and Los Angeles: University of California Press, 1972, 12-15).

73. Natorp, *Die logischen Grundlagen*, 266, 326.

74. [*Ibid.*, 83: "When we attribute existence to an object, this is in a certain sense a tautology. That existence accrues to the object means no more than that it acquires full objecthood."]

75. [Kant, *Critique of Pure Reason*, 126 (B 125).]

76. [*Ibid.*, 137 (A 110).]

77. [See Franz Brentano, *Psychologie vom empirischen Standpunkt*, ed. Oskar Kraus, Hamburg: Meiner, 1971, II, 38-82, and Natorp, *Die logischen Grundlagen*, 37, for comparable critiques of the notion of judgment as connection.]

78. [*The Logic of Hegel* 299 (par. 166 Zusatz).]

79. Hegel, *Enzyclopädie*, 133, par. 167 (*The Logic of Hegel*, 300).

80. Bolzano [*Wissenschaftslehre* I, 141-42; Bolzano gives the example of a triangle with three right angles (*Theory of Science*, 37-38).]

81. Hegel, *Enzyclopädie*, 135, par. 133 (*The Logic of Hegel*, 242).

82. George Frederick Stout, *A Manual of Psychology* (1899), repr. *Significant Contributions to the History of Psychology*, IX, Washington: University Publications of America, 1977, 120-22. [Stout drew on Carl Stumpf, *Tonpsychologie* I, Leipzig: Hirzel, 1883 (repr. Amsterdam: Bonset, 1965).]

83. *Ibid.*, 122-24.

84. [James, *Principles of Psychology* I, 258-65.]

85. [Bergson, *Creative Evolution*, 8, 11, 14 (*Oeuvres*, 499, 501, 503).]

86. [Rickert, *Gegenstand der Erkenntnis*, 174-75.]

87. Hermann Cohen, *Kants Theorie der Erfahrung* (1871), Berlin: Bruno Cassirer, 1925, 399. [Nishida uses the second edition, Berlin: Düm-

mler, 1885. The following quotations from Cohen's *Logik der reinen Erkenntnis* may provide some idea of his views: "The incorrect notion that thought, as unification, consists in a process of *ordering*, rests on the basic prejudgment that thought receives its material from *sensation*, and that its task is merely to work on this material. Against this, we think of plurality as a *unity* to be generated...and we hold that the activity of thought generates its content. The whole, indivisible content of thinking must be a product of thinking, and the whole, indivisible activity of thinking is that which forms the content. This unity of production and produced is demanded by the concept of pure thought....We are not concerned with the psychological content and psychological process of thinking. Pure thought is not representation and cannot be conceived in terms of a process in consciousness." "The origin of something cannot be found in that something itself. Judgment must therefore not shy away from an adventurous detour, if it wishes to trace the origin of the something. This adventure of thought is presented by *nothingness. On the detour of nothingness judgment exhibits the origin of the something*." "In a letter to Arnauld (1690) Leibniz says: 'Each of these substances contains in its nature the law of the continuation of the entire series of its operations'....For a general characterization of thinking let us note the expressions 'operations' and 'the law of operations.' We wish to designate continuity as the law of operations for thinking and judging....*Continuity is a law of thought*. As such it is first and foremost *independent of sensation*....Continuity is the law of thought governing *elements which are conceived and demanded not as given, but as to be produced*....In virtue of continuity, all the elements of thought, insofar as they may qualify as elements of knowledge, are generated from the origin....Being itself must receive its origin through non-being. Non-being is not to be thought of as a correlative concept to being, but, as relative nothingness (*mē on*), denotes the spring-board whereby the leap in virtue of continuity must be carried out." "The production of pure thought cannot begin with the *thing* ...from apparent *nothingness* must the 'something' be derived to receive a true origin....The origin is not properly a category, but rather a law of thought....'Origin' denotes the basic law of thought more unequivocally and more comprehensively than 'continuity.' The latter arose in the context of the problems of mathematics. That it referred to origin remained unclear. The basic demand of origin affects all forms of pure thought, but fits mathematics, a rigorous and exemplary form of pure thought, most exactly" (58-60, 84, 91-93, 119). For a critical discussion of Cohen's theory of the origin, see Natorp, *Die logischen Grundlagen*, 23-29.]

88. Leibniz writes: "In corporeal things there is something besides extension, and indeed prior to it" [*Mathematische Schriften*, ed. C. I. Gerhardt, repr. Hildesheim, 1962, VI, 70; frequently quoted by Cohen].

89. Cohen, *Kants Theorie der Erfahrung*, 398. [The immediately preceding sentences read: "In the first edition of the *Critique of Pure Reason* the 'principle which anticipates all perceptions, as such' is: 'In all appearances sensation, and the *real* which corresponds to it in the object (*realitas phaenomenon*), has an *intensive magnitude*, that is, a degree' [*Critique of Pure Reason*, 201, A 106]. The mistake here is the 'and.' Sensation does not intrinsically possess intensive magnitude and besides this in addition the reality of the object corresponding to sensation. For sensation is no more than the expression of a relation of consciousness to its content, as intuition is another such expression, and thinking another. As principles, extensive and intensive magnitude are meant to determine objects. But sensation in itself is not an object."]

90. [See Kant, *Critique of Pure Reason*, 184 (B 183).]

91. [*Ibid.*, 197 (B 202).]

92. Cohen, *Theorie der Erfahrung*, 387 ["Extensive quantity is a comparison quantity.... Comparison presupposes a something which exists in and for itself, as well as being provided for the purposes of the comparison"].

93. [Kant, *Critique of Pure Reason*, 194 (B 196).]

94. [*Ibid.*, 204 (B 211).]

95. [Cohen, *Logik der reinen Erkenntnis*, 422-24.]

96. [*Ibid.*, 90, 92]

97. [*Ibid.*, 62.]

98. [*Ibid.*, 29, 53, 54, 60, 145.]

99. [*Ibid.*, 29.]

100. Cohen, *Kants Theorie der Erfahrung*, 531-32, 537. [Cf. *Logik der reinen Erkenntnis*, 417: "At Fichte's hands, the Kantian conditions of possibility become the conditions of self-consciousness. Self-consciousness is now the magic formula with which he imagines he can master all the problems of nature. *Light and air* he brings forth

from self-consciousness. Thus self-consciousness becomes the fountainhead of the possible."]

101. [Fichte, *Werke* I, 525.]

102. [*Ibid.*, 462; *Science of Knowledge*, 37.]

103. Max Frischeisen-Köhler, "Das Zeitproblem," *Jahrbücher der Philosophie* 1 (1913) 129-66; here, 142. [This essay is influenced by Natorp's *Die logischen Grundlagen.*]

104. [See Wundt, *Grundriss der Psychologie*, 45-46.]

105. [See Frederick Copleston, *A History of Philosophy*, Garden City, New York: Image Books, IV, 316 and VI i, 30-31.]

106. [Cohen, *Logik der reinen Erkenntnis*, 129.]

107. [Wundt, *Grundriss der Psychologie*, 56-91.]

108. [*Ibid.*, 34-35.]

109. [*Ibid.*, 107-10.]

110. [Max Planck, *Die Einheit des physikalischen Weltbildes*, Leipzig: Hirzel, 1909].

111. [Wundt, *Grundriss der Psychologie*, 34.]

112. [Edward Bradford Titchener, *A Text-Book of Psychology*, New York: Macmillan, 1913, 52: "A sensation...may be defined as an elementary mental process which is constituted of at least four attributes— quality, intensity, clearness (!) and duration." Also among Nishida's books: Titchener, *Lectures on the Experimental Psychology of the Thought Processes*, New York: Macmillan, 1909.]

113. [Natorp, *Allgemeine Psychologie*, 46, cf. *Einleitung in die Psychologie nach kritischer Methode*, Freiburg: Mohr, 1888, 17.]

114. Max Raphael, *Von Monet zu Picasso*, Hanau: Clauss und Feddersen, 1909, 33.

115. Broder Christiansen, *Philosophie der Kunst*, 2nd ed., Berlin: Behr, 1912, 79-82.

116. Konrad Fiedler, "Der Ursprung der künstlerischen Tätigkeit," *Schriften über Kunst*, ed. Hans Marbach, Leipzig: Hirzel, 1896 (ed. Hermann Konnerth, Munich: Piper, 1913, I, 183-236). [Here are some passages alluded to by Nishida: "The meaning of expressive activity can only be that some spiritual content reveals its presence in the motion of a bodily organ; or rather expressive activity can and should be seen as a developmental stage of a psychophysical process; just as the bodily process which begins with the excitation of sensitive nerves reaches a new phase of development in externally perceptible movement, so does the psychical process (which we are conscious of as the

accompanying inner side of that total life-process) know a development which it can attain in no other way in this activity of expression." "A glance into our interior workshop reveals a restless
becoming and passing away, an infinity of processes in which the elements of all being appear in the most various forms at the most various stages of their development. . . . Now, we feel the need, and are
conscious we have the ability, to withdraw from this condition full of
intimations, in which the infinity of being presses tirelessly upon us
. . . [by thought]." "[But] an experience of color has as such not the
slightest affinity with its verbal denotation. . . and even if thought
concentrates its entire force on experience and resolves not to stray
one step from the actuality of the senses. . . [we still find that] in its
exact just as much as in its speculative form knowledge can never
command any other material of actuality than what it has developed
as word and sign!" "When I say, 'The tree is green,' I fail utterly to
touch the infinity of possible representations in which a green tree can
appear in my consciousness." "We observe as a matter of fact a relative independence of thinking and representation. . . as very different
processes which factually belong together in our consciousness, . . . a
belonging together which is both physical and psychical" (193-94,
198-99, 202-05, 219, 224). "As long as we are only seeing, the world
can appear only as finite, never as infinite. And yet there is an infinity
which has nothing to do with the realm of thought, and which reveals
itself purely as an infinity of the visible world. Only the artist and
those who can follow him stand before this infinity. It is opened up
only where the effort to develop received representations to an ever
higher clarity and distinctness takes its origin in the perception of the
eye" (ed. Marbach, 309, as quoted in *Zenshū* III, 112-13).]

117. [Cohen, *Logik der reinen Erkenntnis*, 100-01; Natorp, *Die logischen
Grundlagen*, 14-16.]

118. [Bertrand Russell, (probably) *An Essay on the Foundations of Geometry*, Oxford University Press, 1897, 136; Nishida incorrectly refers to
Scientific Method in Philosophy.]

119. [Bergson, *Creative Evolution*, 359 (*Oeuvres*, 774).]

120. Art too is an infinite advance; Max Raphael says that if one asks a
painter when his work will be completed he may very well answer
with a wry smile, for art always begins anew.

121. [Brentano, *Psychologie* I, 124-28.]

122. "We can readily distinguish a weight of 12 grams from a weight of 10

grams, while a weight of 11 grams could neither be distinguished from the one nor the other. Such a statement, translated into symbols, may be written A = B, B = C, A ‹ C. This would be the formula of the physical continuum as crude experience gives it to us, whence arises an intolerable contradiction that has been obviated by the introduction of the mathematical continuum. This is a scale of which the steps. . . are infinite in number, but are exterior to one another instead of encroaching on one another as do the elements of the physical continuum" (*The Value of Science*, 42; *Valeur de la science*, 61).

123. Poincaré, *Science and Hypothesis*, 114.

124. Bergson, *Matter and Memory*, 246-53, (*Oeuvres*, 324-29).

125. [For Bolzano's "propositions in themselves" see *Theory of Science*, 20-31.]

126. Brentano, *Psychologie* I, 129 ["We can say that mental phenomena are the only ones which have an actual, in additional to an intentional, existence. Knowledge, joy, and desire really subsist; color, tone, and temperature are only phenomenal and intentional"].

127. Kazimierz Twardowski, *Zur Lehre vom Inhalt und Gegenstand der Vorstellungen*, Vienna: A. Hölder, 1894.

128. [Elsewhere Nishida refers to Georg Cantor, *Beiträge zur Begrundung der transfiniten Mengenlehre, Gesammelte Abhandlungen*, ed. Ernst Zermelo, Hildesheim: Olms, 1966. Among his books are found the French and English translations: *Contributions to the Founding of the Theory of Transfinite Numbers*, trans. Philip E. B. Jourdain, Chicago and London: Open Court, 1915; *Sur les fondements de la théorie des ensembles transfinis*, trans. F. Marotte, Paris: A. Hermann, 1899.]

129. Wundt, *Grundriss der Psychologie*, 262.

130. Bolzano [*Theory of Science*, 61-67.]

131. Brentano [*Psychologie* I, 124.]

132. Wilhelm Schapp, *Beiträge zur Phänomenologie der Wahrnehmung*, 2nd ed., Erlangen: Philosophische Akademie, 1925, 15. [Nishida refers to the 1st ed., Halle: Niemeyer, 1910.]

133. [Reference not traced, but see *Darstellung der Wissenschaftslehre aus dem Jahre 1801*, *Fichtes Werke* II, 1-163, and *Die Bestimmung des Menschen*, *ibid.*, 227: "My intellectual faculty seems to move inwardly this way and that, passing quickly from one thing to another; in short, it appears to me as the *drawing of a line.*—A particular thought is a point on this line."]

134. Tätigkeit schlechthin [*Fichtes Werke* I, 237-38 (*Science of Knowledge*, 211)].
135. [Reference not traced, but see *Fichtes Werke* I, 213-15 (*Science of Knowledge*, 192-93) and 346-65.]
136. Hegel, *Enzyclopädie*, 163, par. 181; *The Logic of Hegel*, 314.
137. Husserl, *Ideen*, 59-60, par. 28 (*Ideas*, 54-55).
138. As Husserl observes, if the perception of a certain color is unclear, it does not follow that the conceptual consciousness concerning that color is unclear.
139. [Bolzano, *Theory of Science*, 61-62; Brentano, *Psychologie* I, 112-28.]
140. [Natorp, *Allgemeine Psychologie*, 46, 53; 54-55: "In the actual life of consciousness this distinction [between content and object, equated by Natorp with the distinction between presentative and representative consciousness] shows itself to be a thoroughly fluid one. As soon as I make a content, deemed to be immediately present, an object for myself, and relate myself to it in questioning and answering (judging), I clearly, in that very process, take up my standpoint outside it. Thus it is at once no longer present to me as my immediate experience, but stands over against me. I 'relate' myself to it, that is, it is only representatively present for me."]
141. [Alexius Meinong, "Über Gegenstandstheorie," *Gesammelte Abhandlungen* II, Leipzig: J. A. Barth, 1913 (*Gesamtausgabe*, Graz: Akademische Verlagsanstalt, II, 1971), 481-535.]
142. [Husserl, *Logische Untersuchungen* II, ed. Ursula Panzer, *Husserliana* XIX, Hague: Nijhoff, 1984, 574 (VI par. 10); *Logical Investigations*, trans. J. N. Findlay, London: Routledge and Kegan Paul, 1970, 701. Nishida refers to the 1st ed., Halle: Niemeyer, 1901.]
143. Husserl, *Investigations*, 537, V par. 2 (*Untersuchungen*, 358).
144. *Ibid.*, 559, par. 11 (*Untersuchungen*, 387).
145. Husserl, *Ideen*, 200-24, parr. 87-96, (*Ideas*, 211-35).
146. Husserl, *Investigations*, 586, V par. 20 (*Untersuchungen*, 429).
147. Acts of the same quality and having the same object can differ in intentional essence, as in the case of the representations of an equiangular and an equilateral triangle (*Investigations*, 588, V par. 20; *Untersuchungen*, 429). (A further problem is posed by Husserl's claim that only the world of consciousness is experienced and that we can never have direct experience of the world of things. Since the world of consciousness means only the world of "inner evidence," he avoids being trapped in a dogmatic distinction between the mental and the material worlds.)

148. [Husserl, *Investigations*, 565-66 (*Untersuchungen*, 396-97).]
149. [Husserl, *Untersuchungen*, 443-67, V parr. 23-29 (*Investigations*, 598-616).]
150. [Brentano, *Psychologie* I, 181.]
151. [*Ibid.*, 179.]
152. Analogously, it is impossible for us to apprehend the world merely as color, and to ignore the solid existence of the colored things we perceive. As Schapp observes, the crossbar of the window pane is not a flickering colored shape such as we see in the after-image it leaves, but something solid and heavy [*Beiträge*, 16; Augustine, *De trinitate* XI 3, is the source of this topos].
153. [Husserl, *Ideen*, 43, par. 18 (*Ideas*, 36).]
154. Husserl, *Investigations*, 785, VI par. 45 (*Untersuchungen*, 671).
155. Theodor Lipps, *Bewusstsein und Gegenstand*, Leipzig: Engelmann, 1907, 23-24.
156. Cf. Gerhard Kowalewski [perhaps *Grundzüge der Differential- und Integralrechnung*, Leipzig and Berlin: Teubner, 1909, or *Die klassischen Problem der Analysis des Unendlichen*, Leipzig: Engelmann, 1910; see also Cohen, *Das Prinzip der Infinitesimalmethode und seine Geschichte*, 4th ed., *Werke* V, Hildesheim: Olms, 1984, 32.]
157. [According to Kant, but not Cohen.]
158. [Charles Émile Picard [*Das Wissen der Gegenwart in Mathematik und Naturwissenschaft*, Leipzig and Berlin: Teubner, 1913 (quoted in German); *La science moderne et son état actual*, Paris: Flammarion, 1906.]
159. [*Creative Evolution*, 290, 295: "Life appears in its entirety as an immense wave which, starting from a center, spreads outwards, and which on almost the whole of its circumference is stopped and converted into oscillation: at one single point the obstacle has been forced, the impulsion has passed freely. It is this freedom that the human form registers. Everywhere but in man, consciousness has had to come to a stand; in man alone it has kept on its way." "As the smallest grain of dust is bound up with our entire solar system, drawn along with in in that undivided movement of descent which is materiality itself, so all organized beings, from the humblest to the highest, from the first origins of life to the time in which we are, and in all places as in all times, do but evidence a single impulsion, the inverse of the movement of matter, and in itself indivisible" (*Oeuvres*, 720, 724).]
160. [*Ibid.*, 36, 331-32 (*Oeuvres*, 520, 752-53). For the reference to Paris (etchings, not photographs), see "Introduction à la métaphysique,"

Revue de métaphysique et de morale, 1903 (La pensée et le mouvant
(1934); The Creative Mind, trans. Mabelle L. Alison, New York: Philosophical Library, 1946, 200-02; Oeuvres, 1403-05).]

161. [Spinoza, Ethica, ed. J. van Floten and J. P. N. Land, Hague: Nijhoff,
1914, I, def. iii.]

162. Schapp distinguishes between "sehend meinen" (belief based on seeing) and "urteilend meinen" (belief based on judging). When I see a
piece of pottery and suddenly realize that it is really a piece of bacon
rind, although in both cases I see in the same way, my belief in the
first case is based on seeing, in the second on judgment; in the first
case I simply combine externally the fragment of pottery and the object, whereas in the second I cognize and judge the object [Beiträge,
95-105]. Is not this in effect a difference in the logical contexts of a
single essence?

163. [Husserl, Ideen, 91-94, par. 44 (Ideas, 94-98).]

164. Though psychologists strictly distinguish physical stimulus from psychological sensation, in thinking of the latter in terms of comparative
intensity they already equiparate it with the physical. In fact, physical
phenomena do not exist apart from sensory experience.

165. [Cohen, Logik der reinen Erkenntnis, 433: "In the geometrical possibility realized by Gauss...consciousness justified the hypothesis of
imaginary numbers in spatial intuition. Consciousness criticized the
methods of pure thought, and united number with space. This union
had already been accomplished in analytic geometry, but seemed impossible for the new kind of number....Thus consciousness appears
as a higher authority for thought, demanding and effecting the unification of methods in mathematics." See Carl Friedrich Gauss, A Biography by Tord Hall, trans. Albert Forderberg, Cambridge, Mass. and
London, 1970, 25-28, for Gauss's method of representing complex
numbers geometrically. The square root of minus one is an irrational
number; a complex number contains an irrational number as one of
its constituents. For Hankel, see Hermann Hankel, Vorlesungen über
die complexen Zahlen und ihre Functionen, Leipzig: L. Voss, 1867
(among Nishida's books).]

166. [Ibid., 179, 186-88; 193-94: "The category of time has produced the
unities of plurality, and thus produced in pure thought the content
that otherwise passed for the given. But time and its products are in
turn a presupposition with which space operates....In the judgment
of allness space is perfected as a category. Allness is not plurality, in
which time is perfected....In time the points lie outside one another

and the extent of their series is not to be thought of as a line. Only anticipations occur in time. . . . Nothing has permanence there except the monotonous mode of generation. . . . Allness comes to the rescue of this inconclusive relativity.]

167. [Kant, *Critique of Pure Reason*, 93 (B 75).]

168. [Cf. "What is rational is actual and what is actual is rational," *Hegel's Philosophy of Right*, trans. T. M. Knox, Oxford, London, and New York: Oxford University Press, 1967, 10 (*Grundlinien der Philosophie des Rechts*, ed. Johannes Hoffmeister, Hamburg: Meiner, 1955, 14); Cohen, *Logik der reinen Erkenntnis:* "Being must be referred to *an origin of itself.* And how could this origin, which must lie beyond being, lie elsewhere than in thought?" "The self-sameness of being is a reflex of the activity of thought" (31, 94).]

169. Cohen, *Logik der reinen Erkenntnis*, 154.

170. [*Ibid.,* 420, 424, 428: "Possibility is the place of the emergence of consciousness as a category." "In all its pure products . . . consciousness activates itself as possibility." "When there is a question of possibility, it is always connected with one of these four senses of consciousness" (thought, will, art, freedom).]

171. [Karl Georg Christian von Staudt's *Geometrie der Lage*, Nuremberg: F. Korn, 1847, contributed to the freeing of projective geometry from its Euclidean substrate.]

172. Russell, *Foundations of Geometry*, 123.

173. Hegel, *Enzyclopädie*, 206, par. 254.

174. [Cohen, *Logik der reinen Erkenntnis*, 179, 186-87.]

175. [*Ibid.,* 194-96.]

176. Hegel, *Wissenschaft der Logik* I, 107.

177. [Hegel, *Enzyclopädie*, 108, par. 88 (*The Logic of Hegel*, 163). The reference is to the categories 'being' and 'nothing.']

178. Spinoza [*Ethica* I, def. vi.]

179. David Hilbert, *Grundlagen der Geometrie*, 7th ed., Leipzig and Berlin: Teubner, 1930, 3 (*The Foundations of Geometry*, trans. E. J. Townsend, Chicago: Open Court, 1902).

180. Julian Lowell Coolidge, *The Elements of Non-Euclidean Geometry*, Oxford: Clarendon Press, 1909.

181. [Hilbert, *Grundlagen der Geometrie*, 4-5.]

182. Poincaré, *Science and Hypothesis*, 37-38.

183. [Cf. Luigi Cremona, *Elements of Projective Geometry*, trans. Charles Lendesdorf, 3rd ed., Oxford: Clarendon, 1913.]

184. [Hilbert, *Grundlagen der Geometrie*, 3.]

185. [*Ibid.*, 30.]

186. [*Ibid.*, 3 (phrasing changed in 7th ed.).]

187. [Hegel, *Enzyclopädie*, 349-54, parr. 424-39, but in particular the *Zusätze* of the 1845 edition which refer to "self-consciousness which is immediate, simply self-identical, and at the same time and contradictorily, is related to an external object" (*Philosophy of Mind*, 166).]

188. Wundt, *Grundriss der Psychologie*, 130.

189. *Ibid.*

190. [Bergson, *Matter and Memory*, 86, 88 (*Oeuvres*, 223, 224).]

191. [Bergson, *Creative Evolution*, 218-20 (*Oeuvres*, 664-66).]

192. [Bergson, *Matter and Memory*, 88 (*Oeuvres*, 224).]

193. [Meinong, "Gegenstandstheorie," 488-94.]

194. Wundt, *Grundriss der Psychologie*, 46-51.

195. [Poincaré, *Science and Hypothesis*, 114, 127.]

196. [Cf. Johann Friedrich Herbart, *Lehrbuch zur Einleitung in die Philosophie*, ed. K. Häntsch, Leipzig: Meiner, 1912, 181-268; Herbart's "reals" are discussed in Lotze, *Metaphysik* (1879), Leipzig: Meiner, 1912, 48-62, 371-74 (*Metaphysic*, trans. Bernard Bosanquet, Oxford University Press, 1887, I, 57-74; II, 47-50) and in Windelband, *A History of Philosophy*, New York: Harper Torchbooks, 1958, II, 584-87.]

197. [Gustav Robert Kirchhoff, *Analytische Mechanik*, 1, cited by Rickert in *Die Grenzen der naturwissenschaftlichen Begriffsbildung* (1902), 5th ed., Tübingen: Mohr, 1929, 208. Nishida uses the 2nd ed. (1913).]

198. [Wundt, *Grundriss der Psychologie*, 227.]

199. [Lotze, *Metaphysic* II, 128-35 (*Metaphysik*, 440-45); cf. *Metaphysic* II, 146: "We are never justified in speaking of a merely mechanical development of life, as if there were nothing behind it. There is something behind, viz. the combining movement of the absolute, the true activity that assumes this phenomenal form" (*Metaphysik*, 455).]

200. [*Ibid.*, I, 165 (*Metaphysik*, 137): "There cannot be a multiplicity of independent Things, but all elements, if reciprocal action is to be possible between them, must be regarded as parts of a single and real Being."]

201. [*Ibid.*, 256-58 (*Metaphysik*, 216-18): "We do not in the least traverse this perception (of space), which is endowed with such self-evidence; but only the allegation of a being that underlies it, which must be inaccessible to perception and so cannot share its self-evidence.... Space would lose nothing of its convincing reality for our perception if we admitted that it possesses it only in our perception."]

202. "absolute Tätigkeit" [*Fichtes Werke* I, 127 (*Science of Knowledge*, 124)].

203. [*Metaphysic* II, 317 (*Metaphysik*, 602). Nishida refers to Lotze, *Grundzüge der Metaphysik*, Leipzig: Hirzel, 1883 (*Outlines of Metaphysic*, trans. George T. Ladd, Boston: Ginn, Heath and Co., 1881), for what precedes, but this appears to be incorrect.]

204. Heinrich Hertz, *The Principles of Mechanics*, New York: Dover Publications, 1956, Introduction.

205. [Lotze discusses the "seat of the soul" in *Metaphysik*, 574-82 (*Metaphysic* II, 283-93).]

206. [Lotze, reference not traced.]

207. "*Le passé est passé*" [from Maeterlinck, immediately before the passage referred to in the following note].

208. Maurice Maeterlinck, *Le temple enseveli* (1902), Paris: Charpentier, 1910, 208.

209. Oscar Wilde [*De Profundis*, London: Methuen, 1913 (repr. of 1905 ed., Dawsons of Pall Mall, 1969), 125-26; also referred to in *A Study of Good*, 184-85.]

210. [*Fichtes Werke* I, 277 (*Science of Knowledge*, 244-45); Kant, *Kritik der praktischen Vernunft* (*Werke*, ed. Weischedel, VI, 242-44).]

211. [Bergson, *Matter and Memory*, 196-97 (*Oeuvres*, 293).]

212. [Lotze, *Metaphysik*, 268-302 (*Metaphysic*, I, 315-56).]

213. *Schlechthin tätig* [*Fichtes Werke* I, 140-41, 250 (*Science of Knowledge*, 135, 221).]

214. Hegel, *Enzyklopädie*, 192-93, parr. 232-35 (*The Logic of Hegel*, 370-73).

215. *The Logic of Hegel*, 267 (*Enzyklopädie*, 142, par. 147).

216. [Max Stirner (Johann Kaspar Schmidt), *Der Einzige und sein Eigentum*, Leipzig: Reclam, 1893, 429; *The Ego and His Own*, trans. Steven G. Byington (1907), New York: Libertarian Book Club, 1963.]

217. [Jacob Boehme, *Six Theosophic Points*, Ann Arbor: University of Michigan Press, 1971, 5-13. Among Nishida's books: Boehme, *The Way to Christ*, London: J. M. Watkins, 1911; *The Aurora*, trans. John Sparrow, London: J. M. Watkins, 1914; Julius Hamberger, *Die Lehre des deutschen Philosophen Jakob Böhme*, Munich: Literarisch-artistische Anstalt, 1844.]

218. [Pseudo-Dionysius Areopagite, *The Divine Names and the Mystical Theology*, trans. John D. Jones, Milwaukee: Marquette University Press, 1980, 109: "cause of *being* to all; but itself: non-being" (*Patro-*

logia Graeca, III, col. 588B). Nishida possessed *The Works of Diony-sius the Areopagite* I, trans. John Parker, London: James Parker, 1897.]

219. [Rickert, *Grenzen der naturwissenschaftlichen Begriffsbildung*, 303-39.]

220. [Bergson, *Creative Evolution*, 9 (*Oeuvres*, 499).]

221. [For the inadequacy of both teleology and mechanism see Bergson, *ibid.*, 34-62, 98-102 (*Oeuvres*, 519-40, 570-73).]

222. [Epictetus: *The Discourses*, trans. W. A. Oldfather, Loeb Edition, 1925, I, 335.]

223. [Johannes Scotus Eriugena, *De divisione naturae, Patrologia Latina*, CXXII, 463-66, 596-97. Eriugena considers the ten Aristotelean categories, to which he adds those of possibility and impossibility. This edition of Eriugena is among Nishida's books, but he has marked his copy of Ludwig Noack's translation, *Johannes Scotus Erigena über die Einteilung der Natur*, Leipzig: Dürr, 1870 and 1874; the markings cover the first 48 pages (= *De divisione* I 1-49).]

224. Johannes Huber, *Johannes Scotus Erigena*, Munich: Lentner, 1861, 190. [Nishida marked pages 158-210, which deal with the foundations of Erigena's system. Also in Nishida's collection: Theodor Christlieb, *Leben und Lehre des Johannes Scotus Erigena*, Gotha: Besser, 1860.]

225. [Eriugena, *Expositio in caelestem hierarchiam*, 103C (quoted by Huber, 184-85, underlined by Nishida) and *De divisione*, 452C. Eriugena reduces the ten categories to those of rest and motion, 469, 597; in *A Study of Good*, trans. V. H. Viglielmo, Tokyo: Japanese Government Printing Bureau, 1960, 175, Nishida quotes a similar paradox from Augustine, referring to Joseph Storz, *Die Philosophie des heiligen Augustinus*, Freiburg: Herder, 1882.]

226. [*The Transmission of the Lamp (Ching-te chuang-teng lu)*, fasc. 5.]

227. [*The Record of Lin-chi*, trans. Ruth Fuller Sazaki, Kyoto: Institute for Zen Studies, 1975, 5.]

228. [Eriugena begins *De divisione* (441-42) by dividing nature into "what creates and is not created" (God as first cause), "what is created and creates" (the primal causes), "what is created and does not create" (the created universe), and "what neither creates nor is created" (God as the end of all).]

229. Eriugena, *Liber de praedestinatione, Patr. Lat.* CXXII, 360, 364.

230. [Descartes, *Meditationes de prima philosophia*, ed. Artur Buchenau, Leipzig: Meiner, 1913, 26-39 (third meditation).]

231. [*Fichtes Werke* I, 119; *Science of Knowledge*, 116-17: "Self and not-self, as related and opposed through the concept of their capacity for mutual limitation, are themselves both something (namely accidents) in the self as divisible substance; posited by the self, as absolute, illimitable subject, to which nothing is either equated or opposed."

232. [*The Diamond Sutra* (Chinese version); Edward Conze translates the Sanskrit thus: "The Bodhisattva...should produce an unsupported thought, i.e. a thought which is nowhere supported" (*Buddhist Wisdom Books*, New York: Harper and Row, 1972, 47-48).]

233. [This account is reminiscent of Augustine, *De civitate dei* XI 23, *The Library of Nicene and Post-Nicene Fathers*, ed. Philip Schaff, Grand Rapids, Michigan: Eerdmans, 1956: "They say that souls...sinned by abandoning God; that, in proportion to their various sins, they invited different degrees of debasement from heaven to earth, and diverse bodies as prison-houses; and that this is the world, and this the cause of its creation, not the production of good things, but the restraining of evil. Origen is justly blamed for holding this opinion" (= *The City of God*, trans. Marcus Dods, Edinburgh: Clark, 1913; Nishida possessed a copy). See *Origen on First Principles*, trans. G. W. Butterworth, New York: Harper and Row, 1966, 40-41, 71-75, 239-42 (*De principiis* I 4.1; II 8.4; III 5.4-5); Origen's views in fact show the influence of Plato, *Phaedrus* 246C (the soul losing its wings).]

234. [Augustine, *Confessions* XIII 2-5; *De Genesi ad litteram* I 11,14: God created the world because of his own goodness. Nishida is perhaps influenced here by [Jean Félix] Nourrisson, *La philosophie de saint Augustin*, 2nd ed., Paris: Didier, 1866 (repr. Frankfurt: Minerva, 1968), I, 335: "c'est qu'il a trouvé bon de le créer" (underlined by Nishida). In Nishida's copy I 132-219 (psychology), 321-41 (creation), and II 1-88 (happiness and the good, the two cities) have been marked. Nishida also studied C. Bindemann, *Der heilige Augustinus*, Berlin: Hermann Schulze, 1844-69; Theodor Gangauf, *Des heiligen Augustinus speculative Lehre von Gott dem Dreieinigen*, Augsburg: B. Schmid, 1865 (he marked 209-95, on created, psychological triads as indices of the divine Trinity); Willi Kahl, *Die Lehre vom Primat des Willens bei Augustinus, Duns Scotus und Descartes*, Strasbourg: Trübner, 1886 (he marked 15-42 and 113-16, on Augustine and Descartes); Otto Zänker, *Der Primat des Willens vor dem Intellekt bei Augustin*, Gütersloh: C. Bertelsmann, 1907.]

235. [Cf. Rickert, *Kulturwissenschaft und Naturwissenschaft* (1910), 4th-

5th ed., Tübingen: Mohr, 1921, 35-38, 60-65 (*Science and History*, trans. Arthur Goddard, Princeton: Van Nostrand, 1962).]

236. [Origen on God as creator: *De principiis*, Praef. 4, II 1.4-5. (*Origen on First Principles*, 2, 77-80).]

237. [Augustine, *De trinitate* XV 22.]

238. [Cf. Hegel, *Wissenschaft der Logik* II, 13-18 (reflection as a presupposing of the immediate).]

239. ["You can, because you ought to" (*"Du kannst, denn du sollst"*) comes from Goethe-Schiller, *Xenien*, which alludes to K. Chr. E. Schmidt's *Versuch einer Moralphilosophie*, Jena, 1790; see *Goethes Werke*, ed. C. H. Beck, I, 220, 637. For the reference to Bergson see *Time and Free Will*, 173 (*Oeuvres*, 114).]

240. [Kant, *The Moral Law*, trans. H. J. Paton, London: Hutchinson, 1976, 99-100: "A world of rational beings (*mundus intelligibilis*) is possible as a kingdom of ends, possible, that is, through the making of their own laws by all persons as its members" (*Werke* VI, 72).]

241. [Hegel, *Enzyclopädie*, 131, parr. 123-24 (*The Logic of Hegel*, 230-31).]

242. [Augustine, *De civitate dei* XII 22; XIV 11; *De Genesi ad litteram*, XI 6, 8, 20.]

243. [Rickert, *Gegenstand der Erkenntnis*, 371-83; the category of givenness is more fundamental than those of space, time, and causation.]

244. [Poincaré, *Valeur de la science*, 167. (*Value of Science*, 125).]

245. [Kant, *Critique of Pure Reason*, 233-36 (B 257-62).]

246. Adolf von Hildebrand, *Das Problem der Form in der bildenden Kunst*, 5th ed., Strasbourg: J. H. E. Heitz, 1905, 33; Nishida also had *The Problem of Form in Painting and Sculpture*, trans. Max Meyer and Robert Morris, New York and London: G. E. Stechert, 1907 (repr. 1945).]

247. [Lipps, *Bewusstsein und Gegenstand*: the conscious ego is "the immediately experienced ego...the phenomenal ego, the ego-phenomenon, ego-appearance [which] lodges in every conscious experience as such"; " 'I' as objectification of my consciousness" in contrast to body or "soul" (9, 42).]

248. [Natorp, *Allgemeine Psychologie*, 19-20, 189-213; "Reconstruction of the immediate in consciousness from that which has been formed from it, whether the objectivations of science or those of everyday pre-scientific representation...restores to rigid concepts their movement...leads the objectified back to the stage of subjective givenness

...in a complete and pure reversal of the procedure of objectivating knowledge" (192-93). See *Einleitung in die Psychologie*, 88-103, and Cassirer, *Philosophy of Symbolic Forms* III, 51-57.]

249. [For this symbolism see Novalis, *Heinrich von Ofterdingen*, Stuttgart: Reclam, 1965. Nishida's edition: *Werke*, ed. Wilhelm Bölsche, Leipzig: Hesse und Becker, 3 voll.]

250. [Nishida's source here is Wihelm Bousset, *Hauptprobleme der Gnosis*, Göttingen, 1910 (repr. 1973), p. 127; in his diary for Jan. 1, 1917, he notes that he is reading "Gnosis" (*Zenshū* XVII, 342).]

251. [Rickert, *Grenzen der naturwissenschaftlichen Begriffsbildung*, 258-82.]

252. [Rickert, *Kulturwissenschaft*, 118-32, classes phylogenetic biology and psychology among the disciplines intermediary between the two extremes of history and natural science.]

253. [Augustine, *De civitate dei* I 35; XIV 28; XVIII 49-51; and especially *De vera religione* 27 (underlined by Nishida in Nourrisson, *Philosophie de saint Augustin* II, 76). For Augustine one cannot belong to both cities. Nishida may have gathered this mistaken impression from Nourrisson, II, 45: "mélange et confusion des deux cités par un commerce d'iniquité."]

254. [Bergson, *Matter and Memory*, 102, 113: "The past appears indeed to be stored up, as we had surmised, under two extreme forms: on the one hand, motor mechanisms which make use of it; on the other, personal memory images which picture all past events with their outline, their color and their place in time." "While motor apparatus are built up under the influence of perceptions that are analysed with increasing precision by the body, our past physical life is there: it survives ...with all the details of its events localized in time." (*Oeuvres*, 234, 241).

255. [Spinoza, *Ethica* V, prop. xxxvi.]

256. Meinong, "Bemerkungen über den Farbenkörper und das Mischungsgesetz" (1903), *Gesammelte Abhandlungen* I, 1914 (*Meinong Gesamtausgabe* I, 1969), 495-576.

257. Hegel, *Phänomenologie des Geistes*, ed. Johannes Hoffmeister, Hamburg: Meiner, 1952, 79-89 (*The Phenomenology of Spirit*, trans A. V. Miller, New York: Oxford University Press, 1977; cf. *Enzyclopädie*, par. 175, Zusatz; *The Logic of Hegel*, 308: "The subject, receiving, as in the Singular Judgment, a universal predicate, is carried out beyond its mere individuality."

258. [*Tōjō ungetsu roku* II.]
259. Saint-Cyran [Jean Duvergier de Hauranne, Abbé de Saint-Cyran. This is the epigraph to Nourrisson's *Philosophie de saint Augustin.* The source is given as Fontaine, *Mémoires pour servir à l'histoire de Port-Royal,* Cologne, 1753, II, 58 (Nourrisson, II, 194). Saint-Cyran said: "Saint Augustine is the first of the Latin Fathers. All his words overflow from his virtue. His books issue from the heart. *Unde ardet, inde lucet."*]
260. [Kant, *Critique of Pure Reason,* 135 (A 105).]
261. [*Ibid.,* 156 (B 137).]
262. [Cf. Windelband, *Einleitung in die Philosophie* (1914), 3rd ed. Tübingen: Mohr, 1923, 236: "Herein and herein alone lies the truth of our knowledge: that in it we produce objects which in terms of form and content indeed belong to the real, and yet in their selection and ordering emerge from it as new formations. . . . One might designate the marshaling and shaping of these objects in the human noetic process by the name of appearance, *appearance,* however, which in this case is determined not qualitatively, but *quantitatively,* since it can signify nothing other than the essence, and only a selection therefrom."]
263. [Heraclitus, frag. B 89, in Kathleen Freeman, *Ancilla to the Presocratics,* Oxford: Blackwell, 1952, 30 (slightly modified).]
264. [Cf. Hegel, *The Philosophy of History,* trans. J. Sibree, New York: Dover, 1956, 220: "That the Spirit of the Egyptians presented itself to their consciousness in the form of a *problem,* is evident from the celebrated inscription in the sanctuary of the goddess Neith at Sais: '*I am that which is, that which was, and that which will be; no one has lifted my veil'.* . . . In the Egyptian Neith, truth is still a problem. The Greek Apollo is its solution; his utterance is: '*Man, know thyself.'* " See also Novalis, *Die Lehrlinge zu Sais,* Stuttgart: Reclam, 1966.]
265. Hermann Minkowski, *Peter Gustav Lejeune Dirichlet und seine Bedeutung für die heutige Mathematik,* Leipzig, 1905 [Dirichlet succeeded Gauss at Göttingen.]
266. Bergson, *Matter and Memory,* 183-85 (*Oeuvres,* 284-86).
267. [John Stuart Mill, *An Examination of Sir William Hamilton's Philosophy, Collected Works* IX, 1979, 179-95.]
268. [Galatians 2:20 (RSV); also quoted in *A Study of Good,* 158.]
269. [Matthew 10:39; also quoted in *A Study of Good,* 163.]
270. ["Kulturbewusstsein" cf. Cohen, *Logik der reinen Erkenntis,* 17-18, 609-12; "Wille zum Kulturleben" (Fichte), reference not traced.]

Index